Carbondale and Edwardsville

The Poet Without a Name:

Gray's *Elegy* and the

Problem of History

HENRY WEINFIELD

SOUTHERN ILLINOIS UNIVERSITY PRESS

94 93 92 91   4 3 2 1

Library of Congress Cataloging-in-Publication Data

Weinfield, Henry.
    The poet without a name : Gray's Elegy and the problem of history
    / Henry Weinfield.
        p.   cm.
    Includes bibliographical references and index.
    1. Gray, Thomas, 1716–1771.   Elegy written in a country
    churchyard.   2. Pastoral poetry, English—History and criticism.
    3. Literature and history.   4. Romanticism—England.   I. Title.
    PR3502.E53W45   1991
    821'.6—dc20   90-9892
    ISBN 0-8093-1652-8   CIP

The paper used in this publication meets the minimum requirements of
American National Standard for Information Sciences—Permanence of
Paper for Printed Library Materials, ANSI Z39.48-1984. ∞

In memory of my father,
Mortimer Weinfield (1912–1987)

Contents

Acknowledgments

MY SINCERE thanks to the friends and colleagues who, in one way or another, have shared in the development of this study, from its inception as my doctoral dissertation through the various vicissitudes it has undergone in the course of becoming a book. At the City University of New York Graduate Center, the late Frank Brady went over the original manuscript with meticulous care, Angus Fletcher was unstinting in his generosity, and Allen Mandelbaum was an unfailing source of support, as indeed he has remained over the years. My dear friend Stuart Liebman was a constant interlocutor from the beginning: his insights are everywhere mingled with my own and his analytical rigor alerted me to many an ill-conceived thought or phrase. Other friends who provided intellectual companionship along the way and to whom I owe a tremendous debt of gratitude include William Bronk, Daniel Feldman, Norman Finkelstein, David Katz, Laury Magnus, Dale Ramsey, Gale Sigal, and Walter Stiller. Paul Fry and John Shawcross, in reviewing the manuscript, offered penetrating insights and helped me to hone my argument. Curtis Clark, my editor at Southern Illinois University Press, had the courage to believe in a project that some might have regarded as eccentric and was steadfast in guiding it through the shoals of academe. I was fortunate also in being the beneficiary of the expertise and patience of Susan Wilson, managing editor of the Press, and Ruth Kissell, the copyeditor of the book.

My gratitude to my wife, Joyce, pertains to another order of magnitude altogether and cannot be put into words.

Introduction

THIS BOOK is a study of Gray's *Elegy* from the dual standpoint of literary history and literary theory. Its central argument—and this will explain why I have devoted an entire book to a poem of only 128 lines—is that the *Elegy* constitutes an important turning point or watershed in the history of English poetry. In making this claim, I am of course aware that Gray's status in the canon is currently rather tenuous, not to say peripheral, and that the *Elegy* itself, although generally acknowledged as a beautiful poem, has rarely been considered a particularly original one. I argue, however, that in the *Elegy* certain themes that are of fundamental importance to the tradition as a whole are fully articulated for the first time, in a way that was not previously possible, and, as a result, acquire a resonance that they did not previously have. Specifically, where the thematic constellation of poverty, anonymity, alienation, and unfulfilled potential—or what I refer to as "the problem of history"—was not central to earlier poets, this thematic constellation is directly confronted in the *Elegy*, and in a way that not only has a profound impact on subsequent poets but also obliges us to reinterpret certain aspects of the previous tradition through the terms that the *Elegy* itself establishes.

The "problem of history" of my title has little to do with history in the ordinary sense, either with past events or their interpretation. Rather, it is a double or circular metaphor that is intended to encompass a particular "myth of concern" (in Northrop Frye's phrase), one that is characterized by the utopian impulse toward perfection and that is reflected, albeit in a submerged fashion, in the pastoral tradition (although from the Renaissance to the eighteenth century, the entire poetic tradition may be considered under the rubric of the pastoral). From

the standpoint of this myth of concern, history is simultane-
ously the sphere in which man experiences the loss of paradise
(i.e., deprivation) and in which (and through which) he must
struggle to establish or to recover (depending on whether one
looks forward or backward in time to the New Jerusalem or to
the Golden Age or the Garden of Eden) the Earthly Paradise,
whose loss is what occasioned history, and hence the problem
of history, in the first place. In short, the problem of history (in
the sense of task or telos) is to overcome the problem of history
(in the sense of deprivation, or the thematic constellation to
which I referred earlier).

The myth of concern I have adumbrated is, of course, deeply
embedded in a good deal of the poetry of the English tradition
and in a way that transcends generic distinctions. It is consistent
not only with Christian millennialism but also with the various
secular humanist extensions of Christian millennialism, includ-
ing (at least in theory) the Marxist-Hegelian vision of a social
harmony predicated on the elimination of scarcity, on the one
hand, and the forms of domination and alienation, on the
other—a social harmony that is to be achieved at the end of
history and as the end of history. In English poetry, it is often
associated (though perhaps somewhat narrowly) with a Protes-
tant or "displaced Protestant" or "Miltonic-Romantic" tradi-
tion, whose central text is *Paradise Lost* and whose central
moment occurs when the angel Michael tells Adam that in the
fullness of time "the earth / Shall all be paradise, far happier
place / Than this of *Eden*, and far happier days" (12.463–65).

A corollary to my argument that the problem of history is
fully articulated in the *Elegy* for the first time is that the *Elegy*
represents the symbolic dissolution of the pastoral in what one
might call its transcendental formulation. For if the problem of
history *emerges* in the *Elegy*, this is because it had previously
been submerged in the pastoral and precluded from emerging by
the pastoral. The transcendental world of the pastoral, although
motivated by the problem of history, is insulated from the prob-
lem of history. Consequently, as long as the pastoral maintained
its hold on the literary imagination, the problem of history could

not be confronted directly, could not emerge into the light of day.

This aspect of my argument will seem difficult to fathom if a rigid distinction is made between georgic and pastoral and if the pastoral is narrowly defined as a genre involving "the imitation of the action of a shepherd, or one considered under that character" (this is Pope's definition in his "Discourse on Pastoral");[1] for in this case, the *Elegy* would clearly belong to the georgic rather than to the pastoral tradition. Indeed, it will be noted in this regard that the *Elegy* is written in quatrains and thus corresponds in form to neither of the two main strains of eighteenth-century pastoral: the heroic couplet strain that takes its impetus from Pope and the blank verse strain that descends from Milton. However, not only are the georgic and pastoral genres completely intertwined in practice, but the fact that Virgil regarded his own *Georgics* as in part a corrective, or necessary addition, to his *Eclogues*[2] is itself a preliminary indication of a historical problematic that, I would argue, finally comes to fruition in Gray's *Elegy*. Gray did not write a set of georgics and a set of pastorals—that is, a set of poems focusing realistically on the problems confronting labor and a set of poems presenting an idealized vision of the Earthly Paradise—precisely because, for the first time in the history of poetry, the two sets of concerns could be brought into alignment with each other and dealt with as a single set of concerns. The *Elegy* is thus at once a profoundly realistic and a profoundly visionary poem, and it is precisely because it is *not* a pastoral, in the narrow sense of Pope's definition, that it is able to represent the symbolic dissolution of the pastoral.

The historic *task* of the pastoral (if one may so employ the term) consisted in its confrontation with the problem of history in both the positive and the negative senses that I have outlined. This is to say that the pastoral, as a mode or genre, is historically constituted simultaneously by the necessity of confronting the problem of history and by the fact that the problem of history cannot be resolved in practice, given the historical juncture at which the pastoral originates. The vision of the Earthly Paradise vouchsafed by the pastoral, a vision that is predicated on some version of the Golden Age myth, is thus simultaneously a transcendental solution to the problem of history and a way of circumventing the problem of history entirely. This is a conception that I shall develop in greater depth in chapter 4. For the moment, however, it should simply be borne in mind that the pastoral, in my understanding of the term, is a mode or genre that is fundamentally constituted by the problem of history and only secondarily, or contingently, one that focuses on the lives of shepherds. The question of why this particular historical content should have seized upon the *figure* of the shepherd as its formal vehicle (for I regard the shepherd as essentially a trope) is one to which I can supply none but the most speculative of answers and to which I think no clear answers are immediately forthcoming, but the fact that the question has not previously arisen in exactly this form is interesting in itself and may perhaps indicate how successful the pastoral was in camouflaging its real subject matter. One might hypothesize that *originally* (assuming that it is possible to speak in terms of origins) shepherds and the animals they tended came to be associated with such "pastoral" qualities as gentleness and peacefulness, that these associations culminated in a link between a particular content and a set of formal expectations and conventions, and that the resulting genre then acquired a momentum of its own. (The biblical story of Cain and Abel may testify to the antiquity of these associations, whose roots may lie in the increased potential for violence unleashed by the Agricultural Revolution.) Be that as it may, the point of departure of my own argument is simply that the pastoral (that is, a kind of poetry involving shepherds) was historically constituted by the task of representing the problem of history in what one might call its submerged form and that in this sense it is appropriate to speak of the *Elegy* as representing the symbolic dissolution of the pastoral.

Such, at any rate, may serve to situate the central argument propounded by this study, at least as far as the poem's relationship to the pastoral and the problem of history is concerned, but the development of this argument is only one aspect of what the study as a whole attempts to accomplish. My aim in this book is, first and foremost, to arrive at an interpretation of the *Elegy* that is fuller, deeper, and more compelling and accurate than any that has yet been set forth. Given the current environment of scepticism in which criticism now finds itself, a statement of this kind will seem either naive or arrogant. However, despite the enormous amount of critical ink that has flowed on the subject of the *Elegy* (some of it extremely interesting and informative), I would argue that the poem has never really been understood. Of course, there are different levels of understanding, but with a poem as densely allusive and richly complex as the *Elegy*, more is required than can be encompassed by the short essay—and up to now, the poem has been dealt with only in this form. If the length of the present study is justified, it is because of what one might call the *elasticity* of a certain type of lyric poetry, a quality that enables a poem of only 128 lines to "speak volumes," as it were. Confronted by a poem of this kind, the task of the critic is to perform something of the archeologist's labor so as to "see a world in a grain of sand," as Blake said.

A second aim of this study is to examine the theoretical premises and paradigms underlying previous criticism of the *Elegy* and, by so doing, to develop an overview of the problems and dilemmas confronting formalist criticism in general. The purpose of this aspect of the study is in part propaedeutic: to clear a space for my own interpretation of the poem. However, because the *Elegy* served as a kind of locus classicus for so many of the theoretical preoccupations that absorbed the New Critics, by paying close attention to the existing criticism on the poem we not only can gain insight into the nature of these theoretical preoccupations but also can develop something of a historical understanding of why the New Criticism coalesced as a movement and wherein its limitations as a methodology lay.

Finally, the study aims to resituate the poem historically in terms of its relationship to the poetic canon and also against the

larger historical background. The general conception of Gray is
as a minor poet, and the period in which he wrote has been
labeled "post-Augustan" or "pre-Romantic," the "Age of John-
son" or, more recently, the "Age of Sensibility." But if the *Elegy*
represents a turning point in the history of English poetry, as I
have suggested, then what does that say about our received
assumptions and categories—indeed, about our understanding
of the poetic canon as a whole? How does it affect our under-
standing of Romanticism or even of Modernism? "No poet, no
artist of any art," wrote Eliot in "Tradition and the Individual
Talent," "has his complete meaning alone. . . . The existing
monuments form an ideal order among themselves . . . [and] for
order to persist after the supervention of novelty, the *whole*
existing order must be, if ever so slightly, altered." Eliot had the
new work of art in mind when he wrote this passage; but, in a
sense, it makes no difference whether the work in question is a
new one or one that is being presented in a new light, for in both
cases the same reshifting of alignments that Eliot describes is
bound to occur. And since to assert that the *Elegy* represents a
turning point in the history of English poetry is tantamount to
arguing that its significance to literary history has been re-
pressed, I am confronted with the problem not only of realigning
and reinterpreting a number of received categories but also of
explaining why the interpretation I put forth has not previously
been delineated.

The study unfolds in the following manner. The first two
chapters deal with various questions of evaluation and interpre-
tation that have arisen in the critical literature, thus laying the
theoretical foundations for the interpretation and the hermeneu-
tic strategy that is then developed in chapter 3. By far the longest
chapter in the study, chapter 3 is a phenomenological reading
of the poem that attempts, through a stanza-by-stanza analysis,
to delineate as fully as possible the manner in which the poem
unfolds. Finally, chapters 4 and 5 build on the argument gener-
ated in previous sections to focus on the poem's relationship
to the poetic canon, with particular reference to the pastoral
tradition. Chapter 4 extrapolates from the thematic analysis

of chapter 3 to present a theoretical overview of the poem's relationship to the pastoral and to reflect on some of the consequences of the dissolution of the pastoral in the eighteenth century. Finally, chapter 5, focusing on Wordsworth's complexly ambivalent relationship to Gray, deals with one important way in which the terrain encompassed by the *Elegy* opens out on Romantic and even Modernist poetics.

The various ways in which formal and ideological factors have been intertwined in the criticism of the poem constitutes an important subplot of the present study. Since its publication in 1751, the *Elegy* has been one of the most popular poems in the language; yet, as I demonstrate in chapter 1, criticism has been under a kind of strange compunction to devalue the poem—so as to avoid confronting the discrepancy between the poem's popularity and the perception of Gray as a minor poet. Not only has there been a failure to recognize the poem's originality, as I noted earlier, but there has also been a tendency to attribute its popularity to a variety of extrapoetic factors. And yet, ironically, there has been almost no investigation of its thematic dimension. Indeed, the neglect of the thematic dimension, which was a characteristic of the New Criticism generally, is also largely responsible for the failure of interpretation to arrive at a coherent understanding of the poem, as I argue in chapter 2. From the 1920s to the 1960s, a number of attempts to resolve the problem of structure and meaning posed by the *Elegy* were set forth, but these interpretive readings were severely hampered both by their neglect of the poem's complex thematic dimension and by their commitment—in spite of the New Critical preoccupation with ambiguity—to a narrow hermeneutic model governed by the Aristotelian principle of univocity. Consequently, as I suggested earlier, in my analysis of the abortive attempts of formalist criticism to resolve the problem of interpretation posed by the *Elegy*, the reader will discern an incipient critique of the formalist method generally.

A further aspect of the theoretical subplot I have mentioned has to do with the relationship of rhetorical and other formal issues to ideological ones. It has often been noted that the New

Criticism tended in a conservative direction, although it some-
times camouflaged its ideological biases under the guise of "ob-
jective" formal concerns. All critics impose their ideological
leanings on the texts they examine, of course, and the formalists
were prone to do this with the *Elegy*. Through their analyses of
its imagery and even of Gray's use of such devices as personifi-
cation, they turned a poem that is deeply committed to the
Enlightenment ideal of progress, a poem whose philosophical
roots are Neoplatonist and humanist, into one that expresses
an attitude of despairing quietism. Of course, the reader will
have gleaned something of my own philosophical predilections
through this brief précis, and perhaps a countervailing distortion
as well.

The long third chapter, in which I bring out the themes noted
earlier, and which is written as a stanza-by-stanza analysis of
the *Elegy*, constitutes a kind of experiment in practical criti-
cism. The New Criticism tended to develop a "spatial" analysis
of the text, in which the various issues submitted for examina-
tion were telescoped, as it were, and abstracted from the "tempo-
ral" process of the poem's unfolding. This had the advantage of
concision, but it also led to the neglect of the thematic dimen-
sion of the work. My own interpretive method, by contrast, is
geared to the temporal process of the poem's unfolding. Poems,
like musical compositions (*ut musica poesis*), have a dual rela-
tion to time: they cannot be read "all at once," and yet their
end is contained, as by necessity, in their beginning. In effect,
therefore, my procedure has been to read both forward and back-
ward: forward to grasp the poem's unfolding, and backward to
grasp how in the process of unfolding it reflects on what has
come before. In those cases in which the poem seems to warrant
it, I have grouped several stanzas together into sections; in other
cases—especially toward the middle of the poem, where Gray's
discourse becomes astonishingly dense—I have treated each
stanza singly. The procedure I have employed is an unusual
one, but I believe that there would have been no other way to
encompass the extraordinary complexity of the poem's dialectic.
For the *Elegy* seems to me to be not only a philosophical poem

but one whose "meaning" is temporally grounded in the poem's struggle to arrive at meaning. Broadly speaking, the poem's method of progression may be considered dialectical in the sense that Gray's attempt to arrive at truth obliges him to consider various conflicting perspectives that develop out of one another—with the result that the poem's scope becomes increasingly broadened and at the same time more finely delineated. For this reason, the poem's meaning cannot simply be extracted from a spatial conception of the text as a static entity; it can only be reached through a point by point contact with the poem's unfolding.

If the *Elegy* has a subject, this is perhaps nothing less than the problem of locating meaning and value in human existence generally. But from another point of view, it is possible to discern two basic subject areas in the poem, as well as two basic modalities in terms of which these areas are being developed. The *Elegy* obviously confronts the problem of death, but this problem is completely entwined with the problem of "death-in-life," or what I have referred to as the problem of history. The dialectical enmeshing of these problems, together with the myriad ramifications that proceed from them, is mediated by the poem's contrast between two social classes: the "rude Forefathers of the hamlet" and those to whom Gray sometimes refers as "the Proud." The problem of death impinges on both classes, of course, and, as such, provides the frame for the timeless or universal verities that Gray attempts to articulate; but the problem of "death-in-life" is more clearly slanted toward those buried in the country churchyard and, as such, provides the frame for the sociohistorical side to the poet's dialectic. What is truly extraordinary is the way in which these enormously complex areas and modalities are both delineated and synthesized as the poem unfolds. But this bare and overly schematic outline hardly encompasses the richness of Gray's discourse.

As I demonstrate in chapter 3, the *Elegy* bears an antithetical relationship to the heroic, elegiac, and pastoral traditions. However, as I have indicated, I am especially concerned with the theoretical issues posed by the pastoral because of its relationship to the problem of history. Accordingly, chapter 4 develops a theoretical overview of the pastoral as a utopian response to the problem of history. The emergence of the problem of history in the *Elegy*, I suggest, is not only tantamount to the dissolution of the old pastoral but coincides with the advent of several new forms, including an antipastoral and a demotic pastoral tendency.

The perspective of chapter 4 thus leads directly to the concluding chapter of my study, in which I turn to the question of Wordsworth's relationship to Gray. As the title of the chapter, "Wordsworth and the Reconstitution of the Pastoral," indicates, I regard Wordsworth as representing a tendency that is antithetical to that of Gray in the *Elegy*. At the same time, however, I argue that the *Elegy* exerted a profound, indeed a formative, influence on Wordsworth. My discussion of the nature of this influence and of the complex poetic and ideological reasons why Wordsworth found it necessary to distance himself from Gray brings the study to a close.

I have dwelt at some length on the poem's thematic dimension, but equally important to my analysis is its relationship to language and to the literary tradition. The breadth and the density of Gray's philosophical argument are achieved through a power of condensation that may be unequaled in English poetry, and the extent of Gray's originality, some features of which I have tried to sketch in here, really only emerges against the background of his relationship to the tradition. If the *Elegy* had been a philosophical treatise, it would have comprised volumes. But what we have is something much better: a poem of 128 lines in which Gray poured the wealth of his knowledge, his vision, and his mastery over his craft.

The Poet Without a Name:
Gray's *Elegy* and the
Problem of History

Chapter 1

Popularity, Resonance, Originality: The Question of Evaluation

Since its publication in 1751, Gray's *Elegy* has been one of the most popular poems—if not *the* most popular poem—in the English language. Its success was almost immediate, and by the century's close it had penetrated the consciousness of virtually the entire educated reading public. The story that General Wolfe read it to his troops before the Battle of the Plains of Abraham in 1759 is, even if apocryphal, an indication of how deeply embedded in the popular imagination the poem had become only a few years after its publication. During the nineteenth century, it was called "the typical piece of English verse, our poem of poems";[1] and as recently as 1968, the editor of a collection of essays on the poem could still remark that it is "frequently referred to, with some truth, as the best known poem in the English language."[2] Its popularity would seem to have waned in recent years, perhaps because of the disappearance of the "common reader" and perhaps for ideological reasons as well; significantly, however, we continue to refer to it simply as "*the* Elegy," as if to pay deference to the centrality of its position in the canon.

Of course, the popularity of a poem is not necessarily a reflection of its intrinsic value—although there are now some critics who would deny that there is such a thing as intrinsic poetic value. But in the case of the *Elegy*, this is an issue that deserves to be raised from the outset because of a series of paradoxes with which it is connected. For one thing, the question of popularity is in a sense *thematized* in the poem in the form of a fame-anonymity dialectic. For another, Gray's style is the very anti-thesis of a "popular" style, in the sense in which we have come to speak of a popular style—although in actuality, of course, there is no style that has proven to be more enduring, and hence more popular, than Gray's in the *Elegy*. Gray's diction—always elevated, lyrical, and refined—was criticized by Dr. Johnson as being "remote from common use."[3] Wordsworth repeated Johnson's criticism and made Gray a special target of attack in the Preface to *Lyrical Ballads.* Yet the poet who strove to "imitate, and, as far as possible, to adopt the very language of men" produced no poem that so captured the popular imagination as Gray's *Elegy.*[4]

The thematic and stylistic paradoxes I have broached will be taken up in subsequent chapters, but there is yet a third paradox I want now to consider, and this concerns the issue of canon formation. For in spite of the enormous popularity of the *Elegy* with "common readers" (and the distinction, admittedly, is tenuous but, in my view, nevertheless valid), Gray himself has generally occupied a rather peripheral position in the English poetic canon. The critical consensus, perhaps since Matthew Arnold, is that he is a minor poet, not only because of the paucity of his output but for other reasons as well. However, if the popularity of the *Elegy* were taken as a reflection of its intrinsic value, then not only would Gray's position in the canon have to be revised, but that revision would also call into question a number of other received assumptions and categories of literary history and theory, including perhaps the question of Romanticism itself.

Criticism has never been troubled by the discrepancy between Gray's status in the literary hierarchy and the popularity of his greatest poem, however, because it has always attributed the popularity of the *Elegy* to extrapoetic factors—to the poem's putative subject, to the generic feeling-state it is supposed to evoke in readers, or to its presumed reliance on a set of precursors. The image of Gray as a minor and not very original poet has led to the assumption that the *Elegy* owes its popularity to extrapoetic factors, while the assumption that the *Elegy* owes its popularity to extrapoetic factors has confirmed critics in their preconceptions about its author. Thus, criticism has proceeded in a circle.

Equivocal Responses to the *Elegy:* Arnold, Richards, Wimsatt, Hough

The tendency to attribute the *Elegy*'s popularity to extrapoetic factors is exemplified by Amy L. Reed's study of 1924, *The Background of Gray's Elegy,* which was once considered the standard treatment of the poem. Reed describes her approach as an attempt "to explain the furore created by Gray's *Elegy* in 1751 on the theory that the poem came before its audience not as the representation of novel thought but as the perfectly adequate expression of a widespread popular feeling, the 'melancholy' of the first half of the eighteenth century."[5] Not surprisingly, the *Elegy* disappears into the morass of its "historical background" in this study. But the tendency exemplified by Reed does not begin with her: it can be traced to Matthew Arnold's essay on Gray, which is still probably the most influential piece of criticism on the poet ever written. Arnold's theme, the reader will recall, is that "Gray, a born poet, fell upon an age of prose."[6] In his discussion of the *Elegy,* Arnold finds an opportunity to emphasize this point by mentioning an anecdote originally reported by Sir William Forbes in his *Life of Beattie* (1806). During a visit to Scotland in 1765, Gray apparently was quoted as saying that the *Elegy* "owed its popularity entirely to the subject, and that the public would have received it as well if it had been written in prose."[7] By way of Arnold's essay, then, Gray's remark became a critical commonplace.

It would be difficult to disentangle the various ironic nuances in Gray's remark—and in any event, the *Elegy* does *not* owe its popularity to its subject, or to the beauty of its versification, or to any aspect in isolation. Gray's bitterness might have been occasioned by the disappointing reception of his Pindaric odes. Be that as it may, a poet who had labored upwards of five years

on a poem, as Gray had on the *Elegy*, could not have intended
a remark of this kind to be taken literally. Few poets have placed
so great an emphasis on poetic craft as Gray; to anyone who has
studied his work, it is clear that the "morality of craft" was
almost a religion for Gray—and this is the real reason for his
paucity of output, not because he "fell upon an age of prose."
But Arnold's motivation in repeating the remark was clearly to
temper the popular enthusiasm for the *Elegy*. Thus, he writes:
"The *Elegy* is a beautiful poem, and in admiring it the public
showed a true feeling for poetry. But it is true that the *Elegy* owed
much of its popularity to its subject, and that it has received a
too unmeasured and unbounded praise."[8] Arnold was too astute
a critic not to be aware that if the popularity of the *Elegy* were
merely a function of its subject, then a hundred poems would
be equally popular. Nevertheless, by taking Gray's remark seri-
ously, he seems to be saying that the poem has nothing very
original to offer and that it does not really depart from the realm
of the commonplace. The *Elegy*, he tells us, is a "beautiful"
poem, but in his use of the term, beauty is merely a formal
quality that does not impinge upon content.

Poetry being a verbal art, Arnold's statement begs the question
of whether there can be beauty in poetry that is unconnected to
thought. But in any event, insofar as twentieth-century critics
have attempted to evaluate the *Elegy*, they have tended to do so
along the dualistic lines laid down by Arnold. This is true even of
the New Critics—the "heresy of paraphrase" notwithstanding.
Thus, I. A. Richards remarks:

> The *Elegy* is perhaps the best example in English of a good
> poem built upon a solid foundation of stock responses.[9]

And thus, W. K. Wimsatt:

> Perhaps we shall be tempted to say only that Gray transcends
> and outdoes Hammond and Shenstone simply because he
> writes a more poetic line, richer, fuller, more resonant and
> memorable in all the ways in which we are accustomed to
> analyze the poetic quality.[10]

And thus, Graham Hough:

> The greatness of the *Elegy* . . . no one has ever doubted, but many have been hard put to it to explain in what its greatness consists. It is easy to point out that its thought is common-place, that its diction and imagery are correct, noble but unoriginal, and to wonder where the immediately recognizable greatness has slipped in.[11]

The same separation of form and content that obtains in Arnold's remarks on the *Elegy* is present in those by Richards, Wimsatt, and Hough. Presumably, Richards's reader would have to have two kinds of responses to the poem, which he would then have to balance in one way or another: a series of "stock" (i.e., generalized) responses and a series of "poetic" (i.e., particularized) responses. And the same reductio ad absurdum could be applied to the comments by Wimsatt and Hough. For just as Arnold would have been hard-pressed to explain why the *Elegy* is a "beautiful" poem and Richards, why it is a "good" one, so Wimsatt and Hough would be unable to say why Gray writes a more "poetic" or "resonant" line than Hammond or Shenstone, or wherein the poem's "immediately recognizable greatness" consists. If one drives a wedge between form and content, there is simply no basis for making aesthetic judgments about the formal or stylistic properties of a poem, because words have meanings. There is probably as much "figuration" as such in the poems of Hammond and Shenstone (whom Wimsatt mentions solely because they employ the elegiac quatrain) as there is in the *Elegy*, but Hammond and Shenstone are pedestrian writers while Gray is an extraordinary one. However, since Wimsatt finds nothing in the content or conceptual development of the *Elegy* to distinguish it from the elegies of Hammond and Shenstone, he is obliged to resort to mystical categories to record his intuition of Gray's superiority.

The very fact that Gray should be placed in the same company as Hammond and Shenstone is indicative of the tendency of criticism to assume that the "subject" of the *Elegy* (on which its popularity is supposed to depend), as well as its relationship to a particular genre and to poetic tradition generally, can be taken for granted as being given from the outset. But what *is* the subject of the *Elegy?* Curiously, this question has never really been asked, much less seriously explored, because of the assumption that what the poem is saying is obvious. There are, of course, many poems, especially in the eighteenth century, that do present themselves (at least superficially) in terms of a detachable subject: "The Vanity of Human Wishes," for example, is clearly *about* what its title signifies—which is not to suggest that it is lacking in complexity. But in the case of the *Elegy,* the situation is quite different, for the poem's thematic development is far too complex to permit any sort of a priori reduction. Although such topoi as the inevitability of death and, indeed, the vanity of human wishes, can be extracted from the *Elegy,* the poem contains other themes that are at least as important, and some of its themes are in conflict with others. Yet somehow, without having investigated the matter, criticism has come away with the notion that what Gray is saying in the *Elegy* is not particularly original; hence, that whatever beauty the poem possesses is largely a function of Gray's admitted stylistic mastery; and finally, that for these reasons the poem's popularity may be attributed to extrapoetic factors and to the lack of discernment of ordinary readers.

Dr. Johnson on the *Elegy*

The first important piece of criticism on the *Elegy* is contained in Samuel Johnson's "Life of Gray" (1781). Although Johnson disliked most of Gray's poetry, his remarks on the *Elegy* are extremely laudatory. What has not generally been recognized, however, is that Johnson's response to the poem is diametrically opposed to that of the critical mainstream since Arnold; for in his discussion of the *Elegy,* Johnson stresses not only its *resonance* (as most commentators after him have done) but also its *originality:*

> In the character of his *Elegy* I rejoice to concur with the common reader; for by the common sense of readers uncorrupted with literary prejudices, after all the refinements of subtilty and the dogmatism of learning, must be finally

decided all claim to poetical honours. The *Church-yard* abounds with images which find a mirrour in every mind, and with sentiments to which every bosom returns an echo. The four stanzas beginning "Yet even these bones" are to me original: I have never seen the notions in any other place; yet he that reads them here persuades himself that he has always felt them. Had Gray written often thus it had been vain to blame, and useless to praise him.[12]

The passage is extremely interesting, not only for its explicit observations but for its implicit concerns as well. Almost as if he were anticipating and diagnosing the arguments of future critics (who do not seem to have been aware of this, however), Johnson suggests that although certain of the "notions" expressed in the *Elegy* are original to the poem, they strike such a powerful chord that the reader "persuades himself that he has always felt them." In other words, the reader will be unaware that he is reading something original and will actually tend to think the very opposite is the case. From this point of view, what we might call the *resonance* of the *Elegy*—and by extension, poetic resonance in general—is a function not of "stock responses" but of originality, a term that means both discovering something new and returning to origins. The distinction is clearly a fundamental one, both for how we evaluate the *Elegy* and for critical theory in general.

In his comments on the *Elegy*, Johnson observes that the experience of the common reader is more to be trusted than the dogmatic theories of a learned elite. This emphasis on the common reader was one of the cardinal tenets of a critic who tended to regard poetic value pragmatically, as deriving from the consensus of the reading public over the course of time.[13] And in the case of the *Elegy*, since Johnson was responding to the poem of a contemporary, his emphasis on the experience of the common reader is especially striking.

Not only do Johnson's remarks anticipate and counter, in a rather uncanny way, both the arguments of later critics and the patronizing attitude that some of them have adopted toward the *Elegy*, but they may also be read as miming an important concern of the poem itself: its castigation of the contempt of the

great and proud for those of inferior social status—as expressed,
for example, in the following well-known lines:

> Let not Ambition mock their useful toil,
> Their homely joys, and destiny obscure;
> Nor Grandeur hear with a disdainful smile,
> The short and simple annals of the poor.
>
> (29–32)

Of course, this is not to say that Johnson's common reader
should be identified with Gray's rustics but rather that the
attitudes of the two writers converge on a specific moral issue.
In prefixing a remark of a general nature to his discussion of
the *Elegy*, Johnson was foregrounding an important thematic
concern of the poem itself.

Bloom's Argument Against Johnson

The question, however, is whether Johnson was accurate
in finding the four stanzas he mentioned original. We may ask
this question with Harold Bloom, for whom the problem of
originality is, of course, a central concern. In *The Anxiety of
Influence*, the initial manifesto of the theoretical position he
began developing in the 1970s, Bloom disputed Johnson's con-
tention by pointing out that in the passage Johnson regarded as
original Gray was leaning on a number of "precursors." A close
examination of Bloom's argument will help to open up the
problem of originality, both in itself and as it pertains to Gray:

> Swift, Pope's *Odyssey*, Milton's Belial, Lucretius, Ovid, and
> Petrarch are all among Gray's precursors here, for as an im-
> mensely learned poet, Gray rarely wrote without deliberately
> relating himself to nearly every possible literary ancestor.
> Johnson was an immensely learned critic; why did he praise
> these stanzas for an originality they do not possess? A possi-
> ble answer is that Johnson's own deepest anxieties are openly
> expressed in this passage.[14]

Just as Richards reduced the *Elegy*'s resonance to "stock re-
sponses," so Bloom reduces it to the poem's "precursors" in

literary history. But since Bloom chides Johnson for allowing his anxieties to distort his judgment, we might ask why he does not explain how the precursors he mentions prevent the stanzas from being original. Indeed, if Bloom had entered into a discussion of the sources, this would not only have defeated his argument but also would have pointed up a rather telling ambiguity at the heart of his theory of poetic influence.

It should be noted, first of all, that Bloom's conception of poetic originality is entirely different from Johnson's; indeed, one could say that the two critics approach the issue at different levels. By conflating these two levels, Bloom makes it seem as if he had evidence in hand that would refute Johnson's contention, but in actuality this "evidence" is irrelevant, not only to the level at which Johnson is approaching the issue of originality but to the level at which Bloom is doing so as well. The odd thing about all of this, moreover, is that the argument Bloom employs against Johnson is antagonistic to his own theoretical position.

Johnson, we recall, had referred to the "notions" expressed by the stanzas—that is, to their ideational content. It might be said that he was concerned not so much with the issue of *poetic originality* (which is a more modern preoccupation) as with *originality of thought* manifested in poetry. However, as a theorist who is interested in the problem of poetic influence, Bloom conceives of poetic originality as being specifically mediated by the poetic tradition of a given language. That, of course, is the reason he has proven to be one of the more interesting literary theorists of recent years. Consequently, in his view (and it is interesting that Bloom makes this crucial assertion in the context of his argument against Johnson, in a passage I shall quote in a moment), poetic originality is a phenomenon that can be equated with *individuality of tone.* What Bloom means by individuality of tone is the *intangible* quality that permeates a poet's entire work, giving it its own peculiar resonance and setting it apart from the work of other poets—the poet's *signature,* as it were. In other words, where Johnson had approached the issue of originality from the standpoint of content, in Bloom's formulation the dimension of style is salient. And, as will become clear when we examine the stanzas ourselves, the "sources" to which Bloom alludes are linked to the *Elegy* mainly in terms of the stylistic axis of the poem's style-content dialectic.

Now, it could be argued that since style and content are ultimately inseparable (for what is style?), the evidence that Bloom cites would not necessarily be invalid, even though it is geared to his own conception of originality rather than to Johnson's. But the problem with Bloom's formulation is that precisely *because* style and content are inseparable, it would be impossible to argue that a poet lacked individuality of tone solely on the basis of verbal or syntactical echoes, even if those echoes constitute what critical theory would now term the "traces of intertextual relationships." Because individuality of tone is an intangible quality, it cannot be denied solely on the basis of such echoes or traces; for if the poet is an original one in this sense, then his verbal "borrowings" (the term is not necessarily accurate) are a subsumed aspect of his style, and if he is not original in this sense, then even if he were to invent a new language, it would not answer the charge.

A simpler way of saying this, perhaps, is that if Bloom had been consistent with his own theoretical premises in his argument against Johnson, he would have asserted that the *Elegy* is a poem that lacks individuality of tone. But such an assertion would have exposed the weakness of Bloom's position, for the one aspect of the *Elegy* that has never been questioned is its *resonance.* And what is resonance but individuality of tone?

Immediately after the passage quoted above, Bloom expresses his own anxiety at having confused originality of *thought* with *poetic* originality by attempting to enlist Johnson in his attack on Gray:

> Johnson, who hated Gray's style, understood that in Gray's poetry the anxiety of style and the anxiety of influence had become indistinguishable, yet he forgave Gray for the one passage where Gray universalized the anxiety of self-preservation into a more general pathos. Writing on his poor friend, Collins, Johnson has Gray in mind when he observes: "He affected the obsolete when it was not worthy of revival; and he puts his words out of the common order, seeming to think,

with some later candidates to fame, that not to write prose
is certainly to write poetry." Johnson seems to have so com-
pounded the burden of originality and the problem of style,
that he could denounce style he judged vicious, and mean by
the denunciation that no fresh matter was offered. So, despite
seeming our opposite, when we neglect content and search
for individuality of tone in a new poet, Johnson is very much
our ancestor.[15]

Whether or not Johnson had Gray in mind in his remarks on
Collins, Bloom's argument is specious for several reasons. First
of all, when Johnson criticized poetry that "affected the obso-
lete," as he sometimes did, he was only tangentially concerned
with the issue of originality; he was much more disturbed—as
his famous discussion of *Lycidas* shows—by what he regarded
as the insincerity and facticity of such poetry.[16] Be that as it may,
while Johnson disliked Gray's style in most of his poetry, he ex-
plicitly made an exception of the *Elegy!*

Of course, there is no denying that Gray's poetry is replete
with allusions and echoes, but this, in itself, is no argument
against its being original, either in Bloom's sense or in Johnson's.
The fact that *all* poetic texts bear traces of earlier texts might be
used as an argument against the concept of poetic originality in
general, but in this case the argument would apply to all poets,
not only to those whose relationship to the tradition is as highly
mediated as Gray's. To be sure, in some moods Bloom will argue
that "there are *no* texts but only relationships *between* texts,"[17]
but he maintains an ambivalent attitude toward this extreme
deconstructionist (not to say, reductionist) tendency because, as
a general rule, he does not wish to negate the existence of the
individual subject, whether it be the poet or the poem.

Indeed, the peculiar thing about Bloom's argument, as I pre-
viously suggested, is that it is antagonistic to his own theory.
That the traces of a poet's "precursors" in his poetry do not
necessarily militate against the originality of that poetry has
nowhere been argued more forcefully than in Bloom's writings
on poetic influence. This may not always be apparent because
Bloom's master concept is *poetic strength* rather than original-
ity; his is a gnostic rather than a noetic theory of influence. But
in practice it would be impossible to disengage the two concepts

from each other because poetic strength, as Bloom employs the notion, is the establishment of poetic priority in relation to the tradition as a whole. Indeed, since in Bloom's view, poets achieve poetic strength by wrestling with their precursors, the fact that traces of these precursors may be found in "strong poems" poses even less of a threat to his theory than it would to one that stressed originality more overtly. For within the terms of Bloom's theory, the issue of poetic strength hinges not on whether traces can be discerned in a particular poem, but rather on whether the poem *subsumes* (or, in Bloom's lexicon, "transumes") its precursor texts or whether it is *consumed* by them.[18]

Are Gray's stanzas "consumed" (for this is the real question) by the precursors Bloom mentions? There is no scientific way of deciding, but we can examine the sources themselves by turning to Roger Lonsdale's annotated edition of Gray's poetry, which Bloom himself seems to have consulted. First, here are the stanzas:

> Yet ev'n these bones from insult to protect
> Some frail memorial still erected nigh,
> With uncouth rhimes and shapeless sculpture deck'd,
> Implores the passing tribute of a sigh.
>
> Their name, their years, spelt by th'unletter'd muse,
> The place of fame and elegy supply:
> And many a holy text around she strews,
> That teach the rustic moralist to die.
>
> For who to dumb Forgetfulness a prey,
> This pleasing anxious being e'er resigned,
> Left the warm precincts of the chearful day,
> Nor cast one longing ling'ring look behind?
>
> On some fond breast the parting soul relies,
> Some pious drops the closing eye requires;
> Ev'n from the tomb the voice of Nature cries,
> Ev'n in our Ashes live their wonted Fires.
>
> (77–92)

There are a number of general observations that can be made about the "sources" mentioned by Bloom and cited by Lonsdale (but "sources" is a misleading term in this context). First of all, one of the sources is in prose and three are in other languages, so clearly those four could have no bearing on the question of individuality of tone and hence on the issue of originality at the level at which Bloom is confronting it. Second, none of the sources has any real bearing on the "notions" expressed by the stanzas—that is, on the actual tenor of Gray's thought. The passage from Swift cited by Lonsdale, which happens to be in prose, is somewhat more closely connected than the others to the insights Gray is developing, but it is very obvious that Gray's perspective is diametrically opposed to Swift's in this case. Finally, with the exception of the Swift, the sources are connected to the *Elegy* only by way of phrasal echoes or borrowed metaphors that do not impinge on the poem's tone but are easily incorporated by Gray; in the case of the passages from Lucretius, Ovid, and Petrarch, of course, the "echoes" and metaphors are further distanced by the linguistic divide.

From the standpoint of Bloom's theoretical premises, the two sources from the English poetic tradition that Lonsdale cites are the most interesting items to consider. In Pope's *Odyssey* (11.89–90), Elpenor tells Odysseus, who has descended into the Underworld: "The tribute of a tear is all I crave, / And the possession of a quiet grave." Lonsdale relates these lines to line 80 of the *Elegy:* "Implores the passing tribute of a sigh." And in *Paradise Lost* (2.146–51), we have Belial's famous question, which the editor relates to the stanza beginning "For who to dumb Forgetfulness a prey":

> for who would lose,
> Though full of pain, this intellectual being,
> Those thoughts that wander through Eternity,
> To perish rather, swallowed up and lost,
> In the wide womb of uncreated night
> Devoid of sense and motion?

It would be easy to say merely that although these two passages have some connection to the general problem of death and annihilation that Gray is confronting in the *Elegy*, they obviously are remote from the tenor of Gray's thought. Very few readers would have picked up the echo from Pope's *Odyssey*.

More, perhaps, would have heard the echo from Milton in Gray's stanza because of the resonance of Belial's rhetorical question; but even so, Gray's stanza is obviously not "consumed" by Milton.

But that is not the primary point that needs to be made in regard to the two passages. On the contrary, whether or not Gray was aware of echoing them, the existence of the echoes indicates that there *is* an important connection between the *Elegy* and the passages from Pope and Milton. It would take a close reading of the poem to bring this connection to light, but in considering why Gray should be echoing two such remote texts, one begins to get at least a glimpse of the nature of his originality.

In the passages from Pope's *Odyssey* and *Paradise Lost*, the confrontation with death and annihilation occurs in an *epic* context: the evocation of the sublime is in both cases staged in terms of heroic action. In the four stanzas from the *Elegy*, however, as in the poem as a whole, the context is very far from being a heroic one; the scene is a country churchyard and the poet is meditating on the graves of anonymous rustics. Yet in the *Elegy*, as I shall argue in chapter 3, the heroic is not irrelevant but is retained from an antithetical perspective, for part of what is "mourned" in the poem is the loss of the heroic. It is ultimately for this reason that traces from the epic tradition can be discerned in the four stanzas, as elsewhere in the poem.[19] Far from militating against Gray's originality, these traces offer a glimpse of what Bloom would call the *clinamen*, the creative swerve that enables strong poems to carve out a metaphysical space for themselves.[20]

Although it is in prose, the passage from Swift that Lonsdale cites deserves to be considered because here is at least a convergence of context and subject matter. In "Thoughts on Various Subjects" (1735), Swift writes: "There is in most people a reluctance and unwillingness to be forgotten. We observe even among the vulgar, how fond they are to have an inscription over their grave. It requires but little philosophy to discover and observe that there is no intrinsic value in all this; however, if it be founded in our nature, as an incitement to virtue, it ought not to be ridiculed."

If Gray was influenced by the notions expressed in this passage, which is not very likely, the influence would obviously have been antithetical. And once again, the connection between the two writers is an indication of Gray's originality—as well as an indication of a more general shift in sensibility that seems to have occurred around the middle of the eighteenth century. Nowhere is the plight of the poor rendered with greater empathy and power than in Swift's "Modest Proposal," but neither Swift nor any of the other Augustans would have found any "intrinsic value" in the fact that the "vulgar" should also desire to be remembered after death. This is precisely the attitude Gray is reacting against in the *Elegy*, as in the lines previously quoted:

> Let not Ambition mock their useful toil,
> Their homely joys, and destiny obscure;
> Nor Grandeur hear with a disdainful smile,
> The short and simple annals of the poor!
>
> (29–32)

The question remains as to whether any positive evidence can be mustered to corroborate Johnson's insight that the four stanzas are original. Obviously, we will never know what Johnson had in mind, and in any event I would argue that the poem's originality consists not in any particular detail but rather in Gray's total conception. But as a point of departure, let us recall the second of the four stanzas that Johnson had singled out:

> Their name, their years, spelt by th'unletter'd muse,
> The place of fame and elegy supply:
> And many a holy text around she strews,
> That teach the rustic moralist to die.
>
> (81–84)

The word "elegy" has a tremendously ironic resonance in this context: it seems to leap off the page, and for an extremely interesting reason. First of all, what these lines are conveying, more or less explicitly, is that the names and years on the tombstones *take the place* of a fuller memorial to the individual. But precisely because the inscriptions are *merely nominal*, they only serve, ironically, to emphasize, first, the *anonymity* of those buried in the country churchyard and, second, the contrast between those who are lost to history and those whose *presence* is symbolically maintained by fame and elegy. Because they are lost to history, moreover, those who lie buried in the country churchyard cannot—*as individuals*—be the subjects for an elegy. And yet they are the subject of Gray's *Elegy*, which thereby redefines its own tradition at the same time that it expresses, self-reflexively, its awareness of the loss of the elegiac occasion. Thus, the primary subject of the *Elegy* is not the loss of the particular individual through death but, in an ironic reversal, the loss, for the majority of humanity, of the potential for individuation in life. This theme is obviously of major significance, yet it does not emerge prior to the *Elegy*, and in the stanza quoted above we have at least a glimpse of the creative process through which it emerged.

That Gray himself was conscious of the dialectical ironies he was charting is corroborated by the fact that in its initial version neither the title of the poem nor the stanza we have been discussing contained the word "elegy." In the Eton Manuscript (see appendix B), the poem was entitled "Stanza's Wrote In a Country Church-Yard," and in the version that has come to be known as the *Stanza's*, Gray had originally written: "The Place of Fame, & *Epitaph* supply" (my italics). In the process by which the *Stanza's* became the *Elegy*, the poetics of loss was extended to encompass what I have termed the "problem of history." This reshaping of traditional thematic and generic material has profound ramifications for the history of English poetry.

Chapter 2

Structure and Meaning: The Formal Problem of Interpretation

T HE NOTION that the *Elegy* is lacking in originality and that its popularity can be attributed to extrapoetic factors has naturally had a strong impact on how the poem has been interpreted. It is not so much that "the most popular poem in the English language has received curiously little attention," as F. W. Bateson remarked in 1950,[1] as that the approach to the poem has been mainly confined to a relatively narrow formal problem. Until recently the formalist approach was the prevailing one in Anglo-American criticism, of course; and from the standpoint of that general method, it is quite true, as Frank Brady asserts, that "few poems have been interpreted in such widely divergent ways" as the *Elegy.*[2] Indeed, in some respects the *Elegy* served as the locus classicus for a range of theoretical issues that were among the most salient to the New Criticism; as a result, much of the interpretive literature is interesting not only for the light it sheds on the poem but in relation to larger critical issues. Yet the tendency of much of this literature to treat the poem as if it were a kind of elaborate puzzle may not, in the end, have increased our appreciation of its richness or of its importance to the tradition in very large measure.

In the manner in which it both continues and departs from nineteenth-century assumptions, the modern approach to the *Elegy* presents something of a paradox. During the nineteenth century, as Lonsdale observes, discussion of the *Elegy* "tended to be pre-occupied with such matters as Gray's sources, the location of the churchyard and Gray's relationship to the 'Age of Reason', and to attempt little more critically than general appreciation of Gray's eloquence along the lines of Johnson's tribute."[3] There were exceptions, of course, but most critics during the period tended to take the poem's meaning for granted. Thus, commenting on the fact that Wordsworth professed to find it unintelligible, Hazlitt dryly remarked: "It has, however, been understood."[4]

From this perspective, Richards's notion that the *Elegy* is built upon a foundation of stock responses is merely a negative extension of the nineteenth-century view. But here is where the modern situation poses additional complexities. For at the same time that critics have continued for the most part to disregard what the *Elegy* is *saying*—that is, to disregard its philosophical content and thematic development—early in the century they began to focus their attention on the poem's *structure* and on what might be called its *surface meaning,* which had come to seem problematic. The contradiction between these two attitudes exemplifies the artificial separation of poetic surface from poetic depth that Paul de Man, in his seminal essay "Form and Intent in the American New Criticism," described as a characteristic of the formalist approach generally. As a result of that separation, de Man suggests, the temporal dimension of the poem, its "struggle with meaning," is lost, and the question of form, which "is never anything but a process on the way to its completion," becomes reified as a static entity.[5] Although the various attempts to resolve the formal problem posed by the *Elegy* have resulted in interpretations that are sometimes diametrically opposed to one another, these attempts have all been hampered by the separation of surface from depth noted by de Man. In analyzing them, I shall therefore be obliged to come to terms with some of the theoretical consequences of formalist criticism generally.

The present chapter does not, however, undertake to resolve the formal problem posed by the poem but only to present a critical overview of the various attempts that have been made to resolve it. Although in one sense the assumption that the poem poses a formal problem of interpretation is a consequence

of the artificial separation of surface from depth noted by de
Man, that problem—even considered in itself—cannot be re-
solved as long as the separation is maintained. What is required
is an analysis of the poem's thematic development, and this will
be attempted in chapter 3.

The Formal Problem of Interpretation
(From a Formalist Standpoint)

The formal problem posed by the *Elegy* hinges on certain
ambiguities in the text of the standard version of the poem (see
appendix A). These ambiguities, it is important to note from the
outset, are less prominent—or at least have been *conceived* as
less prominent—in the draft of the poem contained in the Eton
Manuscript (appendix B), to which I alluded at the end of chapter
1. That "version" of the poem (if indeed Gray ever considered
it as such) is generally referred to as the *Stanza's*. The Eton
Manuscript is entitled "Stanza's Wrote In a Country Church-
Yard," but the manuscript also contains most of the revisions
that Gray eventually incorporated in the final text of the *Elegy*.

The basic problem posed by the standard version centers on
Gray's use of pronouns. The first-person singular appears for the
first and last time in stanza 1:

> The Curfew tolls the knell of parting day,
> The lowing herd wind slowly o'er the lea,
> The plowman homeward winds his weary way,
> And leaves the world to darkness and to me.

Through the next twenty-two stanzas the poem is written en-
tirely in the third person; however, in lines 93–94 we have the
following apostrophe:

> For thee, who mindful of th'unhonour'd Dead
> Dost in these lines their artless tale relate.

In the context of the final thirty-two lines of the *Elegy* (97–128),
the ambiguous references of lines 93–94 pose a problem for

interpretation of the poem as a whole, and thus these lines
provide the crux of the formal problem.

In the Eton Manuscript there are four stanzas following line
72 that Gray eventually rejected, although he made use of some
of the material from these stanzas for the standard version. For
reasons that have to do with both the logic of the text itself and
the physical state of the manuscript, it is plausible to assume
that Gray originally intended these stanzas to form the poem's
conclusion.[6]

> The thoughtless World to Majesty may bow
> Exalt the brave, & idolize Success
> But more to Innocence their Safety owe
> Than Power & Genius e'er conspired to bless
>
> And thou, who mindful of the unhonour'd Dead
> Dost in these Notes thy [corr. to their] artless Tale relate
> By Night & lonely Contemplation led
> To linger in the gloomy walks of Fate
>
> Hark how the sacred Calm that broods around
> Bids ev'ry fierce tumultuous Passion cease
> In still small Accents whisp'ring from the Ground
> A grateful Earnest of eternal Peace
>
> No more with Reason & thyself at Strife;
> Give anxious Cares & endless Wishes room
> But thro' the cool sequester'd Vale of Life
> Pursue the silent Tenour of thy Doom.

If Gray had concluded the poem with these stanzas (and there
are some critics who wish that he had), it would have been
natural to link the references in the fifth and sixth lines above
to the poet (or, more properly in formalist terms, the narrator)
and his poem (or, again, the narrator's utterance). But in the
context of the standard version, the pronominal references of
lines 93–94 are more tenuous and, from an aesthetic point of
view, more problematic. For in the process of revising and ex-
panding the poem, Gray made the following changes: he changed
the grammar of the reference in line 93 to the accusative case
("And thou" becoming "For thee"); introduced a hypothetical

"kindred Spirit" (line 96), who is represented conditionally as inquiring after the fate of the "thee," and a hypothetical "hoary-headed Swain" (line 97), who is represented as informing the "kindred Spirit" of this fate in lines 98–116 (which are set off in quotation marks); and finally, of course, created the "Epitaph" to the "Youth to Fortune and to Fame unknown" (lines 117–28), who is probably (but not necessarily) associated with the "thee" of line 93. Thus, Gray's revision incorporates certain at least quasi-dramatic elements (some commentators, indeed, have conjured an entire dramatis personae, complete with settings and props) that render whatever "natural" assumptions we might otherwise have entertained in regard to the references—and hence the poem's structure and meaning—problematic.

This, then, is the crux of the formal problem posed by the *Elegy*—at least from the formalist perspective in terms of which that problem has generally been presented. The perspective has, of course, conditioned the nature of the critical response to the poem, and, as a result, certain underlying assumptions have gone unexamined. For example, virtually all of the commentators have agreed that whereas the pronouns in lines 93–94 of the *Elegy* are problematic, the corresponding ones in the *Stanza's* clearly refer to Gray himself (or to the "narrator," in formalist terms), and it is on that basis that the *Stanza's* have so frequently been foregrounded and contrasted to the *Elegy* in the critical discussion—sometimes, indeed, as if they constituted a separate and even superior poem. From a more structuralist-oriented point of view, however, the status of pronominal "shifters" is always somewhat open to question, and since, in the *Stanza's* as well as in the *Elegy*, the pronouns are distanced by the second person, it could be argued that their referentiality is problematic already in the earlier version. This, of course, would vitiate the force of the contrast between the two versions. The distinction we are entertaining would not seem to be of paramount importance at this stage, for our concern is with the *Elegy*, after all, and both formalism and structuralism (however they are ultimately defined) would agree that in the *Elegy*, at any rate, the ambiguities pose a problem. But as will later become clear, the overly delineated contrast that has habitually been drawn between the *Stanza's* and the *Elegy* is indicative of a conflict within formalism itself—and one, moreover, that has had a determining impact on how the *Elegy* has been interpreted.

In its purely theoretical aspect, the formal problem posed by the *Elegy* raises a number of issues that we shall have to confront. But the reason that the formal problem has assumed such prominence in the critical discussion has less to do with the purely theoretical issues it raises than with the dissatisfaction with the standard version that some critics have felt since early in the century. That dissatisfaction fueled the modern critical debate and, therefore, before turning to the larger theoretical issues involved, we should examine how the debate unfolded.

Shepard's Biographical Hypothesis

The modern controversy over the *Elegy* was initiated by Odell Shepard in 1923.[7] Like several other critics after him, Shepard felt that the *Elegy* is inferior to the *Stanza's* in regard to structure and tone, but at the same time he found himself confronted with an interpretive dilemma. On the one hand, he argued, in "the only easy and natural reading" of the *Elegy*, the "Youth to Fortune and to Fame unknown" of the "Epitaph" must stand for Gray himself (349); on the other hand, with this interpretation "the tone of the entire second part . . . is that of the sentimental and lachrymose self-pity which most boys put behind them in the early part of adolescence" (350). Furthermore, Shepard found it hard to believe that so reticent a man as Gray would have indulged in self-revelation: "For a man to memorialize his own sincerity and generosity would be less a mark of . . . passion than of execrable bad taste. Here, then, lies our problem—strong evidence in the text of the *Elegy* that Gray has done a thing which it seems highly improbable that such a man could have done. One feels like defending Gray against himself" (351).

Shepard's remarks are typical of the reaction against Romanticism of the period in which they were written, and from our present vantage point they may strike us as somewhat ludicrous. But if it were really necessary to identify the Youth of the "Epitaph" with Gray himself, as in Shepard's "only easy and natural reading," then one could easily agree that some principle of taste had been violated. Of course, everything in the *Elegy* cries out against so slavish an interpretation of the text; and yet, because Shepard is caught on the horns of a dilemma, his reaction is as extreme as it is. For while he denounces the possibility that Gray is indulging in self-revelation, he retains the naive assumption that the poet's "I" is an unmediated extension of his actual presence. In other words, he is trapped within a conception of what constitutes poetic language that is at odds with his social and ideological assumptions. For this reason we can discern in his remarks the seeds of what will later emerge as the formalist tendency to view the "I" in terms of a persona or invented narrator. This latter tendency, however (and as we shall see, it has problems of its own), does not yet exist as an alternative for Shepard, and thus the dilemma he confronts remains intractable in strictly formal terms.

Those critics who would deny that the *Elegy* is a coherent work of art have generally done so on the basis of Shepard's "only easy and natural reading," but as Shepard himself finds this reading contradicted by his impression of Gray the man, he boldly sets out to "defend Gray against himself." Unfortunately, the task of defending Gray's character can only be accomplished at the expense of pointing out his deficiencies as a poet, for since the text itself is self-revelatory, it is necessary to show that Gray's *intentions* were otherwise. Accordingly, Shepard goes in search of "those flaws of structure which occur when a poet lays a manuscript aside for so long that he forgets his original mood or intention, or when he tries to weld into one piece separate scraps of work originally composed with no single whole in mind" (352). What he comes up with, essentially, is that there are two "seams" in the *Elegy:* one between the twenty-third and twenty-fourth stanzas (i.e., immediately before the crucial pronominal ambiguities we noted earlier) and one between the "Epitaph" and the rest of the poem (352). Shepard's argument is merely circular: it is intended to show that the *Stanza's* constitute a poem that is "better rounded off than the *Elegy* of the standard text" (358), but it merely asserts that the seams, in and of themselves, are indicative of flaws of structure. The question is whether these seams (if one wants to refer to them as such) are justified by the poem as a whole. To deal with this question adequately, one would have to examine the *Elegy* from the standpoint of its thematic development, but as Shepard's analysis is restricted to the poem's surface—where the concept of structure is merely a static abstraction—his assertion carries no force.

Be that as it may, Shepard's attempt to explain the flaws of structure he has adduced then gives rise to the central hypothesis informing his article. What Shepard proposes, in essence, is that the "Epitaph" was originally written as a separate poem commemorating Gray's friend Richard West, who died in June 1742. Thus, according to Shepard's conjecture (for which, as he admits, there is not the slightest shred of evidence), there would have been a period during which Gray had two different pieces of work on his table—the poem on West and the *Stanza's*. However:

> In going over his papers, as we know that he did at Walpole's suggestion in 1747, Gray would see that although these two poems were concerned with two different persons they dealt with fairly similar subjects and were in the same stanza and mood. Now the evidence of patching that we have seen in the 24th stanza and the established fact that an earlier conclusion of the *Elegy* was abandoned to make way for another totally different conclusion make it seem a plausible suggestion that Gray set to work to join these two poems, that all of the present *Elegy* from the 19th stanza to the Epitaph is really a sort of bridge thrown between two pre-existing piers. In this suggestion we have a considerable extension of our original hypothesis [i.e., that the "Epitaph" was originally a separate poem commemorating West]. It involves the supposition that Gray fused together not only two poems but two personalities. (360)

Shepard presents the *Elegy* as a hopelessly inept performance, but it is difficult to imagine that any poet, let alone one so committed to problems of craft as Gray obviously was, could be so obtuse as to fail to recognize—for several years—the connections between two compositions dealing with similar subjects and in the same stanza and mood. However, although Shepard maintains that the two pieces were initially unconnected, he then proceeds to suggest that both were probably begun during the summer of 1742 and that, consequently, the *Stanza's* may also "be associated in some way with West's death" (362). In other words, we are asked to believe that the "seams" in the *Elegy* result from the fusion of two unconnected poems but that these poems (which are in the same stanza and mood) were begun around the same time and were both associated with the death of West!

The question of when the *Elegy* was begun has never been settled and has been a much debated issue among scholars.[8] Shepard's assumption that it was begun in 1742 is based entirely on the testimony of William Mason, Gray's friend and executor. We have no way of knowing whether Mason had firsthand knowledge of the originating circumstances of the *Elegy;* however, the case for dating the poem from 1742 is not strong, and on the basis of the available evidence the likelihood is greater that the poem was begun several years later.[9] Moreover, as Herbert W. Starr pointed out in a critique of Shepard's article, there is nothing in Gray's correspondence or in the manuscript record to suggest that the "Epitaph" ever existed as a separate poem. Starr observes that if it had originally been conceived as a separate poem commemorating West or if it was intended to refer to West in the context of the completed *Elegy,* it is strange that Gray did not acknowledge this to Horace Walpole, who, after all, had also been an intimate friend of West.[10]

But to argue on the basis of the biographical record, as Shepard's opponents have done, is really to miss the point. Since the biographical record is inconclusive, the possibility argued by Shepard that Gray had personal reasons for suppressing the West connection cannot be ruled out.[11] And there is no reason *not* to assume that West would have entered into Gray's feelings during the composition of the *Elegy*. He was Gray's closest friend, after all, and a poet of promise who died at the age of 25 before his promise could be fulfilled. Moreover, as Shepard hastens to point out (though this does not necessarily prove his hypothesis), Gray's "Youth to Fortune and to Fame unknown" echoes a line from West's *Monody on Queen Caroline,* in which West had referred to himself as "A muse as yet unheeded and unknown" (370). But the issue is not whether Shepard's hypothesis in regard to the originating circumstances of the *Elegy* is plausible but whether it is *valid* as far as interpretation of the poem is concerned. In order to interpret the Youth as a reference to West, who is never, of course, named in the poem, we would have to transfer the locus of meaning from the text itself to the poet's hidden consciousness. Moreover, the *intentional fallacy* appears in a particularly glaring light in Shepard's hypothesis, for the intentions it ascribes to Gray are actually in direct contradiction to the text itself. If the Youth of the "Epitaph" is identified with Richard West (or with anyone else, for that matter), then clearly he is no longer *unknown*. It is also possible, however (and this is the direction my own reading of the poem will take), that Gray's intentions are *literally* embodied in the figure of the "Youth to Fortune and to Fame unknown" and that the latter is not a person but, precisely, a *figure*.

Shepard's hypothesis is no longer taken seriously, but it should be noted that the hypothesis has important implications for how we conceive of the poem generically and for how we place it in the tradition. For example, Shepard remarks that the identification of the Youth of the "Epitaph" with Richard West "enables us to place Gray's poem definitely among the elegies, such as *Lycidas* and *Thyrsis,* which mingle general reflection with the grief of personal bereavement" (372). In other words, the *Elegy* should be classified as a pastoral elegy on the model of *Lycidas* (not that the latter is noted for "the grief of personal bereavement"). But the notion that the *Elegy* was modeled on *Lycidas* was a received idea long before Shepard wrote his article, and it may have predetermined his hypothesis in regard to the poem's genesis. Interestingly, most critics have concluded that the *Elegy* was modeled on *Lycidas*, including those whose approach to the formal problem is diametrically opposed to Shepard's. Shepard, of course, does not elaborate on the nature of the relationship between *Lycidas* and the *Elegy*, but in order to have done so, he would have had to probe the thematic development of Gray's poem. For the same reason, my own discussion of this issue must be postponed until chapter 3—where I shall argue that the *Elegy* constitutes a radical departure not only from *Lycidas* but from the pastoral tradition generally.

The Formalist Strategy of Depersonalization

Shepard's article makes it clear that the formal problem posed by the *Elegy* is inextricably bound up with the question of taste and hence with ideological considerations. Indeed, the formal problem comes into focus only as a result of Shepard's perception that some principle of decorum is violated by the "only easy and natural reading" of the poem. Shepard's reaction is obviously a defensive one—partly against his own "Romantic" conception of poetic expression, according to which the poet's "I" is an unmediated extension of his actual presence; but this reaction is not entirely idiosyncratic, for in the ensuing debate over the *Elegy* the problem of decorum will be a constant against which the various attempts to resolve the formal issues posed by the poem will be played out.

From this perspective, it stands to reason that the attempt to arrive at a nonproblematic reading of the *Elegy* would have adopted the strategy of depersonalizing the poem and, indeed, such was the case. The hypostatization of a narrator or persona as a mediating link between the poet and the poem—not only for overtly dramatic poems, such as Browning's monologues, but even for what we loosely refer to as "lyric" poems as well—was, of course, a cornerstone of the New Criticism, and despite the attempt of contemporary critical theory to move beyond formalism, it continues to play a dominant role in practical criticism. Thus, a strategy aimed at depersonalizing the *Elegy*, particularly in light of Shepard's ambivalent reading, would have been sanctioned by the climate of opinion in which the New Criticism arose. But perhaps it is equally true that the New Criticism was itself occasioned by the inability of the older "Romantic" or biographical criticism to resolve the kinds of issues posed by the *Elegy.*

On the face of the matter, it would seem that the problem of decorum foregrounded by Shepard's reading simply vanishes as soon as a dramatic conception of the narrator is postulated, for in this case it is no longer the poet who is identified with the Youth of the "Epitaph" but rather a "speaker" who is the poet's invention. Seizing on this possibility, R. S. Crane argued as follows:

> The *Elegy* is an imitative lyric of moral choice . . . representing a situation in which a virtuous, sensitive, and ambitious young man of undistinguished birth confronts the possibility of his death while still to "Fortune and to Fame unknown."[12]

The problem is more complicated than this, however. For as Yvor Winters subsequently observed:

> If we try to rescue the youth to Fortune and to Fame unknown by saying with Professor R. S. Crane that the poem is a dramatic monologue spoken by an imagined youth of the place and period, we shall have to imagine a local rustic who could have written a long poem in this language, or we shall have to imagine a youth all but indistinguishable from Thomas Gray, who (with very bad taste) inserted himself into the conclusion of a poem about people very different from himself.[13]

As Winters suggests, Crane's reading leads either to an absurd situation or to one in which the problem of decorum is merely postponed. The notion that the *Elegy,* with its contrasting reflections on the rich and the poor, could be spoken by a local rustic is, of course, absurd. Crane was probably arguing the second of Winters's alternatives, according to which the narrator would belong to the same social class as the poet. But in this case, either the problem of decorum is displaced onto the narrator, if one conceives of him primarily as the *speaker* of the poem, or it falls back upon the poet, if one conceives of the narrator as a *character* in an invented drama. For if one conceives of the narrator only as the speaker, then he is a mere redundancy, and if one conceives of him as a character, then one has to question why the poet would have conflated a character capable of sophisticated reflections with the illiterate peasants of his poem. But in any event—and one could argue that this must often be the case when a dramatic structure is artificially imposed on a lyric poem—it is apparent that the mere hypostatization of a narrator does not resolve the problem.

Ellis's "Stonecutter" Interpretation

A more thoroughgoing and elaborate attempt to resolve the formal problem in dramatic terms was made by Frank Ellis in an article entitled "Gray's *Elegy:* The Biographical Problem in Literary Criticism."[14] Ellis's polemical thrust in this article was directed against the "biographical fallacy"—the notion that a poem can be read as an autobiographical document. At the outset Ellis indicates that the *Elegy* was "chosen as the vehicle for this argument because it has long been censured for its intrusive biographical detail" and because "adverse criticism of a purely formal nature, namely that the poem lacks a coherent structure, can so clearly be seen to rest on the assumption that the poem is excessively autobiographical" (971). However, Ellis maintains a somewhat ambivalent attitude toward the biographical problem; for although he denies that the poet's experience can be reconstructed from his poem, which is what Shepard had attempted to do, he nevertheless believes that "the reconstruction of the poet's experience from diaries, letters, accounts of friends, and public records, may illuminate his poetry" (971). The latter premise, seems, on the surface, to be a more reasonable one than the former, but in practice the two may lead to identical results, and Ellis's attempt to elucidate Gray's biography is not really more convincing than Shepard's had been. However, it should be noted that whereas Shepard's interpretation had been entirely dependent on his biographical hypothesis,

Ellis's may be considered on its own merits, in spite of the fact that he links it to biographical speculations of his own. Ellis's theory about the poem's origins must be taken into account, however, for on the basis of this theory he develops certain insights into the poem's thematic concerns that are both interesting in themselves and connected to his attempt to resolve the formal problem.

One of the more flagrant examples of the biographical fallacy in criticism of the *Elegy* is the obviously absurd notion that Gray was actually in a country churchyard when he wrote the poem. This idea was originally put forward in an article published in 1783 that purported to be a continuation of Johnson's criticism but was eventually traced to John Young, a professor of Glasgow University (Ellis, 991). The reason Ellis mentions this theory, however, is to suggest that, on the contrary, Gray was in London when he began the *Elegy* and that the poem was conceived in the summer of 1746 under the impact of the trial of the Scottish lords implicated in the Jacobite rebellion of 1745.[15] Ellis's argument is extremely tenuous, to say the least. Although Gray's correspondence indicates that he was impressed by the pageantry and solemnity of the trial and although the *Elegy* may have been begun during this period, there is nothing to prove that it originated under the impact of the trial. Moreover, even if we assume that Ellis is correct, his attempt to read the poem in light of the trial, by combining phrases from Gray's correspondence and from accounts of the trial with phrases from the *Elegy*, is completely lacking in specificity and hence unconvincing. The philosophical reflections that Gray develops in the *Elegy* are much too generalized to be linked to a single experience, and there is no reason why Gray could not have developed his perspective on ambition prior to the trial, since it is clearly consonant with Christian ethics.

Ellis's biographical speculations are thus of little importance in themselves, but, interestingly, they enable him to focus on the poem's fame-anonymity dialectic—a thematic concern that is certainly crucial to the *Elegy*, as will become apparent in Chapter 3. In the context of his overall interpretation, however,

Ellis's treatment of this theme is beset with an additional series of methodological difficulties. Having hypostatized an experiential point of origin for the poem, he then proceeds to treat what is legitimately a *thematic* concern as if it were a *structural* principle organizing the entire poem—a principle, moreover, whose existence would enable us (1) to elucidate the process by which the *Stanza's* became the *Elegy* and (2) to resolve the ambiguities posed by the standard version. Ellis's analysis is extremely ingenious, as we shall see, but in this analysis, a construct pertaining to the thematic level is displaced and accommodated to a genetic hypothesis, on the one hand, and an overt structural conception, on the other. These accommodations coincide, respectively, with the *biographical fallacy* (although Ellis warns against it) and with what might be termed the *dramatic fallacy*, which is related to the biographical fallacy by antithesis. Where the biographical fallacy treats the poem as an autobiographical document, the dramatic fallacy not only hypostatizes a "speaker" but turns this construct into an independent character. The two fallacies are antithetically related, for in both, meaning is displaced from the poem to an actual speaking presence.

Ellis's ambivalent relationship to the biographical problem manifests itself, first of all, in the overly delineated contrast he draws between the *Stanza's* and the *Elegy*. I noted earlier that this strategy is typical of the formalist approach to the poem, but what lies behind it, we can now see, is a swing of the pendulum between the biographical and dramatic fallacies, as criticism attempts to maintain its logocentric premises. Ellis thus continues a tendency that was already present in Shepard's discussion, although his conclusions, to be sure, are diametrically opposed to Shepard's. Although he rejects the more extreme consequences of a biographical reading (e.g., the notion that Gray was actually present in the churchyard), he nevertheless asserts that the *Stanza's* "were originally an 'artless Tale' about Thomas Gray" (981) and that the four rejected stanzas from the Eton Manuscript "unequivocally identify the speaker of the poem as Thomas Gray" (980).[16] Moreover, although he suggests that "nothing else of Gray's public or private experience [besides his reading of *Lycidas*] could be inferred from the *Stanza's* in the absence of internal documents" (982), he makes copious use of such documents to interpret the *Stanza's* as a record of Gray's struggle with ambition. In other words, as far as the *Stanza's* are concerned, what we are given is a standard biographical reading in which meaning is consistently referred to its origins in Gray's life.

Although Ellis makes use of the term "speaker" in his discussion of the *Stanza's* (as in the passage quoted above), it is clear that since he identifies the speaker with Gray, this is an empty category as far as the *Stanza's* are concerned. However, by positing a speaker already in the *Stanza's*, Ellis is setting the stage for his interpretation of the *Elegy*, which is where his argument takes a radical turn. For what Ellis argues is that Gray, disturbed by the personal nature of the *Stanza's*, "depersonalized them entirely" in his revision by imposing a dramatic structure on the poem (985). Elevating the theme of anonymity to an overt structural principle, Ellis suggests that the *Elegy* "is a poem which achieves total 'anonymity' despite its subjective genesis" (986).

The crux of Ellis's argument hinges (as one might expect) on his interpretation of the problematic pronouns of lines 93–94 ("For thee, who mindful of th'unhonour'd Dead / Dost in these lines their artless tale relate"). In Ellis's view, these pronouns do not refer to the narrator and to the *Elegy* itself but rather to a "Stonecutter" and to the lines that this "rustic artist" inscribes on the tombstones of the poor.[17] Ellis infers the presence of this "Stonecutter" from stanzas 21–22, which are among those Johnson had singled out for attention. However—and this is an interesting slip—Ellis quotes these stanzas from the Eton Manuscript rather than from the *Elegy*, as he should have done:

> Yet even these Bones from Insult to protect
> Some frail Memorial still erected nigh
> With uncouth Rhimes, & shapeless Sculpture deckt
> Implores the passing Tribute of a Sigh.
>
> Their Names, their Years, spelt by th'unletter'd Muse,
> The Place of Fame, & Epitaph supply

> And many a holy Text around she strews,
> That teach the rustic Moralist to die.

Line 82 in the standard edition reads: "The place of fame and elegy supply"—not "Epitaph" as in the Eton Manuscript. But Ellis gives the latter text because it better accords with his interpretation, according to which the Stonecutter, who inscribes epitaphs on the headstones of the poor, becomes in turn the "Youth to Fortune and to Fame unknown" of the *Elegy*'s "Epitaph."

With the hypostatization of the Stonecutter as an actual presence in the poem, the rest of Ellis' dramatic scenario falls easily into place:

> But who was there among the illiterate peasantry on whom the rustic artist could rely for a similar office? Who, in short, would write the epitaph-writer's epitaph?
>
> Gray assigns this role to a literate outlander, the Spokesman of the poem, the "me" of line 4. But in order to introduce the *Epitaph* into the poem, a further dramatic complication had to be invented. Gray imagines that after the village Stonecutter is dead and buried, another melancholy wayfarer ("Some kindred Spirit") will enter the churchyard seeking to learn of the Stonecutter's fate. Still another peasant ("some hoary-headed Swain") will be able to tell the Enquirer of the irregular life of the Stonecutter and point to the *Epitaph* written by the Spokesman and now fixed over the Stonecutter's grave.
>
> (985)

Thus, in Ellis's scenario, there are four independent characters: the "Spokesman," who in one sense is "simply the vehicle of the poem" but, as the author of the "Epitaph," is also a character in his own right; the "Stonecutter," who is the Youth of the "Epitaph"; the "kindred Spirit," who is also the "friend" referred to in the "Epitaph" (line 124); and finally, the "hoary-headed Swain."

The advantage of Ellis's reading is that it resolves the pronominal ambiguities in a way that is consonant with the principle of decorum: "Shifting the reference from the Poet to the peasants and the peasant-poet fully satisfies the requirement of impersonality" (986). Unfortunately, however, as John H. Sutherland demonstrated in a critique of Ellis's interpretation, this reading simply does not hold up under scrutiny:

> It does violence to grammar and to logic to read "thee" as referring to a stonecutter who is not even mentioned in the poem—whose existence is only indirectly suggested by the abstract phrase, "th'unletter'd muse." Similarly, one must stretch common sense to the limit to make "these lines" refer to "uncouth rhimes" mentioned four stanzas before— rhymes which are described as being so short and rough that they provide nothing more than "names" and "years" instead of "fame" and "elegy."[18]

Moreover, as Sutherland points out, the Stonecutter theory accords rather poorly with the actual description of the Youth in the "Epitaph." Line 119, for example, reads: "Fair Science frown'd not on his humble birth," and this alone would suggest that the Youth cannot be identified with the illiterate peasantry. To be sure, Ellis attempts to meet this objection by reading "Science" as "native intelligence" (1003), but as Sutherland observes, Gray must have meant "knowledge gained as the result of education." The latter usage, which is the primary eighteenth-century meaning of "science," occurs frequently in Gray's writing, while the former is not recorded in the *OED*.[19]

In addition to Sutherland's objections, there is another problem that might be raised. In order to imagine the Spokesman as the author of the "Epitaph" on the Stonecutter—and Ellis asserts that the "Spokesman . . . is as much a creature of Gray's imagination as Caliban is of Shakespeare's" (991)—it is necessary to include him (as Ellis does in the passage quoted earlier) "among the illiterate peasantry." But in this case, we are asked to believe that a poem notable for its reflections on the lives of the poor could be spoken by an illiterate peasant—which is the absurd consequence that Winters had drawn from Crane's interpretation of the *Elegy* as an "imitative lyric." Ellis, to be sure, does not make very much of this aspect of his interpretation; indeed, at another point in his argument he contradicts himself by observing that "the Spokesman . . . obviously derives from a social class and milieu different from that of the 'rude' peasants whom he describes" (989). But the contradiction is endemic to Ellis's argument, for if the Spokesman belongs to a different social class, then why would the Stonecutter have relied on him "for a similar office?" Ellis wants the Spokesman to be both an actor in a dramatic scenario and "simply the vehicle of the poem," but this is impossible.

In an attempt to preserve the dramatic core of Ellis's interpretation, Morse Peckham suggested that not the Spokesman but the "friend" of line 124 of the "Epitaph" ("He gain'd from Heav'n ['twas all he wish'd] a friend") should be regarded as the author of the "Epitaph." (Ellis, as we noted, had identified the friend with the kindred Spirit of line 96.) Thus, where Ellis conceives of the Spokesman as, in effect, an actor in a dramatic scenario, Peckham views this scenario as entirely a projection of the Spokesman's imagination. He proposes that the Spokesman

> imagines the local Stonecutter-Poet whose function it is to compose epitaphs and carve them, imagines an inquirer who will ask about him [i.e., the Stonecutter] after his death sometime in the future, imagines the Swain who will be asked, imagines the epitaph that will be written for the Stonecutter, and imagines the Friend who will write it and who, perhaps, will succeed him as village epitaph-writer and carver.[20]

With Peckham's Rube Goldberg-like apparatus for interpreting the poem, it is unnecessary to conceive of the Spokesman as a peasant; on the other hand, this interpretation makes it necessary to attribute the "Epitaph" to another erstwhile poet. Of course, there is nothing in the *Elegy* to suggest that the friend of line 124 has been gifted with poetic talent, but with a Spokesman of such vivid imagination, anything is possible! And, of course, the Spokesman would himself be a product of Gray's imagination. Indeed, in Peckham's view, Gray has been so zealous in depersonalizing the poem that the real author of the *Elegy* is not Thomas Gray but the Spokesman!

> It is not Gray who wrote an elegy in Stoke Poges, but an imaginary poet invented by Gray who composes a poem in an unidentified graveyard. Gray imagines the anonymous Poet, who is the Spokesman.[21]

Of course, if Ellis's conception is vulnerable to the criticisms of Sutherland, Peckham's is all the more so. But in any event, with Peckham's interpretation we have reached a situation of infinite regress, in which the attempt to "depersonalize" the poem could lead to an indefinite number of further mediations.

The Grammatical Problem: A Parenthesis

Sutherland was obviously concerned to refute Ellis's interpretation, but—and this is interesting in regard to the milieu in which both critics were working—he nevertheless agrees with Ellis that by changing the pronouns Gray depersonalized the poem. At the same time, however, Sutherland notes that "there is no real evidence that Gray wishes to change the reference of either 'thee' or 'these lines.' "[22] Indeed, as I suggested earlier, there is no objective basis for the assumption that Gray depersonalized the poem, since the problematic pronouns are already distanced by the second-person in the *Stanza's*. But there *is* a discrepancy between the two "versions," and this discrepancy points to what in fact is an objective problem in the text of the *Elegy*, although one that has apparently been overlooked. The discrepancy, and the problem it reveals, is not one of *voicing*, as the critics have assumed, but simply of *grammar*.

Let us again compare the two "versions":

> And thou, who mindful of the unhonour'd Dead
> Dost in these Notes their artless Tale relate
> By night & lonely Contemplation led
> To linger in the gloomy walks of Fate
>
> Hark how the sacred Calm that broods around . . .
> (Stanza's)

> For thee, who mindful of th'unhonour'd Dead
> Dost in these lines their artless tale relate;
> If chance, by lonely contemplation led,
> Some kindred Spirit shall inquire thy fate,
>
> Haply some hoary-headed Swain may say . . .
> (Elegy)

There is no reason to interpret the shift to the accusative case as a sign that Gray has changed the reference and thereby depersonalized the poem, and even if we were to assume that he is addressing a "Stonecutter" (or some other figure) in the *Elegy*, why should the accusative be more appropriate than the vocative? But, then, why *did* Gray change "And thou" to "For thee"? There is a real mystery here because, while the corresponding lines in the *Stanza's* pose no difficulty, the grammatical organization of stanza 24 in the *Elegy* is problematic. The shift to the accusative case, together with the semicolon after "relate," indicates that "For thee" is part of the predicate of a missing clause—and this is very peculiar in a poet such as Gray. Disregarding the semicolon, we could, perhaps, read "For thee" as the object of "inquire"; but since "inquire" already takes "thy fate" for its object, the syntax would be doubled and extremely awkward with this reading. And if we search for the missing predicate in the stanzas immediately preceding, we shall search in vain:

> For who to dumb Forgetfulness a prey,
> This pleasing anxious being e'er resigned,
> Left the warm precincts of the chearful day,
> Nor cast one longing ling'ring look behind?

> On some fond breast the parting soul relies,
> Some pious drops the closing eye requires;
> Ev'n from the tomb the voice of Nature cries,
> Ev'n in our Ashes live their wonted fires.

> For thee, . . .

The grammatical organization of stanzas 22 and 23 is complete; and although the ear naturally turns back to line 85 because of the repetition of "For," the connection is merely an aural one because in line 85 the word is a conjunction and in line 93, a preposition. Thus, we are left with a grammatical quandary.

Gray is a master, and we may take it on faith that there are no unwitting solecisms in his verse. However, while there is no basis for the assumption that he depersonalized the references, there is, objectively, a grammatical problem in stanza 24—and this is the *real* problem posed by the *Elegy* in formal terms. And this problem, as we shall see, can be resolved. But the solution is so entirely bound up with the poem's thematic development that at this point it would be incomprehensible and must therefore be postponed.

Bronson's Argument and the Principle of Univocity

The major advantage of Ellis's "Stonecutter" interpretation, as we noted, is that it resolves the formal problem posed by the *Elegy* in a way that is consonant with the requirements of "decorum." As Sutherland demonstrated, however, the interpretation is untenable on internal grounds. Thus, criticism would seem to have been thrown back upon the objections to the *Elegy*'s structure and tone that were initially voiced by Shepard. Ellis had been aware that "adverse criticism of a purely formal nature, namely that the poem lacks a coherent structure, can . . . be seen to rest on the assumption that the poem is excessively autobiographical" (971). However, not all of the commentators who approached the *Elegy*, both before and after the appearance of Ellis's article, were as concerned with the problem of decorum as he was. The reason for this is that if one interprets the poem as an "imitative lyric," in Crane's sense, then the problem of decorum is circumvented—although not, as Winters pointed out, done away with. Thus, Cleanth Brooks in 1947 and Frank Brady in 1965, equating the "Narrator" with the "thee" of line 93 and the Youth of the "Epitaph," offered interpretations of the *Elegy* in which the issue of decorum was not seen as a serious problem. Arguing that the *Elegy*'s structure is determined by its contrast between the graves of the rich and the poor, Brooks, in what is probably the best-known treatment of the poem, suggested that the "narrator" differs from both classes in that he chooses to be buried in the country churchyard whereas the poor have no choice in the matter.[23] Similarly, but with somewhat different consequences, Brady argued that the

poem's conclusion provides the necessary contrast to its reflec-
tions on the poor; for just as the "narrator" has his own perspec-
tive on the poor, so too they have a perspective on him.[24] Both
of these interpretations provide justifications for the relation-
ship of the final thirty-two lines to the preceding ninety-six;
however, it should be remembered that the poem's structure
needs justifying only in the context of the problem of decorum
and that the mere hypostatization of a Narrator does not set the
problem to rest.

The problem was directly confronted by Bertrand Bronson,
however, in an article entitled, appropriately enough, "On a
Special Decorum in Gray's *Elegy*." Bronson not only equates
the "me" of line 4 with the Youth of the "Epitaph," but he
suggests that the "Epitaph" was consciously intended as a per-
sonal memorial and, furthermore, that Gray was fully aware of
the difficulties this would entail. Thus, according to Bronson,
the chief difficulty the poet faces in the *Elegy* is

> how to devise a memorial in the form of inscriptional verse
> for oneself that shall be perfectly serious and emotionally
> sincere; that shall be neither objectionably self-abasing nor
> apparently self-satisfied; neither too cold and impersonal to
> communicate emotion nor too revealing of private emotion
> or self-commiseration.[25]

Bronson's argument as to how Gray triumphs over the poem's
"inescapable egocentricity" (172) is really very simple. Focusing
on the problematic twenty-fourth stanza, he notes that

> for nearly ninety lines the poet had, as it were, disembodied
> himself, diffusing his identity in generalized, impersonal
> statement. . . . He has so long ceased to mention himself
> that we have been projecting into his lines our own train of
> thought all this while. It seems, therefore, perfectly natural
> to be addressing another as "thee." This transference is surely
> one of the subtlest effects in our literature. For now, we
> join the poet in addressing himself in the second-person,
> continuing the identification as we imagine "some kindred
> spirit" inquiring about *us* . . . The supposed answer [to the
> "kindred Spirit's" inquiry] is further insulated from the man,

> Gray, by being attributed to an imaginary stranger, unknown both to him and to us, so that we are not aroused from our meditative imagining, nor divided from the poet. When, finally, the summary epitaph comes, it is still further removed from reach of Gray's apparent personal responsibility by being read on a headstone, unauthored, possessed of lapidary detachment and finality. (175–76)

In other words, Bronson feels that what begins as a personal statement nevertheless acquires *universal* connotations. From his point of view, then, it might be said that the entire controversy over the *Elegy* is misdirected. For if the reader projects himself into the poem in the way Bronson suggests, it would follow that analysis should begin from *this* premise rather than from the supposedly "objective" issues of referentiality and so forth. Thus, Bronson is able to justify the poem's structure and tone from within the terms of Shepard's "only easy and natural reading," but without resorting to biographical speculations and without interpolating a dramatic context as the other critics had found it necessary to do. In effect, his is a phenomenological reading of the poem *avant la lettre*.

Bronson's conclusions seem to me to be substantially correct, and in chapter 3 I shall demonstrate that the principle of universality he implicitly adduces is, in fact, grounded in the *Elegy*'s thematic development. However, Bronson's approach is divided between the formalist assumptions he maintains in common with the other critics and his feeling that our actual experience of the poem flies in the face of those assumptions. On the one hand, he maintains that the poem's conclusion is virtually an "autobiographical document" (176), and on the other, he suggests that we do not experience it in this way. But what is ultimately at issue in Bronson's interpretation—and hence the doubleness of his approach—is the *principle of univocity* on which critical interpretation has traditionally been founded.

To Aristotle in the *Metaphysics*, "Not to have one meaning is to have no meaning." This, in essence, is the principle of univocity, and it is easy to see that it is the underlying assumption of all the criticism on the *Elegy* we have examined—including Bronson's interpretation, though more ambivalently in his case. Until recently, of course, the principle of univocity was an unquestioned (and usually unconscious) tenet of criticism in general—and this, paradoxically, in spite of the emphasis that the New Critics placed on ambiguity. As applied to the *Elegy*, this principle would suggest that the "thee" of line 93 must refer to a specific individual in order for the poem to be coherent. The problem, however, as we have seen, is that any attempt to provide a univocal solution to the ambiguities posed by the text must either arrive at Shepard's conclusion, that the poem is deficient in regard to structure and tone, or, if it seeks to justify the poem, must do so on the basis of some idea or construct that is not in the text itself—and hence the tendency of so much of this criticism to swing between the biographical (or intentional) and dramatic fallacies. All of this is a consequence of the need to maintain the principle of univocity. On the other hand, it must be admitted that Bronson's non-univocal conclusion raises the question of whether interpretation that is not governed by Aristotelian logic can be rigorous or whether it must resign itself, as the Deconstructionist School would suggest, to the mere "play of ideas." Between these two extremes, there is, perhaps, a middle course that can be charted. As applied to the *Elegy*, such a course would suggest that the poem's meaning ultimately depends on our *inability* to assign fixed referents to the problematic pronouns and, furthermore, that this inability is an aspect of Gray's poetic intention. But in order to establish whether this is in fact the case, we shall have to pay close attention to the poem's thematic development.

Given the acceptance of the principle of univocity by formalist criticism generally, as well as the separation of poetic surface from poetic depth that goes along with it, it is easy to see why the debate over the *Elegy* came to a halt in the 1960s and why so little of substance was written on the poem thereafter. Bronson's divided approach indicates that while criticism no longer had any room to maneuver within a univocal theoretical orientation, it was not yet ready to free itself from that orientation. Yet in spite of the extensive interpretive literature that had accumulated on the *Elegy* by that point, the richness of the poem's struggle with meaning had not really been mined at all. Like the "gem of purest ray serene" of the fourteenth stanza, the *Elegy* was in danger of sinking deeper into the "dark unfathom'd caves of ocean."

Chapter 3

A Reading of Gray's *Elegy*

Stanzas 1–4

The Curfew tolls the knell of parting day,
The lowing herd wind slowly o'er the lea,
The plowman homeward plods his weary way,
And leaves the world to darkness and to me.

Now fades the glimmering landscape on the sight,
And all the air a solemn stillness holds,
Save where the beetle wheels his droning flight,
And drowsy tinklings lull the distant folds;

Save that from yonder ivy-mantled tow'r
The mopeing owl does to the moon complain
Of such, as wand'ring near her secret bow'r,
Molest her ancient solitary reign.

Beneath those rugged elms, that yew-tree's shade,
Where heaves the turf in many a mould'ring heap,
Each in his narrow cell for ever laid
The rude Forefathers of the hamlet sleep.

LANDSCAPE AS PRELUDE

IN HIS "Life of Denham," Dr. Johnson refers to "a species of composition that may be denominated *local poetry*, of which the fundamental subject is some particular landscape to be poetically described, with the addition of such embellishments as may be supplied by historical retrospection or incidental meditation."[1] Johnson's reference is to what is now usually called "topographical poetry," and topography, the description of a landscape, is implicitly linked in his definition to topos, or theme; for the prevailing metaphor of such poetry is simply that a particular landscape gives rise to a particular set of reflections.

Since both description and reflection depend on the standpoint of the observer, the issue of topography is also related to that of *perspective.*[2]

The issues of topography and perspective confront us immediately in the opening stanzas of the *Elegy*, for the poem begins with a description of a rural landscape at twilight, but our perspective on what is being described does not become firmly established until the end of the fourth stanza—and our perspective on *why* it is being described, not until much later. The description is of the greatest possible simplicity but is pregnant with undisclosed meaning. We are *thrown* into the landscape, in effect, but we have no way to gauge where we are, until—in cinematic fashion—the focus shifts from background to foreground, from the scene beyond the churchyard to the churchyard itself in which the poet's meditation is (putatively) situated.

The term "landscape" seems appropriate in connection with the opening stanzas, and in fact Gray himself uses it in line 5; but the pictorial analogy is somewhat misleading, for all the elements that compose the scene are in motion—or rather in a kind of *slow motion* that gives the effect of stasis or timelessness. The basic dialectic of motion played off against stasis (about which I shall have more to say later on) lends itself also to a musical analogy, and in fact the pictorial is linked to the musical in the opening stanza by the tolling of the Curfew, which is what seems to set the figures in the landscape—as well as the poem itself—into motion. Ian Jack observes that the *Elegy* is "the poem *par excellence* of recurrent patterns and subtle variations from the norm,"[3] and on the tonal level this is immediately evident in stanza 1, for the *toll*ing of the Curfew reverberates with the *low*ing of the herd winding *slow-ly* o'er the *lea*. We cannot as yet ascertain the significance of the Curfew, or indeed of any of the other symbols presented in stanza 1, for Gray's topoi are at this stage completely embedded in his topography. But pressing the musical analogy further, we might say that this bell will reverberate throughout the poem—like the ground bass of a passacaglia.

Gray's description in stanza 1 has a phenomenological immediacy that is governed by three factors: (1) the use of the present tense; (2) the paratactical symmetry of the clausal construction; and (3) the linkage between the description and the "me" of line 4. The combined effect is to project the reader into the scene and to make him experience the poem from the standpoint of this interior "me." As we noted in chapter 2, this is the only point in the *Elegy* at which the first person pronoun actually appears, but the ensuing reflections will nevertheless be anchored upon it. In order to distinguish this "me" from the poet—and especially since a great many questions hinge on the nature of the pronominal ambiguities—I shall refer to it henceforward in terms of a "lyric-I."

Being almost purely descriptive, the initial four stanzas of the *Elegy* are in the nature of a *prelude* to a meditation that will follow. For the moment, however, we can have no real thematic grasp of what this meditation will encompass, and we must be wary of reading too much from the outset into the images that are presented. But much can already be learned by focusing on the stylistic and rhetorical issues that present themselves for analysis.

Paradoxically, however, part of what is disclosed from the outset is the poem's curious ambivalence about disclosing its meanings—or rather, disclosing them too soon. This is already evident in line 1, where the word "Curfew" has an overly technical, and hence evasive, quality—as if an attempt were being made to limit the significance of the evening bell to its literal meaning. Lonsdale mentions that the curfew, dating from William the Conqueror's time, was still rung at Cambridge when Gray resided there, and he suggests that Gray might have taken the word from *Il Penseroso:* "I hear the far-off Curfeu sound" (line 73).[4] Certainly the *Elegy* follows in the wake of Milton's poem and of the *penseroso* tradition generally, but what concerns us here is that the factual neutrality of "Curfew" is immediately countered by the word "knell" in line 1, which in turn is countered by the phrase "parting day." The issue of death—which would make the Curfew also a *passing bell*—is thus being raised from the outset, but in an ambiguous way, for it is unclear precisely how the connection between death (as such) and the diurnal cycle is being intended. On the surface, it appears that the connotation of death is the vehicle of a metaphor whose tenor is the end of the day, but which of these takes *poetic* priority is another matter. Since the adjective "parting" has a human specificity, "parting day" is a pathetic fallacy—and this makes one wonder whether the diurnal cycle should not be taken as a metaphoric substitution for death rather than the other way round. Not that this ambiguity in itself is unique to Gray, but what is important is that already in line 1 certain questions about the relationship between Man and Nature, as mediated perhaps by the problems of death and consciousness, are implicitly being raised. And these questions will turn out to have not only an ontological but also a political significance in the poem.

It is interesting, therefore, as Norton Nicholls informs us in his valuable memoir of the poet, that Gray "had at first written 'tolls the knell of *dying* day' but changed it to *parting* to avoid the *concetto.*"[5] This is certainly plausible. However, other indications suggest that what Gray wanted to avoid was not merely a conceit as such (and "parting day" is also, though to a lesser extent, a conceit) but any explicit reference to the problem of death. Indeed, none actually occurs until line 36, and throughout the earlier stanzas, the issue is consistently deferred and circumvented by euphemism. This presents us with an enigma—though one whose solution must also be deferred for the present.

DANTE'S PRESENCE AND THE EXPERIENCE OF THE "THRESHOLD"

In any event, what is fascinating is that *both* adjectives— the original "dying" and the revision of "parting"—come from separate passages in the *Divine Comedy*. Gray acknowledged to Nicholls that the opening line of the *Elegy* was imitated from *Purgatorio* 8: 5–6;[6] but as Lonsdale notes, a second passage from Dante, *Inferno* 2: 1–3, stands behind the entire first stanza of

Gray's poem.[7] Both passages are quoted below (with the Mandel-
baum translations), but in somewhat greater length than as they
are echoed by Gray, so as to set them in context:

> Era gia l'oro che volge il disio
> ai navicanti e 'ntenerisce il core
> lo di c'han detto ai dolci amici addio;
>   e che lo novo peregrin d'amore
> punge, se ode squilla di lontano
> che paia il giorno pianger che si more.
>   (*Purgatorio* 8.1–6)

> It was the hour that turns seafarers' longings
> homeward—the hour that makes their hearts grow tender
> upon the day they bid sweet friends farewell;
>   the hour that pierces the new traveler
> with love when he has heard, far off, the bell
> that seems to mourn the dying of the day.[8]

> Lo giorno se n'andava, e l'aere bruno
> toglieva li animai che sono in terra
> da le fatiche loro; e io sol uno
>   m'apparecchiava a sostener la guerra
> si del cammino e si de la pietate
> che ritrarrà la mente che non erra.
>   (*Inferno* 2.1–6)

> The day was now departing; the dark air
> released the living beings of the earth
> from work and weariness; and I myself
>   alone prepared to undergo the battle
> both of the journeying and of the pity,
> which memory, mistaking not, shall show.[9]

What the two passages from Dante share in common is that
both are among the most crucial "threshold moments" in the
Commedia (and a fortiori in all of Western literature). This is to
say that in both passages there is a mystical withdrawal from the
quotidian of "work and weariness" that not only encapsulates
the *moto spiritale* of Dante's poem but is also a prelude to its
central action. In spite of the obvious differences separating the
two poets, it is essentially for this reason that Dante represents

an important point of departure for Gray in the *Elegy*. Of course, in the *Elegy* the transitional experience of the twilight hour is not translated into an objective drama centering on the poet's spiritual progress, as it is in the *Commedia*, for the cultural predicates for such a drama are not accessible to Gray. Nevertheless, the sense of a spiritual quest that Gray derived at least partly from Dante is embedded in the landscape of stanza 1.[10]

In certain important respects, Gray's perspective in the *Elegy* remains firmly grounded in the rationalism of his time, and in a way that would not seem to have allowed for Dante's influence to have taken a very deep poetic hold. The *Elegy* is neither a Christian allegory, such as *Pilgrim's Progress* (which Dr. Johnson compared to the *Commedia*),[11] nor an overtly Dantean poem in the Romantic mode, such as Shelley's *Triumph of Life*. Where the *Commedia* centers on the spiritual progress of Dante himself, though understood as Everyman, Gray is an invisible presence in the *Elegy*; where Dante is vouchsafed a vision of eternity, Gray has no final truths to offer. Nevertheless, the language of the opening stanzas corresponds in certain obvious ways to traditional accounts of mystical experiences, and particularly to the sensorial/spiritual paradoxes that such experiences often emphasize. In Plotinian or Neoplatonic terms (and Gray, as we shall see, is a thoroughgoing Platonist, both in regard to his thought and his poetic practice), in order for the mind to take hold of its true object there must be a removal from the narrow experience of the senses. And since the visual and the visionary are inversely related, the fading of the landscape in stanza 2 is a prelude to meditative *clarity*. In the context of the transitional experience of the twilight hour, however, this process makes itself felt at first as an intensification of the sensorial dimension; for as the landscape *fades on the sight*, it *glimmers*. Moreover, this paradox extends itself also to the oppositions of sound and silence and motion and stasis. The air *holds a solemn stillness:* it is pregnant with latent or undisclosed meaning. And this stillness, being both motionlessness and silence, is intensified, in spite of Gray's qualifying clauses ("Save where . . ."), by the *droning* of the beetle and the *drowsy tinklings* lulling the distant folds. The peculiarity of Gray's description in the first three stanzas is that from a strictly mimetic standpoint the landscape is actually crowded with a plethora of different entities in motion, all of which are connected to different sounds. Yet the impression we derive from these stanzas, partly as a result of their tonal convergences, is, on the contrary, that of silence—or what Eliot, thinking perhaps of Dante, called "the still point of the turning world."

With the transition from stanza 2 to stanza 3, and as a concomitant to the fading of the landscape, Gray's imagery becomes increasingly weighted toward the symbolic rather than the naturalistic pole of literary expression. For while the "mopeing owl" and the "ivy-mantled tow'r" might plausibly appear in a setting such as the one described, they are also, of course, literary conventions that are associated with melancholy and attached to particular generic expectations. In spite of their "conventionality," however, these images are rendered memorable by Gray's mastery over diction and syntax and by his ability to make use of the quatrain form to condense meaning into small formal units. Indeed, as a general rule it seems that as Gray's language moves closer to the symbolic and "purely literary" pole, his syntax becomes correspondingly more complex. The adverbs "now" and "yonder" in lines 5 and 9 are deictics that situate the utterance in terms of the immediate experience of the "lyric-I"; and as I have suggested, this *naturalistic illusion* will be maintained throughout the poem and will be confirmed at important transitional points. However, the archetypal status of Gray's imagery indicates that the naturalistic perspective is above all a framing device for a vision that is essentially *allegorical*, in the sense of being focused on universals and, indeed, on the problem of value itself.

THE GREAT SLEEP OF NATURE

In stanza 4, the ostensible subject of the *Elegy*—insofar as it focuses on those buried in the country churchyard—is finally introduced. The "rude Forefathers of the hamlet" are the

subject of the poem, and the phrase is the grammatical subject
of the stanza, but this subject has been suspended until the final
line of the quatrain in order to heighten its dramatic impact.
This dramatic suspension of the subject is particularly interest-
ing here, moreover, because while the subject itself is plural,
it is referred to initially in the singular ("Each in his narrow
cell . . .").

Although we do not realize this until we come to line 16, the
perspective in stanza 4 has shifted from the landscape beyond
the churchyard to the churchyard itself. The parallel pronominal
phrases of line 13 point us in the direction of the Forefathers,
who are now *heaped up* with Nature, as it were. Being no longer
alive, they are no longer separate entities; yet the fact that
they are referred to initially in the singular emphasizes the
individuality they once possessed. (The problem of individua-
tion, which will loom so large in the poem, is here hinted at for
the first time.) Having departed from life, the Forefathers *sleep
forever:* they are now eternally a part of the perpetual sleep
which is Nature.

Earlier I suggested that already in line 1 certain questions
about the relationship between Man and Nature are implicitly
being raised, and I noted also that in the opening stanzas of the
poem any explicit reference to the problem of death is studiously
avoided. With the introduction of the Forefathers, these issues
begin to take on more substance, for the thematic relationship
between the Curfew and the "passing bell" that would be rung
to toll the knell of a parting life is now clear. The Curfew would
be rung by men, of course, but in a certain sense it is Nature
that rings the changes, and at this point in the *Elegy,* everything
appears to be subsumed by the great sleep of Nature. The rude
Forefathers sleep in the bosom of Nature as they slept at the end
of a day of labor—and this puts the image of the plowman,
plodding homeward his weary way, into perspective. It is not a
question of death, but rather of sleep. Death exists as a problem
only at the point at which consciousness poses the separation
between Man and Nature. In Nature's "diurnal course" (to quote
Wordsworth in "A slumber did my spirit seal"), all things are
perpetually asleep.

The point, then, is that in this opening movement of the poem, there is a very great weariness, a desire for sleep, a desire to be free of labor and therefore of History, a desire to return to where (as in Keats's Nightingale ode) there is consciousness neither of death nor of "hungry generations." One should beware of referring this desire to Gray in autobiographical terms: it merely exists in the poem as universal desire, and it is in this form that we apprehend it.

Stanzas 5–7

The breezy call of incense-breathing morn,
The swallow twitt'ring from the straw-built shed,
The cock's shrill clarion, or the ecchoing horn,
No more shall rouse them from their lowly bed.

For them no more the blazing hearth shall burn,
Or busy housewife ply her evening care:
No children run to lisp their sire's return,
Or climb his knees the envied kiss to share.

Oft did the harvest to their sickle yield,
Their furrow oft the stubborn glebe has broke;
How jocund did they drive their team afield!
How bow'd the woods beneath their sturdy stroke!

THE LIVES OF THE FOREFATHERS:
THE EMBEDDING OF PERSPECTIVES

Serving as a kind of prelude, the opening stanzas of the *Elegy* had situated Gray's meditation in terms of a landscape perceived at twilight and evocative of the crepuscular emotions associated with the *penseroso* tradition generally. But with the introduction of the Forefathers, who sleep forever in their narrow cells, there is an immediate shift of perspective. The melancholy twilight imagery now gives way to the imagery of a cheerful dawn: the swallow replaces the owl, and the "ecchoing horn" the Curfew. The plowman's weariness, permeating the opening stanzas, has been left behind, and everything now partakes of the spirit of a brisk allegro.

The shift of perspective that occurs in stanza 5, however, is not merely a matter of imagery or tonality in an isolated sense but has important philosophical and structural consequences. On the structural plane, stanzas 5–7 take the form of a series of *imaginary tableaux* that together constitute a single poetic movement—one that is both discrete unto itself and at the same time embedded in the perspective of the earlier stanzas. This is not to suggest that the imagery of the first four stanzas is any less "imaginary" in an ultimate sense than that of the following three: we have no way of knowing whether, and to what extent, the opening stanzas reflect an actual experience, and in any event this is not what is important. In the opening stanzas, however, the illusion, at least, is fostered that the "I" is actually present in the churchyard. Given the perspective of the "lyric-I," which has now been established, Gray's evocation of the lives of the Forefathers in stanzas 5–7 constitutes a *secondary* level of representation.

THE *BEATUS ILLE* TOPOS

Each of these stanzas depicts the rural life of the Fore-fathers at a particular time of day and in relation to the activity on which the rhythm of their lives is focused—or in other words, before, after, and during the labor of the day. Although the scene shifts from dawn to evening and finally to the heat of the day, the note that is struck in stanza 5 remains constant, and the picture of the Forefathers that emerges is harmonious in every detail and singularly *devoid* of melancholy. Drawing upon the conventions of the *Beatus ille* ("Happy the man") topos, which derives its name from the opening of Horace's second Epode, Gray has represented the Forefathers in terms of the classical conception of what constitutes a good, happy, and fulfilled life. Of course, Gray's representation of the Forefathers in these stanzas is only a moment in the poem's dialectical progression and thus cannot entirely be taken at face value.

In itself, the description of the dawn in stanza 5 is the very opposite of pathetic; yet, ironically, it is precisely this that determines the stanza's pathos, for the description, of course, is drawn from the perspective of the eternal sleep of the Forefathers, who will never again be roused from their "lowly bed." (The adjective "lowly" points not only to the ground in which the Forefathers are buried but also to their humble social origins, and thus very subtly begins to bring an important thematic burden to light.) By suspending the predicate until the final line of the quatrain, much as in stanza 4 he had suspended the subject, Gray manages to juxtapose feeling-states and perspectives that are nevertheless *discrete* unto themselves. This is what is so remarkable about stanza 5 in particular, although to some extent the general procedure carries over to stanza 7. Thus, when the "no more" of line 20 is finally sounded, it reverberates all the more powerfully against the "for ever" of line 15—as indeed both phrases reverberate, in a symbolic sense, against the tolling of the Curfew. Gathering momentum, the phrase is then repeated at the beginning of stanza 6—though in variation, so as to avoid simple anaphora.

The dramatic effect produced by the suspension of the predicate is amplified by the "recurrent patterns and subtle variations from the norm" of stanza 5. Lines 17 and 18 both contain a subject and a modifying phrase, with the caesura in both cases falling before the preposition, and the resulting parallelism is strengthened by the fact that both lines contain compound adjectives modifying terminal nouns.[12] Simply because line 19 contains two subjects, however, this initial pattern is then broken, and as a result there is an increase in tension that is finally resolved in line 20:

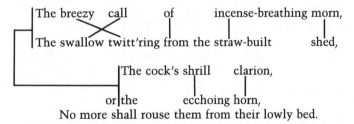

No more shall rouse them from their lowly bed.

The same principle functions on the tonal level, moreover. In "the cock's shrill clarion, or the ecchoing horn," the hard *c*'s,

soft *i*'s, *r*'s, *l*'s, and *o*'s of the two line-halves echo one another;
and in this line both "clarion" and "ecchoing" are trisyllables
that are speeded up and elided to fit a single weak position in
the meter:

clárĭŏn   /   ećchŏĭng

There are moments in the *Elegy* at which Gray's technique
seems almost miraculous for the complexity it is able to balance
and the sheer beauty it is able to sustain. Stanza 5 is surely one
of these.

The scene depicted in stanza 6, as Lonsdale notes, can also
be found in Horace's second Epode, to which we have already
alluded, in Virgil's *Georgics*, and in Lucretius;[13] but in wending
our way through these sources, we come upon a number of
striking ambiguities. First of all, Gray's representation of the
scene is mainly indebted to Lucretius, for it is Lucretius who
renders it from the standpoint of a negated future:

> "No longer will you happily come home
> To a devoted wife or children dear
> Running for your first kisses, while your heart
> Is filled with unspoken gratitude."[14]

The passage is in quotation marks because Lucretius is pres-
enting this pathetic scene only for the purpose of satirizing it.
It occurs in the famous section toward the end of Book III of *De
Rerum Natura* in which the Epicurean poet inveighs against the
fear of death, pointing out that when we engage in maudlin
ruminations over our own death, we absurdly project ourselves
into a future from which we shall be absent—but as if we could
be there to witness it. As far as Lucretius is concerned, "Death /
Is nothing to us" (3.830–31)—in both senses of the statement.

In presenting the same basic scene, but in itself rather than
against the background of a negated futurity, Horace and Virgil
are imitating as well as reacting against Lucretius, for both
present it as an example of rural piety and without the slightest
satirical intention. (Horace, it is true, puts his praise of rural
retirement in the mouth of the usurer Alfius, who has no inten-

tion of practicing what he preaches, and thus the entire second Epode is framed by a satirical intention; but this is another matter, for Horace's description itself is without satirical emphasis.) Since Gray's representation of the scene is also meant, at least initially, to be taken in a straightforward manner, it has probably also passed through the alembic of Horace and Virgil. His debt to Lucretius, however, indicates the presence of a darker undercurrent—which indeed makes itself felt in the manner in which stanzas 5–7 are embedded in stanzas 1–4.

ECCLESIASTES AND THE GEORGICS: ANTITHETICAL VISIONS OF HUMAN LABOR AND DESTINY

We can now begin to come to grips with some of the deeper philosophical issues that are implicitly being posed by the *Elegy* up to this point; for given the tonal contrast between stanzas 5–7 and 1–4—a contrast which in some respects is more pronounced than the one Milton draws in *L'Allegro* and *Il Penseroso*—it is possible to discern an emerging conflict between two antithetical (but partially overlapping) visions of human destiny. Again, the central question has to do with the relationship between Man and Nature, but this primary and all-encompassing dialectic has now become more clearly focused on the mediating issue of *labor*. The terms of this conflict can best be appreciated by aligning the two sections of the poem with two texts from antiquity that focus paradigmatically on the problem of labor from antithetical perspectives: Ecclesiastes and Virgil's *Georgics*.

The feeling-tone of the opening stanzas—notwithstanding the underlying presence of Dante—is clearly dominated by the tendency represented by Ecclesiastes; for given a vision in which everything is subsumed by the cycles of Nature, "What profit hath a man of all his labour that he taketh under the sun?" Human activity, from this perspective, in its attempt to deny the reality of death, is merely "vanity and vexation of spirit." The melancholy vision of Ecclesiastes has obvious affinities in

Greek and Roman literature (Lucretius himself comes to mind)
and many descendants among the moderns. We need not expand
upon this issue further except to say that in its modern version,
as Romantic melancholy, this tendency leads from Gray to Keats
and then to Tennyson, whose greatest poetry is imprinted by it:

> Man comes and tills the field and lies beneath,
> And after many a summer dies the swan.

By contrast with the tendency represented by Ecclesiastes,
Virgil's *Georgics* is the most important, and in some respects
the earliest, elaboration of a *positive* conception of labor in the
ancient world. The eighteenth century understood this very
well, although not always in the most radical sense; thus, it
is not surprising that Gray should have been so profoundly
influenced by this aspect of Virgil. Indeed, as Lonsdale indi-
cates, stanzas 5–7 are fairly littered with echoes of the *Georgics*,
both in the original and in Dryden's translation.[15] To be sure,
the Virgilian ideals of cheerful labor and healthy moderation
can be found in other Roman poets, but in the *Georgics* these
ideals are connected to the possibility of shaping reality in ac-
cordance with human happiness. What is more, they are given
a solid metaphysical basis in a vision of Nature—and human
nature—that is diametrically opposed to either the cyclical vi-
sion of Ecclesiastes or the chaotic atomism of Lucretius. As
Jacques Perret argues in his important study of the poem, "In
no thinker of antiquity except Virgil does one find the idea, so
often implied in the first book of the *Georgics*, that nature, like
human endeavor, is working toward definite ends, and that
contemplation of the universe ought therefore to inspire men
to work."[16]

Virgil's elaboration of a positive conception of labor in the
Georgics has an important bearing on a series of issues we shall
later take up in connection with the pastoral. Indeed, as Virgil
himself informs us (with a certain ambiguous sadness) at the
conclusion of the *Georgics*, the latter poem was written partly
in reaction against the perspective he had previously entertained
in the *Eclogues*:

All this I've sung of cultivating fields,
Of tending flocks and caring for the trees,
While by the deep Euphrates noble Caesar
Thunders triumph, grants the reign of law
To grateful subjects, claims his path to heaven.
All this time sweet Naples nourished me,
Her Virgil, in the flower of humble peace,
In study: I who played at shepherds' songs
In callow youth, and sang, O Tityrus,
Of you at ease beneath your spreading beech.[17]

In the *Georgics*, then, Virgil is concerned with the possibility of making immanent—through a historical process founded on labor—the vision of harmony that is projected in transcendental terms in the *Eclogues* and in the pastoral tradition generally.

It is interesting, therefore, that in turning away from the pessimism of the ancient world, Virgil, as Perret observes, makes use of the myth of the Golden Age. This myth, of course, is central to pastoral tradition and to Virgil's own *Eclogues*; but since it represents the necessity for labor as the consequence of a decline from a previous state of plenitude, its inclusion in the *Georgics* is surprising, to say the least. However, in the *Georgics* Virgil presents the myth not in the original form in which it had been handed down by Hesiod in *Works and Days*, but in a new and optimistic interpretation:

The father willed it so: He made the path
Of agriculture rough, established arts
Of husbandry to sharpen human wits,
Forbidding sloth to settle on his soil.
Before Jove, farms and farmers were unknown;
To mark off or divide the land was wrong,
For things were held in common, and the earth
Brought forth her substance then, more generously,
When none imposed demands upon the ground.
Jove endowed the serpents with their venom,
Commanded wolves to prowl and seas to rise,
Shook honey from the leaves, hid fire away,
Stopped up the streams of wine, so that mankind
By taking thought might learn to forge its arts
From practice: seek to bring the grain from furrows,

Strike out the fire locked up in veins of flint.
Then rivers first bore hollow boats, and sailors
Numbered the stars and named them: Pleiades,
The Hyades, the radiant Northern Bear.
Men discovered how to trap and hunt,
How to circle forests with their hounds;
Some plunged their casting nets deep in broad rivers,
While others trailed their dripping lines at sea.
Harsh iron emerged, and saws with whistling blades
(For earlier, men split their logs with wedges);
Then followed all the civilizing arts:
Hard labor conquered all, and pinching need.

                              (*Georgics*, 1.121–46)

In other words, in bringing an end to the Golden Age, Jupiter is
acting for the benefit of humanity. Virgil's reinterpretation of
the myth thus runs parallel to the (mainly) Protestant doctrine
of the "fortunate fall," which Milton expounds at the end of
Paradise Lost:

                    for then the Earth
Shall all be Paradise, far happier place
Than this of *Eden*, and far happier days.

                              (12.463–65)

But what is striking about Virgil's conception, as Perret's analy-
sis indicates, is not merely that the eschatological vision govern-
ing it is posed in immanent terms but that this vision is predi-
cated on the progressive transformation of Nature through
technology:

> Jupiter is attempting to force man to invent technology, and
> to wrench him from the torpor that would have stifled his
> intelligence. . . . From all this, however, one fact clearly
> emerges: technology and the necessity for labor are not sim-
> ply a *pis-aller*, not a burden man must bear in consequence
> of the universe's gradual decline. On the contrary, the very
> evil against which we must struggle was introduced into the
> world only in order that there be work and technology—and
> this work is conjointly ordained to beautify the world and to
> exalt the human race.[18]

Virgil's conception of labor in the *Georgics* is thus an extremely radical one when considered in relation to its time. But it might also be argued, of course, that his unwavering idealism, coupled with his defense of imperialism, has conservative implications. As L. P. Wilkinson points out, for example, the problem of slavery is never once mentioned in the *Georgics*, despite the fact that when Virgil was writing the poem, the use of slave labor on the large estates (or *latifundia*) had for some time been forcing the peasantry off the farms and had thus created a "lumpen proletariat" in Rome itself.[19] It may be unfair to tax Virgil with a criticism of this kind. A poem that aims at representing a religious or utopian vision should not have to accommodate itself necessarily to the demands of realism; in any event, a polemic against slavery is certainly implicit in Virgil's conception of the nobility of working the soil. However, what is true for Virgil does not necessarily apply to the many imitators of the *Georgics* during the eighteenth century. If most of these now stike us as cloyingly sentimental and fundamentally conservative in spirit, this is an indication of how even the most progressive conceptions can be vulnerable to conservative appropriation.

Gray's representation of the Forefathers in stanzas 5–7 of the *Elegy* comes perilously close to succumbing to the same tendency toward sentimentality that we associate with many eighteenth-century pastorals. However, in the case of the *Elegy* this does not occur, and essentially for two reasons. In the first place, as will become clear when we examine stanza 8, Gray is himself aware of this danger, and his consciousness of the problem as the poem develops will then, from the reader's standpoint, be reflected back upon stanzas 5–7, as a corrective to the overly idealized depiction of labor contained therein. But even before we arrive at stanza 8, the fact that Gray's representation of the Forefathers is embedded in the perspective of the opening stanzas has the effect of distancing us from an ethos that would otherwise appear anachronistic and sentimental. The Forefathers, after all, now belong to the past—not only as individuals but in a generic sense. In other words, what is now *past* is not only the lives of the Forefathers individually, but—given the social transformations of the eighteenth century—the life of the peasantry as a whole, and hence the idealizing mode stemming from Virgil and the *Beatus ille* tradition, in terms of which that "life" (if indeed it ever corresponded to reality) had formerly been represented. To be sure, Gray is drawing upon the moral center of the Virgilian perspective on labor in stanzas 5–7, and he is doing so, as we noted, partly as a corrective to the melancholy temper of the opening stanzas. But, ultimately, he is able to draw upon the Virgilian ethos only because the embedding of stanzas 5–7 has the effect of distancing his representation of the Forefathers from a perspective whose naivete and lack of dimension make it inadequate as a final "resting place" for his meditation. In itself, the Virgilian ethos can only be reaffirmed from the standpoint of its pastness—which is not to deny its meaningfulness to the present. Paradoxically, however, the meaningfulness of this perspective to the present is rendered possible only by the fact that its representation as nostalgia is simultaneously the representation of its annulment.

Stanza 8

Let not Ambition mock their useful toil,
Their homely joys, and destiny obscure;
Nor Grandeur hear with a disdainful smile,
The short and simple annals of the poor.

THE DIATRIBE AGAINST AMBITION AND GRANDEUR AND THE DEMANDS OF REALISM

Ambition and Grandeur have apparently been eavesdropping on the preceding stanzas and are inclined to regard Gray's sermon on the Forefathers with a certain amount of skepticism, not to say levity. For if they know anything at all, these avatars of the upper classes, it is that "useful toil" (of the sort performed by the Forefathers, in any event) happens to coincide with poverty and obscurity. This admittedly rather prosaic fact of life has not yet been entered into the discussion, but from the vantage point of Ambition and Grandeur, it is not entirely unworthy of consideration.

It is through Ambition and Grandeur, therefore—and paradoxically, through the diatribe *against* Ambition and Grandeur—that the somewhat narrow idealism of stanzas 5–7 is, if not entirely repudiated, at least incorporated in a larger vision. The *decorum* of stanza 8 is thus exceedingly complex. On the surface, Gray's diatribe against Ambition and Grandeur is a defense of the ethical and religious values associated with his representation of the Forefathers—that is, a defense of Christian-cum-pastoral *humilitas*. But what emerges from the diatribe is the implicit recognition that the perspective of stanzas 5–7 is too lacking in a sense of historical irony to satisfy the demands of realism. By attacking Ambition and Grandeur, who, as alienated presences, are rather obvious targets, Gray is able to point up the limitations of that earlier perspective without explicitly repudiating it—indeed, while seeming to reaffirm it. Not that Ambition and Grandeur do not deserve whipping: on the contrary, the vehemence of Gray's invective seems to suggest that these cynics, while privately sneering at "the short and simple annals of the poor," would in public be extremely unctuous in support of the pastoral ethos that was projected in stanzas 5–7, since the myth of social harmony projected by that ethos is clearly in their interests. These scions of the eighteenth-century upper classes are not unlike the usurer Alfius, whom we met up with in Horace's second Epode: "When the usurer Alfius had uttered this [his praise of rural retirement], on the very point of beginning the farmer's life he called in all his funds upon the Ides—and on the Kalends seeks to put them out again!"[20]

Nevertheless, although Ambition and Grandeur are alienated presences, Gray's diatribe against them tacitly points up the limitations of the perspective drawn in stanzas 5–7 and at the same time suggests that the problem of value cannot simply be boiled down to a choice between Christian humility and worldly ambition. For the truth of the matter is that "useful toil" and "homely joys" are one thing (although the second of these adjectives has somewhat ambivalent connotations), but poverty and the obscurity that goes along with it (Gray's rhyme conveys this conjunction with absolute precision) are quite another. If the word "poor" strikes a powerful chord in closing the stanza, this is at least partly because the issue of poverty has been significantly absent hitherto; indeed, one might say that in stanzas 5–7, which present a picture of sufficiency, however simple and unadorned, it has been studiously avoided. The reason has something to do with the fact that such polarities as poverty and wealth, obscurity and fame, absence and presence—polarities that now begin to take a firm grip on the poem—are only meaningful from a historical perspective that conceives of the division of men into classes. As long as Nature, corresponding to the abstract idealism of the pastoral, had provided the primary frame of reference, the issue of poverty could only be alluded to by circumlocution and euphemism. Curiously—but this will not become clear until stanza 9—the same holds true for the problem of death itself.

The Problem of "Death-in-Life"

The connection that is established in stanza 8 between "useful toil," on the one hand, and poverty and obscurity, on the other, marks the emergence in the *Elegy*—and in the history of English poetry—of the problem of *alienation*, which is to say, the "problem of history" in its negative aspect. As the poem develops, the problem of alienation will unfold as a counterweight to the problem of death; therefore, for the sake of symmetry (and at the risk of multiplying categories), we may refer to it as the problem of *death-in-life*.

The Role of Personification

In any event, the emergence of the historical aspect of Gray's dialectic in stanza 8, and the shift from a descriptive to a reflective mode, coincides with the first of what will be a series of personified abstractions appearing in the poem. Personification obviously plays a central role in Gray's poetry, but his use

of the figure has never been treated systematically and in fact
has often been misunderstood. The issue of personification is a
complicated one in general, of course, and especially where the
eighteenth century is concerned. For one thing, as Bertrand
Bronson has pointed out, the eighteenth-century custom of capi-
talizing nouns indiscriminately often makes it difficult to dis-
tinguish when personification is being used in the true sense.[21]
Moreover, what we would normally call personification often
functions purely as a *grammatical* figure in the work of the
period. Such is the case, for example, in the opening lines of *The
Vanity of Human Wishes:*

> Let Observation with extensive view
> Survey Mankind from China to Peru

—where the effectiveness of the couplet would actually be di-
minished by an attempt to visualize "Observation" or otherwise
endow it with human characteristics. In Johnson's couplet, "Ob-
servation" is less a being than a capacity or function. By treating
this capacity as a grammatical subject, the poet avoids the neces-
sity of having to stipulate a human agent: he is thus using
personification as a *figure of condensation,* which is one of the
common uses for the figure during the period, and certainly a
valid one. In the hands of weaker poets, of course, personifica-
tion was often an empty rhetorical flourish; but the wholesale
condemnation of the figure, under the aegis of Coleridgean or
symbolist poetic theories, fails to take account of the grammati-
cal possibilities that it affords.

From the outset of Gray's career, his use of personification is
an organic aspect of his technique, inseparable from his deepest
poetic conceptions. The reason for this is simply that the pri-
mary impulse of Gray's poetry is a Platonizing one, a fact that
is immediately evident in the early odes.[22] Indeed, one might
characterize the early odes as representations of *symbolic action*
(to borrow Kenneth Burke's central concept), in which abstract
motivational impulses come into collision with the equally
abstract forces that determine human destiny. This is a moral
poetry of the species rather than the individual, in which the

poet's aim is to derive knowledge of paradigms rather than of particulars. A brief passage from the *Ode on a Distant Prospect of Eton College*, where Gray also makes use of the figure of Ambition, might serve to illustrate the point:

> Ambition this shall tempt to rise,
> Then whirl the wretch from high,
> To bitter Scorn a sacrifice,
> And grinning Infamy.
>
>   (70–74)

Ambition, here, is an abstract impulse within the individual; as such, Gray's figure exemplifies what the sixteenth-century rhetorician Richard Sherry called *pathopoeia:* "whereby the passions of the mind . . . are personified."[23] But this internal impulse is treated as an external agency for the perfectly legitimate reason that it exerts a real impact on human beings: the individual who succumbs to it becomes caught up in forces beyond his control—such, in any event, is the moral tenor of the passage. Personification is obviously central to a Platonizing poetry of this kind, where the emphasis is on the dramatic representation of abstract forces that make individual psychology a microcosm of a cosmic drama. It thus functions simultaneously as a *figure of elaboration*, insofar as it enables the poet to represent these forces from the standpoint of a morally apprehended totality, and as a *figure of condensation*, insofar as it enables him to grasp the particulars of experience in the form of a paradigm.

Gray's use of personification in the early odes differs from his use of the figure in the *Elegy*, however, for in the *Elegy* his field of representation embraces the sociopolitical realm. As a result, personification in the *Elegy* functions not merely in relation to abstract forces within and outside the individual but also in relation to particular *types* and *classes* of individuals. Thus, in line 29, Ambition refers both to the motivational impulse itself, which operates to a greater or lesser degree in all individuals, and also to ambitious *persons*. In the first sense, the figure concretizes an abstraction and, in the second, it functions synecdochically, to summon up a conception of ambitious persons in general. However, in this second sense the figure also has a metonymic function; for since ambition is clearly being associated with wealth and power, it is also associated with the *class* of those who possess them. The overlap of figuration that occurs in the context of Gray's use of personification in the *Elegy* is indicative of the processes of condensation and association that contribute to the poem's resonance. But the role of personification is not limited to these processes of condensation and association. Indeed, it may be considered Gray's master trope in the *Elegy*, for as we shall see, his use of this figure is directly connected to his investigation of the problem of value.

Stanza 9

The boast of heraldry, the pomp of pow'r,
And all that beauty, all that wealth e'er gave,
Awaits alike th'inevitable hour.
The paths of glory lead but to the grave.

Just as in stanza 8 the problems of poverty and obscurity are directly confronted, so in stanza 9 the problem of death is no longer referred to euphemistically as "sleep." "Lowly bed" in line 20 is a metaphor that distances us from the reality of death; "grave" in line 36 is a metonymy that brings us closer to this reality. The dialectically enmeshed problems of "death-in-life" and death thus emerge in successive stanzas and in the context of Gray's polemic against Ambition and Grandeur (and all that these figures imply).

The "Death the Leveler" Topos

The reason, of course, that Ambition and Grandeur are not to have contempt for the poor is that "the paths of glory lead but to the grave." We have here an expression of the "Death the Leveler" topos, which of course is everywhere to be found in the tradition, and which therefore Gray is content to render as a simple truism—as if to indicate by this gesture that *there is nothing more to be said.* The fact that there is a full stop after the third line in the quatrain (and stanza 9 is the only instance in the *Elegy* in which this occurs) intensifies this effect.

BROOKS'S INTERPRETATION

Considered in the abstract, the problem of death would appear to be so weighty as to reduce all other concerns to a merely secondary importance, and most critics have assumed that this is what actually happens in the *Elegy*, which is one reason, perhaps, that its originality has so rarely been recognized. The assumption that Gray's meditation reaches a kind of terminus in the realization that all are equal in the face of death is, in fact, the basis for Cleanth Brooks's interpretation of the poem, to which I alluded at the end of chapter 2:

> The paths of glory lead but to the grave, but so does the path along which the "plowman homeward plods his weary way." The graves are different. . . . But both are graves—the fact of death cannot be glossed over—this is the matter on which Gray's irony exerts its force.[24]

Brooks's argument has ideological implications because the notion that death "is the matter on which Gray's irony exerts its force" tends to nullify the importance of the problem of poverty (or, more broadly, of "death-in-life") in the poem. Logically, of course, Brooks is correct that if the paths of glory lead but to the grave, then so does the plowman's path; but *poetically*, Brooks is wrong, for while the fact of death cannot be glossed over in actuality, as far as the text of the *Elegy* is concerned, this is precisely what the euphemisms of the earlier stanzas have accomplished!

It might be argued that these euphemisms are sentimental, but this would be to view the situation too narrowly. In relation to the "pastoral" perspective of stanzas 5–7 they *are* sentimental, perhaps, but in relation to the poem as a whole they are not. Indeed, there is a sense in which they are actually safeguards against a very real ethical *and* poetic danger that Gray faced in the *Elegy*, precisely because of his confrontation with the problem of death: the loss of a humanist perspective, on the one hand, and the loss of his poem, on the other. For since all paths do lead to the grave, this awareness could lead to the leveling of *everything* connected to this world, and not only the alienated values of Ambition and Grandeur. In this case, everything would become "vanity and vexation of spirit," as it does for the Ecclesi-

astes poet. If Gray had followed this poetic path to its logical
conclusion, as Brooks assumes he has, it would have been impos-
sible for him to develop his material beyond the static dogmas
of a conventional religious attitude. The historical dimension
of his meditation would have been nullified from the outset,
and this would have left none but a religious basis for meaning
and value.

But however primary the "Death the Leveler" topos would
appear to be in the *Elegy*, the fact of the matter is that Gray
articulates it only in a negative context—as a *corrective* to the
attitudes of Ambition and Grandeur, who, by raising themselves
above their fellow human beings in order to maintain the illu-
sion of their invulnerability, become less human in the process.
In other words, the theme serves to strengthen a humanist
perspective rather than to nullify it. For this reason, it is invoked
not for its own sake—and certainly not to revel in the horrors
of the grave, as with much of the poetry of the "Graveyard
School"—but, however paradoxical this might seem, in the con-
text of *larger* ethical issues. This is why, when Gray is referring
to death in relation to the Forefathers, he calls it "soft names in
many a mused rhyme."

Stanza 10

Nor you, ye Proud, impute to These the fault,
If Mem'ry o'er their Tomb no trophies raise,
Where thro' the long-drawn isle and fretted vault
The pealing anthem swells the note of praise.

THE THEME OF MEMORY

In stanza 10, the theme of Memory—which will be associ-
ated with a constellation of issues, including fame, history, and
poetry itself—begins to be developed against the socioeconomic
background of the poem's contrast between the Forefathers and
the "Proud" (i.e., the poor and the rich) and against the meta-
physical background of its examination of the problems of death
and "death-in-life." Memory, which is the traces of the past on

the present, is at once the physical and the metaphysical bridge between life and death, absence and presence; and in the unfolding dialectic of Gray's discourse, it somehow permeates and brings together the various constituents of the poem's search for meaning and value.

Stanza 10 continues the polemic that was begun in stanza 8; but where the latter had evoked the pathos of "the short and simple annals of the poor"—and hence the limitations of the earlier "pastoral" perspective—stanza 10, by contrast, but quite as antithetically, evokes the pomp and solemnity of the funeral rites that commemorate the great and powerful. And here one is confronted with an extraordinary irony: for notwithstanding the admonitions of Christian humility, the trophies raised over the tombs and the pealing anthem swelling the note of praise (the latter having been deflected from God to man) are no mean thing! They are tokens of recognition and of a kind of fulfillment in the world to which, it may be, all human beings would aspire if they could. Again, all of this is evoked from the negative standpoint of the diatribe—and the arrogance of pride is an alienated perspective, of course—but it is evoked nonetheless.

On the surface or representational level of meaning, the Proud are being admonished in stanza 10 not to blame the poor for the fact that the poor will not be remembered by History—and in stanza 12, it will be made clear that the "fault" lies not with anything intrinsic to the poor as individuals but, precisely, with "Chill Penury" (line 51). However, this representational level is undercut by a remarkable sequence of lexical and syntactical displacements. In the first place, the word "tomb" in line 38 is a catachresis in regard to the humble graves of the poor; but the trope makes it possible for Gray to evoke a positive state of affairs through the overt statement of a negative and to do so, moreover, without breaching the poem's decorum. This procedure explains why, in line 39, the adverb "where" can effect a transition for which in actuality there is no grammatical antecedent. The prose sense that "where" condenses would be something like the following: "as it [Memory] does for the great and powerful, who, when they die, have elaborate funerals in great

churches *where . . ."* and so on. The syntax leaps across a seman-
tic chasm because the articulation of what the poor do not have
is really for the purpose of evoking what the rich (but not only
the rich—the unstated reference is meant to include all those
who have symbolic *presence* in the society) do have.

In the figure of Memory in line 38, Gray makes use of personi-
fication in a manner entirely different from that of stanza 8.
Ambition and Grandeur, we noted, represent motives within
the individual as well as ambitious and grandiose persons and
the class to which such persons would belong. Memory, how-
ever, is not meant to be considered as a human faculty in this
context, except insofar as the preservation of historical memory
requires actual human beings: it is rather to be considered as a
transfinite agency, much as in Greek mythology Memory is
depicted as the Mother of the Muses. But what is peculiar about
the personification of Memory is that it turns an effect into a
cause. It is apparent that those who have trophies raised over
their tombs will be *remembered*—that is, by their nations or by
History in general—because that is the function of the trophies.
But why should Memory initiate the process? It might seem
that the personification has a merely ornamental function in
this context, but that is by no means the case. Indeed, the
coinciding of cause and effect in the personification corresponds
to the reality of the situation, which in turn it emphasizes. For
in order for an individual to be remembered by History, that
person would have to have been *present* to his society in a
manner that would have marked him out beforehand as an
individual *to be* remembered. In other words, the memorial
process is both the cause and the effect of its concrete manifesta-
tions—and this is what the figure of personification enables the
poet to represent.

Personification and Value: Brooks's Interpretation Continued

Memory and Ambition are thus both figures of condensa-
tion; but even on superficial examination, it is apparent that the

values associated with the two—and personification is only meaningful, as we shall see, in the context of a system of clearly delineated values—are fundamentally different. Ambition in stanza 8 is plainly a vice, and we are led to take a dim view of it essentially from a Christian ethical perspective. (The fact that we are simultaneously led to see the limitations of that perspective is another matter.) Memory, however, has no such immediately obvious negative connotations but would seem, on the contrary, to be a beneficent agency—especially insofar as we conceive of it as the Mother of the Muses in a humanist context. It is true, of course, that the fame imparted by Memory, although a "good" in itself, often falls to the ambitious—which means that at a subterranean level of analysis, there is an implicit collision between the Christian and humanist perspectives. This conflict of values accounts for the ambivalence of stanzas 8–11, and indeed it will make itself felt throughout the poem. But as far as the personifications themselves are concerned, it is nevertheless apparent that Ambition and Memory do not fall out smoothly on the same ethical plane.

This perspective, it will be noted, runs completely counter to Brooks's influential analysis of how personification functions in the *Elegy*. To Brooks, the personifications "are actually the allegoric figures, beloved by the eighteenth century, which clutter a great abbey church such as that at Bath or Westminster." As such, "they are used ironically. That is to say, they are contrasted with the humble graves of the country churchyard, and they are meant, in contrast, to seem empty, flat, and lifeless."[25] In other words, the personifications are less an aspect of Gray's technique for Brooks than an aspect of the poem's content and a structural principle that serves to delineate its contrast between the rich and the poor. This means that the personifications may be considered monolithically and without regard for their individual value determinations. Interestingly, this allows Brooks to accommodate the *Elegy* to a New Critical perspective, in spite of the well-known nominalist bias of the New Criticism against allegory; for by arguing that Gray adopts an ironical attitude to the personifications, Brooks suggests—although he does not go so far as to make it explicit—that in fact we are not dealing with personification at all in the usual sense, but rather with a kind of *parody* of personification. The implication is that Gray is not concerned with Ambition and Memory as such, but rather with the *personifications* Ambition and Memory.

The strategy behind Brooks's argument is not merely to accommodate the *Elegy* to a nominalist aesthetic framework, however, but also, as was suggested earlier, to a conservative ideological perspective, in keeping with the view that death is the matter on which Gray's irony exerts its force. But in order to comprehend this, we have to examine how the concept of irony that Brooks interposes would operate in regard to the individual personifications themselves.

As it turns out, Brooks's concept of irony is either redundant or incoherent, depending on whether the valences of the personifications in question are negative or positive. The reason has to do with the very nature of personification. Since personification (or, more specifically, *pathopoeia*) treats abstractions as agencies—that is, since it delineates them as forms—any given personification must *already* be constituted within a definite system of formal values and must therefore embody a simple and unambiguous attitude that cannot then be altered by an additional attitude without destroying the poem's internal coherence. This is not to say that ambiguities will not arise as a result of the *context* in which the personification is situated—and our analysis of Memory has already indicated that they do, in fact, arise in the *Elegy*—but rather that the personification itself occupies a definite ethical dimension.

In the case of Ambition in stanza 8 or Flattery in stanza 11, for example—and both are personifications that represent human characteristics—it is clear that irony is *already* given in the appellation itself, so that to assert that Gray regards *those* figures ironically is merely tautological. Flattery is always a vice, and Ambition, when it overwhelms the character, which is precisely what the personification establishes, is similarly vicious. By their very *names*, the two figures announce that they are alienated presences who cannot, therefore, be regarded otherwise than ironically.

Of course, Brooks's argument is not really directed at these figures, but rather at those I have termed "transfinite agencies"—Memory in stanza 10 and Knowledge in stanza 13. Now, Memory imparts fame, and Knowledge imparts itself, and both fame and knowledge are, of course, desiderata, other things being equal; yet if we accept Brooks's argument, we are obliged to regard Memory and Knowledge as metonymic of the upper classes, and hence on the same ethical and social plane as Ambition and Flattery. The implication that follows from this is that fame and knowledge are somehow *bad*—not merely when they are acquired by vicious persons (such as Ambition and Flattery), but bad *in themselves*. Indeed, Brooks goes on to say that "what Knowledge has to give us is associated with madness, not sobriety."[26] And if fame and knowledge are *bad*, then it follows that the poor are better off without them—hence, that they are better off being poor. Not that Brooks is himself arguing that knowledge is bad and poverty good, of course, or even that he is explicitly ascribing so extreme a position to Gray. But if we take his interpretation of the *Elegy* to its logical conclusion, the poem becomes a defense of the status quo under the aegis of Christian humility and pastoral withdrawal from the world. And all of this follows from what is overtly a formal analysis of Gray's use of personification!

That the ideological implications of Brooks's argument are untenable will become clear when we examine the thematic development particularly of stanzas 12 to 15. But what is already clear is that these implications are plausible only if one accepts the reductive terms of Brooks's analysis, according to which not only Ambition and Flattery but also Memory and Knowledge are to be *identified* with the upper classes. It does happen to be true, of course, that Memory and Knowledge are *associated* with the rich and powerful, but that is another matter entirely. For if Memory raises no trophies over the graves of the poor, and if Knowledge fails to unroll her ample page for them, it is not the *fault* of Memory and Knowledge but rather of "Chill Penury." We are not asked to take a dim view of Memory and Knowledge per se, but we are led to the awareness that these abstract functions are controlled by the upper echelons of society and consequently are not available to the poor. The distinction is an important one, for if we accept Brooks's argument that the personifications correspond in toto to the poet's ironical attitude toward the pretensions of the rich and powerful, then what we have done, in essence, is to factor out the problem of poverty— or, more broadly, of "death-in-life"—which is an essential aspect of the poem's dialectic. What this leaves us with, on the one hand, is a rather sentimental poem that espouses the ideology of pastoral withdrawal and, on the other, a nihilistic view of culture as a merely illusory attempt to deny the reality of death.

Stanza 11

Can storied urn or animated bust
Back to its mansion call the fleeting breath?
Can Honour's voice provoke the silent dust,
Or Flatt'ry sooth the dull cold ear of Death?

THE "DEATH THE LEVELER" TOPOS CONCLUDED

Stanza 11 recapitulates and brings to a close the "Death the Leveler" theme that was initially posed in stanza 9. Thus, with respect to the symmetry of this section of the poem, stanza 11 is to stanza 10 as stanza 9 was to stanza 8: in both cases, the reality of death is invoked as an admonition against hubris. But as a result of the emergence of the theme of memory in stanza 10, the nature of the hubris addressed in stanza 11 has to do with the desire of human beings to perpetuate themselves symbolically. This is one of the functions of works of art, and thus the question of art itself is opened up.

In the context of the "Death the Leveler" topos, the incidental ironies of stanza 11 are somewhat obvious. Brooks observes that "the most 'animated' bust (*anima* = breath, soul) cannot call the fleeting *anima* of the dead man back to its 'mansion.' And the mansion receives its qualification in the next line: it is no more than silent dust."[27] We might add that the literal meaning of "mansion" as a great house enriches the metaphor because the rhetorical question pertains to those who hope that their

wealth will insulate them from reality. But again, all of this is
wholly traditional, and the fact that the theme is intrinsically
ironical does not render its statement either interesting or po-
etic. On the contrary, the stanza owes its power to a much
deeper irony and one that is conveyed by the concreteness of
the images in line 41: the fact that the question of art and its
relationship to "immortality" is being posed, albeit by negation.
Even Brooks acknowledges this in a way; after all, his essay is
entitled "Gray's Storied Urn." In stanza 11, the "storied urn"
appears in a negative context, but the connection between Gray
and Keats is less antithetical than it would appear.

Stanza 12

Perhaps in this neglected spot is laid
Some heart once pregnant with celestial fire,
Hands, that the rod of empire might have sway'd,
Or wak'd to extasy the living lyre.

THE PROBLEM OF UNFULFILLED POTENTIAL (1)

In stanza 12, the thematic center of the *Elegy* shifts to the
problem of unfulfilled potential, and Gray's treatment of the
theme is at the heart of his accomplishment in the poem. The
potentiality-actuality dynamic is, of course, fundamental to Ar-
istotle's *Metaphysics* and to his thought generally; so it is highly
significant that during the period in which Gray was at work on
the *Elegy*, he was especially preoccupied with Aristotle. Indeed,
if the scholarly consensus that the poem was begun in the
summer or autumn of 1746 is correct, then it follows that Gray's
involvement with Aristotle coincides with the early stages of
the poem's composition. Writing to Warton in September of
that year, in a letter that contains one of his earliest allusions
to the *Elegy*, Gray notes that Aristotle is "the hardest Author
by far I ever meddled with"; he then immediately adds: "this &
a few autumnal Verses are my Entertainments dureing the Fall
of the Leaf."[28]

Philip Wheelwright's discussion of the potentiality-actuality relationship in Aristotle's philosophy is interesting in regard to the problem of unfulfilled potential as the latter is developed in the *Elegy:*

> If a thing's actual character fulfilled all the implications of its definition—e.g. if man, defined as a rational animal, were in the fullest measure to realize everything that both "animal" and "rational" connote—it would be "complete" and "perfect" (*teleios*) of its kind, and hence divine. But, among mortals at any rate, perfect completeness or complete perfection is never found. In each actual embodiment there is always, to a greater or lesser degree, a "falling short" (*steresis*) of what the thing ideally (i.e. by definition) is.[29]

Wheelwright glosses the Aristotelian *steresis* variously as a "falling short," a "lack of form," a "lack of final character," "incompleteness," "notyetness," "absence," and "privation."[30] Now, this concept—or rather, Gray's derivation of it—is central to the *Elegy*, as we shall see, but its significance will be mediated by other concerns. Thus, in stanzas 12 to 15, the vision of *steresis* is focused specifically in terms of material poverty and social class, but later on in the poem it will be seen in universal terms, as an aspect of the human condition.

The thematic shift that occurs in stanza 12 is immediately evident from the opening word "Perhaps," which indicates that we are now in the realm of pure speculation. But the problem of unfulfilled potential is by no means thematically unmotivated, for it is latent in the poverty-obscurity connection that was established in stanza 8; its salience, however, had been partially suppressed by the "Death the Leveler" focus of stanzas 9 to 11.

In line 13 ("Beneath those rugged elms, that yew-tree's shade"), the demonstrative pronoun had served to root us in the site of the meditation; now, in line 45 ("Perhaps in this neglected spot is laid"), it returns us to the country churchyard. But where in stanzas 5 to 7 the lives of the Forefathers had been represented in terms of pastoral fulfillment—with the pathos at this point deriving from their lives being *no more*—the perspective in stanza 12 has been reversed and the pathos now focuses on the fact that those buried in the country churchyard were, in effect, "buried" during their lifetimes by the conditions of their existence, conditions that made it impossible for them to realize their potential as individuals. Thus, stanza 12 marks a shift in the locus of the poem's central pathos from the problem of death to that of "death-in-life" and, correspondingly, from the sphere of Nature to that of History. These metaphysical counters will eventually be entirely confounded with one another, of course; for the problem of death, for man, is precisely that of not having sufficiently lived, and human nature cannot be considered apart from History. But what is striking is that death, which would normally be considered the *major* focus in the dialectic of loss constituting the elegy as a genre, is here taken over and subsumed by "death-in-life."

THE SUBJUNCTIVE OF THE *Elegy*

As a correlative to the thematic shift described above, the grammatical center of the poem shifts in stanza 12 to the subjunctive mood—to a *might have been* whose pathos is antithetical to the *no more* and *for ever* that had marked the finality of death in stanzas 4 to 6. Those buried in the country churchyard are undifferentiated, having failed to leave a mark on History. The subjunctive, however, enables Gray to maintain a realistic and entirely unsentimental hold on this perspective while at the same time evoking the hypothetical possibility of an individual who *might have* emerged from the generic anonymity of his class: it enables him, in short, to express the real and the ideal, the abstract and the concrete, the present and the absent, simultaneously and in terms of each other.

Gray's use of the subjunctive to express the pathos of unfulfilled potential coincides with his use of synecdoche in stanza 12. The stanza is constructed around two symmetrical instances of this figure. Paradoxically, the reason that synecdoche is employed is that the concept of the individual is itself an abstraction that can only be concretized by being linked to parts of the body that stand in for the whole. But while the heart and the hands stand for the whole individual, they are, in their stark literalness, fragments of the whole; thus, synecdoche is countered by the ironical pathos of a concreteness that was doomed to remain abstract.

The potentiality-actuality relationship developed in stanzas 12 to 15 is extremely ambiguous and difficult to parse. Figuratively speaking, the poet is staring into the *emptiness* of the grave and speculating on a *fullness* that might have been. But does this *might have been* point to a fullness that was destined to remain unknown or to an emptiness that might have been full if other conditions had obtained? Both possibilities are latent, and ultimately the ambiguities are unresolvable because they exist in the realm of pure speculation, for Gray as much as for the reader. Nevertheless, from the standpoint of pure content, at least, the images in stanza 12 are expressive of fullness; thus, we are led to the first of our two alternatives. The force of the images is carried by a latent indicative that is framed by the subjunctive; and if we foreground this indicative, we find that the heart *was* at one time pregnant with celestial fire and that the hands *were* as adept as those that have actually swayed the rod of empire or waked the living lyre to ecstasy.

The feeling of waste is both intensified and mitigated by the suggestion of a fullness that was destined to leave no historical traces. But this interpretation leaves us with two further possibilities: (1) that the potential for creative expression might have existed but creative expression itself never occurred and (2) that creative expression actually occurred but has been lost to history. The latter interpretation is not given in the stanza to the same extent as the former, however, for it is clearly impossible to have swayed the rod of empire while remaining unknown. Yet this interpretation is by no means an empty extrapolation, for to have waked the lyre to ecstasy while remaining unknown—that is, to have been a *poeta ignotus*—is eminently possible. Consider the destiny of Thomas Chatterton, for example—the "marvellous Boy" of Wordsworth's *Resolution and Independence*, who was born in 1752 (the year after the publication of the *Elegy*) and who poisoned himself in 1770, after the so-called forgery of his Rowley Poems was discovered. Chatterton's story suggests that there were forces operating during the period that were opening up new possibilities for expression for members of the working classes while at the same time, of course, repressing those possibilities. It may be that the same historical circumstances that enabled Chatterton to become a poet in the first place ensured that he would not be able to sustain himself as one.[31]

It is important, however, that at this stage of the *Elegy*, the "rod of empire" and the "living lyre"—which are symbolic instruments in the hands of two distinct types of "rounded" individuals—are seen in terms of a basic complementarity. From the balanced perspective of classical humanism, the *via activa* and the *via contemplativa* are parallel paths, for both may lead to fulfillment and greatness and both are dependent on each other. (The paths of glory may lead but to the grave, when considered under the aspect of eternity, but given the limitations of the human condition, they are apparently not wholly to be despised.) The creative process (i.e., "celestial fire") is generic, manifesting itself in various directions, and the perspective on power itself is singularly devoid of melancholy or ressentiment. This is not because Gray has a naive attitude toward power, of course—and we have already seen that such is not the case— but rather because, other things being equal, *presence* (or being) must be seen as a "good" in itself when measured against *absence* (or nothingness). And precisely because Gray is speculating on what might have been from the standpoint of what could not have been, the apparent innocence of this attitude toward history does not strike us as sentimental.

Those buried in the country churchyard are lost to History, but in contemplating their fate Gray is at the same time meditating on the nature of History. To Gray in the *Elegy*, History is more than the chronicle of those who have made an impact on History: it encompasses the problematics of loss and thus enters the domain of lyric poetry—which is something profoundly new in the history of English poetry. Yet it is as a chronicle of those who have achieved renown that History presents itself—and in a sense, one can only conceive of it otherwise by negation.

Gray's use of the subjunctive is of radical significance in this regard, for it enables him to convey presence and the "presence of absence" simultaneously.

Stanza 13

But Knowledge to their eyes her ample page
Rich with the spoils of time did ne'er unroll;
Chill Penury repress'd their noble rage,
And froze the genial current of the soul.

THE PROBLEM OF UNFULFILLED POTENTIAL (2)

The imagery of stanza 12 leads us to interpret the ambiguity of unfulfilled potential primarily from the standpoint of a fullness that failed to leave any trace of itself. But this interpretation, if taken to an extreme, verges on sentimentality, for it implies that extraordinary creative capacities can flourish under conditions of poverty and deprivation. In other words, it conceives of the creative process as being unmediated by social and historical factors—much as, in the pastoral, the poet is represented as a shepherd.

To the extent that such an interpretation is latent in stanza 12, stanza 13 follows as a necessary corrective. For what happens, in effect, is that the subjunctive meets up with an implicit conditional. Indeed, the hands *might have* swayed the rod of empire or waked the lyre to ecstasy *if* (but this is an enormous if) Knowledge had unrolled her ample page and Chill Penury had not frozen the genial current of the soul. From this point of view, the concept of potentiality becomes equivalent to "innate intelligence," or some such abstraction, and hence the *might have been* of stanza 12 no longer underscores a fullness that failed to leave a trace of itself but, on the contrary, an emptiness or poverty that was simply incapable of emerging from its generic confines. That, of course, is true, and, though obvious, needs to be stated explicitly in order to counteract the tendency, on the one hand (the left), to sentimentalize the situation, and on the other hand (the right), to "impute to These the fault" for not having imposed their mark on the world. The simple point being made is that knowledge is a prerequisite to creative power (for knowledge is a kind of power), and under conditions of deprivation, one is deprived also of knowledge.

Knowledge is described as "rich with the spoils of time," which suggests to Brooks that it is being associated with the "ignoble competition . . . of the 'madding crowd.' "[32] But the military metaphor, though perfectly apt, does *not* signify that Knowledge is an alienated presence that should be viewed ironically. On the contrary, if time is understood in both its negative and positive aspects—that is, as embracing both discontinuity and continuity—then it becomes clear that knowledge is that which is simultaneously *won back from time* and *preserved against time,* for it is the basis on which the future is constructed. The personification of knowledge thus emphasizes the sense in which History, as an active process, is predicated on the accumulation of knowledge. History, in this teleological sense, is "man-made" time (for Hegel, man is the inventor of time)—to be set over against mere transience or death. This, of course, is not to suggest that knowledge (with a small "k") must always be viewed in such exalted terms—Gray has no illusions on that score—but rather that Knowledge as a function is being seen in its universal relation to the human enterprise.

If Knowledge has failed to unroll her ample page to the poor, it is not because her riches are merely in the service of the upper classes. Those riches are ultimately in the service of humanity as a whole; but in relation to this issue, a conservative interpretation, such as Brooks's, might easily meet up with a leftist analysis that conceives of knowledge as equivalent to ideology. Both perspectives, however, would be equally misguided. In Marxian terms (as distinct from those of contemporary cultural leftism), Knowledge's riches would constitute use-value—which is immeasurable, since it ultimately corresponds to that which increases the creative capacities of humanity as a whole—while the riches of Ambition and Grandeur would constitute exchange-value. Under conditions in which use-value and exchange-value are in contradiction—that is, in which ex-

change-value *mocks the useful toil* of the producers of value—
Chill Penury is necessarily a member of the dramatis personae.
Knowledge is a kind of power, but its power to distribute the
riches of knowledge can be appropriated by the rich and powerful
and arrested by their servant—Chill Penury.

Stanza 14

Full many a gem of purest ray serene,
The dark unfathom'd caves of ocean bear:
Full many a flower is born to blush unseen,
And waste its sweetness on the desert air.

The connection that has been drawn between obscurity and
poverty, on the one hand, and between unfulfilled potential and
ignorance, on the other, suggests that the *Elegy*, although a lyric
poem without an explicit didactic focus, nevertheless has an
implicit programmatic dimension. Nobody would argue that
the poem does not deplore "Chill Penury," but the ideological
consequences that may be drawn from this will depend on how
one interprets the poem's tone. The crucial issue is whether
one believes that the poem is expressing—and consequently
buttressing—an attitude of *resignation* to a state of affairs that
is intrinsic to the nature of things and therefore as inevitable as
death or whether one believes that it contains an implicit po-
lemic against this state of affairs. The *Elegy* has been interpreted
in both of these directions by critics of opposite political persua-
sions. During the French Revolution, for example, as Frank Ellis
points out, it was translated by revolutionists and monarchists
alike.[33] In the twentieth century, academic critics of a conserva-
tive temper have tended to view it as a conservative poem of
resignation; but, paradoxically, such would also appear to be the
case among critics on the Left—including those who might
at one time have entertained the possibilities of "proletarian
culture."

Much as it is impossible to reduce the subject matter of the
Elegy to a particular construct, so it is equally impossible to
pinpoint the poem's tone in terms of a particular *attitude*. The

reason for this, essentially, is that as Gray's meditation unfolds, the various perspectives it adopts are continually being revised and reinterpreted against one another, so that the major problems of death and "death-in-life" on which it is focused are sometimes congruent with and sometimes antithetical to one another. A "conservative" reading of the poem would argue that these problems are ultimately symmetrical in the *Elegy*; a "Platonic" (or perhaps "Marxist-humanist") reading would argue that they are ultimately asymmetrical and that the poem's tragic emotion is generated not only in terms of that which is inevitable (and hence bounded by Nature) but also in terms of that which is amenable to human intervention (and hence bounded by History).

EMPSON'S INTERPRETATION

William Empson's well-known discussion of stanza 14, in the "Proletarian Literature" chapter of *Some Versions of Pastoral*, represents the classic statement of the position that Gray's tone in the *Elegy* reflects a conservative political outlook. Finding that the *Elegy* "is an odd case of poetry with latent political ideas," Empson argues as follows:

> What this means [stanza 14 as a whole], as the context makes clear, is that eighteenth-century England had no scholarship system or *carrière ouverte aux talents*. This is stated as pathetic, but the reader is put into a mood in which one would not try to alter it. (It is true that Gray's society, unlike a possible machine society, was necessarily based on manual labor, but it might have used a man of special ability wherever he was born.) By comparing the social arrangement to Nature he makes it seem inevitable, which it was not, and gives it a dignity which was undeserved. Furthermore, a gem does not mind being in a cave and a flower prefers not to be picked; we feel that the man is like the flower, as short-lived, natural, and valuable, and this tricks us into feeling that he is better off without opportunities. The sexual suggestion of *blush* brings in the Christian idea that virginity is good in itself, and so that any renunciation is good; this may trick us into feeling it is lucky for the poor man that society keeps him

unspotted from the World. The tone of melancholy claims that the poet understands the considerations opposed to aristocracy, though he judges against them; the truism of the reflections in the churchyard, the universality and impersonality this gives to the style, claim as if by comparison that we ought to accept the injustice of society as we do the inevitability of death.

Many people, without being communists, have been irritated by the complacence in the massive calm of the poem, and this seems partly because they feel there is a cheat in the implied politics; the "bourgeois" themselves do not like literature to have too much "bourgeois ideology."[34]

The passage is extremely interesting on a number of levels. Empson's argument, like Brooks's, is an ingenious one, but if there is a "cheat in the implied politics," it is being perpetrated by the critic, not the poet; for what Empson has done here is to pose his *own* conservative interpretation in the language of the Left. First of all, when Empson remarks that Gray's society "might have used a man of special ability wherever he was born," he is echoing none other than Edmund Burke, the "father of modern conservatism," and he is being disingenuous in the same way that Burke had been in a famous passage from *Reflections on the Revolution in France* (1790):

> You do not imagine that I wish to confine power, authority, and distinction to blood and names and titles. No, Sir. There is no qualification for government but virtue and wisdom, actual or presumptive. Wherever they are actually found, they have, in whatever state, condition, profession, or trade, the passport of Heaven to human place and honor. Woe to the country which would madly and impiously reject the service of the talents and virtues, civil, military, or religious, that are given to grace and to serve it; and would *condemn to obscurity* [my italics] everything formed to diffuse lustre and glory around a state! Woe to that country, too, that, passing into the opposite extreme, considers a low education, a mean contracted view of things, a sordid, mercenary occupation, as a preferable title to command![35]

I have set the phrase "condemn to obscurity" in italics because Burke here, and perhaps in the passage as a whole, is inadver-

tently echoing none other than Gray in the *Elegy*, though from
a point of view that is clearly antithetical to Gray's. But what
is disingenuous (or, in any event, naive) in the remarks of both
Burke and Empson is the assumption that English society in the
eighteenth century (or indeed any other society, for that matter)
made use or could have made use of the "talents and virtues"
of members of the lower classes. In the first place, how would
these talents and virtues have been discovered? Secondly, what
is a talent or virtue in the abstract, when it has not been nurtured
by education? This is precisely the point that Gray is making in
the *Elegy*.

Empson goes on to say that "by comparing the social arrange-
ment to Nature, [Gray] makes it seem inevitable, which it was
not." Here he is subtly echoing the "commodity fetishism"
chapter of *Capital*, in which Marx points out that the economic
"laws" that obtain under capitalism tend to be regarded as
though they were laws of Nature and hence inevitable.[36] But
Gray is *not* comparing the social arrangement to Nature in order
to make it seem inevitable. On the contrary, in the metaphorical
substitutions of stanza 14, he is making use of natural symbols
that *already embody human values* so as to convey something
on the order of an inverted carpe diem theme, which has already
been prepared for by the previous stanzas. Both the gem and the
flower symbolize beauty, purity, innocence, and so on—and, of
course, the gem in particular does not merely embody abstract
values but is valuable in economic terms as well. It is ludicrous
for Empson to argue that "a gem does not mind being in a cave
and a flower prefers not to be picked," because in attacking
Gray's use of the pathetic fallacy he is making use of it himself.
In actuality, of course, neither the gem nor the flower would
have any feelings in the matter at all: they serve to concretize
a human pathos, and they are set in relation to the theme of
unfulfilled potential that has been developed throughout the
poem, and more or less explicitly in stanzas 12 to 13. And as far
as poetry is concerned, the pathetic fallacy is no fallacy at all,
for language simply has no other means of concretizing internal
feeling-states than through external objects.

Empson notes that "the sexual suggestion of *blush* brings in the Christian idea that virginity is good in itself, and so that any renunciation is good"; but, in fact, this verb is a clue to the inverted carpe diem theme that is being developed in the poem. This becomes apparent when we examine stanza 14 against its clearest "source" in the English tradition, Edmund Waller's famous lyric "Go, lovely rose." (The italics, indicating words that are echoed in stanza 14, are mine.)

> Go, lovely rose!
> Tell her that *wastes* her time and me
> That now she knows,
> When I resemble her to thee,
> How *sweet* and fair she seems to be.
>
> Tell her that's young,
> And shuns to have her graces spied,
> That hadst thou sprung
> In *deserts*, where no men abide,
> Thou must have uncommended died.
>
> Small is the worth
> Of beauty from the light retired;
> Bid her come forth,
> Suffer herself to be desired,
> And not *blush* so to be admired.
>
> Then die! that she
> The common fate of all things rare
> May read in thee
> How small a part of time they share
> That are so wondrous *sweet* and fair.[37]

In Waller's lyric, the blushing of the girl is in contradistinction to the blooming of the rose, for the one denotes withdrawal and the other emergence—though perhaps on a deeper level these two antithetical meanings coincide, since there is a suggestion that the girl's loveliness is intensified by her modesty. In stanza 14 of the *Elegy*, the primary meaning of "blush" is clearly "bloom," but something of Waller's delicately ambiguous shading has been retained. The flower's reticence is intrinsic to its beauty, much as the pathos we feel in connection with the unfulfilled potential of the poor is intensified by their having remained "far from the madding crowd's ignoble strife" (line 71). (The Keatsian formula for this will be: "Heard melodies are sweet, but those unheard / Are sweeter still.") But this is very far from saying that the poor "are better off without opportunities" or that "we ought to accept the injustice of society as we do the inevitability of death."

GRAY'S IMPLICIT DIDACTIC FOCUS

The context for Gray's echoes of Waller is the theme of unfulfilled potential that he has been developing in the previous stanzas of the *Elegy*. And one might ask why, if he were expressing an attitude of conservative resignation, he would have evoked this problem in the first place.[38] He might simply have concluded, with Pope in the *Essay on Man* (although we should not hold Pope to this attitude), that "Whatever is, is right" (4.394). But that Gray is not expressing such a view is corroborated by *The Alliance of Education and Government*, a fragment in the Augustan verse-essay mode, which is the only explicitly didactic poem that Gray ever attempted and of vital importance for our understanding of his political philosophy. Begun no later than 1748, and probably abandoned by 1749,[39] the composition of *The Alliance* was overlapped by that of the *Elegy*, and the intimate connection between the two is immediately apparent.[40] Both the subject of *The Alliance* and the pattern of imagery it employs indicate that it ought to be read as a companion piece to the *Elegy* and particularly in relation to stanza 14. The poem's basic argument is given in its title. "I mean to show," wrote Gray to Thomas Warton, "that [education and government] must necessarily concur to produce great & useful Men."[41] Indeed, the poem argues that in order for both the individual and the society as a whole to *flourish*—that is, to fulfill their potential— "equal Justice with unclouded Face" must "scatter with a free, tho' frugal, Hand / Light golden Showers of Plenty o'er the Land." (The last of these lines echoes line 63 of the *Elegy*: "To scatter plenty o'er a smiling land.") In the absence of a system dedicated to this end, "fond Instruction on the growing Powers /

Of Nature idly lavishes her Stores." The organic metaphor is
developed throughout *The Alliance*, not because the social ar-
rangement is being viewed in terms of inevitability, but, on
the contrary, because the flourishing or languishing of human
powers is being viewed analogically as an "organic" process that
is conditioned by the *nature* of the social system. Indeed, from
the very first word of the poem ("As"), it is clear that the entire
conception is built not on an identity between Nature and Soci-
ety but on an *analogy* between them. In the opening lines, the
gem and the flower of stanza 14 make an appearance, and there
are other echoes between the two poems as well; for instance,
the word "genial" in line 3 of *The Alliance* occurs in stanza 13
of the *Elegy*, where it has similar connotations:

> As sickly Plants betray a niggard Earth,
> Whose barren bosom starves her gen'rous Birth
> Nor genial Warmth, nor genial Juice retains
> Their Roots to feed, and fill their verdant Veins:
> And as in Climes, where Winter holds his Reign,
> The Soil, tho fertile, will not teem in vain,
> Forbids her Gems to swell, her Shades to rise,
> Nor trusts her Blossoms to the churlish Skies:
> So draw Mankind in vain the vital Airs,
> Unform'd, unfriended, by those kindly Cares,
> That Health and Vigour to the Soul impart,
> Spread the young Thought, and warm the opening Heart.
> So fond Instruction on the growing Powers
> Of Nature idly lavishes her Stores,
> If equal Justice with unclouded Face
> Smile not indulgent on the rising Race,
> And scatter with a free, tho' frugal, Hand
> Light golden Showers of Plenty o'er the Land:
> But Tyranny has fix'd her Empire there,
> To check their tender Hopes with chilling Fear,
> And blast the blooming promise of the Year.

(1–21)

Clearly, then, a simple comparison of *The Alliance of Educa-
tion and Government* and the *Elegy* disposes of Empson's argu-
ment. But to be fair to Empson, it should be noted that although
stanza 14 has a specific reference to the situation of the poor,

the problem of "death-in-life" that the poem as a whole raises
has a bearing on the human condition in general, over and above
the socioeconomic dialectic. In articulating this side to the argu-
ment, Empson is on firmer ground, although to some extent his
interpretation remains a reductive one even in this regard:

> And yet what is said is one of the permanent truths; it is only
> in degree that any improvement of society could prevent
> wastage of human powers; the waste even in a fortunate life,
> the isolation even of a life rich in intimacy, cannot but be
> felt deeply, and is the central feeling of tragedy. And anything
> of value must accept this because it must not prostitute
> itself; its strength is to be prepared to waste itself, if it does
> not get its opportunity. A statement of this is certainly non-
> political because it is true in any society, and yet nearly all
> the great poetic statements of it are in a way "bourgeois,"
> like this one; they suggest to many readers, though they do
> not say, that for the poor man things cannot be improved
> even in degree.[42]

This is moving, but not quite accurate. It is true, as Empson
observes, that one aspect of the tragic emotion generated by the
Elegy stems from the inevitability of waste imposed upon us
by our finitude. But in the context of stanzas 12 to 14, at least,
the waste that Gray is lamenting is clearly one of *kind* rather
than of degree. The gem and flower remain a gem and flower
even if unperceived (Bishop Berkeley to the contrary), but the
same cannot be said for the human situation, in which the
potentiality-actuality relationship is far more complex and am-
biguous. The heart may have been pregnant with celestial fire
(and from this point of view, the individual was *already* like
the gem or flower), but for lack of the appropriate conditions
the individual was unable to *become* himself (and from this
point of view, the unperceived gem and flower stand in relation
to sheer absence).

Contrary to Empson's assertion, moreover, it is not the articu-
lation of tragic inevitability that is "bourgeois"; what is "bour-
geois" is the *omission* of the tragedy of what is *not* inevitable.
And far from being an accurate reflection of Gray's argument in
the *Elegy*, Empson's final statement in the passage quoted above
is merely tautological; for if things improve for the poor man in

degree, then eventually he ceases to be poor, and this, of course, is a difference in *kind*. Or to pose the matter in Marxist terms: "Quantity becomes quality."

Finally, although Empson's interpretation of the *Elegy* is a conservative one that is couched in the language of the Left, we should note that an adherent of "proletarian literature" would certainly find the poem anathema on ideological grounds. For one thing, Gray is clearly working in the "high style," and he is the very antithesis of a "popular" poet—which is why the enormous popularity of the *Elegy* is so ironical a fact. For another, what Gray is clearly asserting in the *Elegy* is that the conditions of deprivation do not lend themselves to poetic capability. On both accounts, then, Gray could be accused of "elitism." But if he had been able to respond, Gray would have pointed out that the concept of "proletarian literature" is not only a "version" of pastoral that is premised on a sentimental illusion but one that is all the more vicious in accepting deprivation as a normal basis for culture. Ironically, the category of proletarian literature (or its contemporary offshoots) is one that undercuts its own revolutionary doctrine; for if the poor were able to attain to poetry, it would follow that the conditions of deprivation and exploitation did not inhibit them and hence were not wholly to be despised.

Stanza 15

Some village-Hampden, that with dauntless breast
The little Tyrant of his fields withstood;
Some mute inglorious Milton here may rest,
Some Cromwell guiltless of his country's blood.

The theme of unfulfilled potential that has been developed in the three previous stanzas reaches a climax in stanza 15, as a result of the *naming* of three figures who embody different types of greatness and who are symbolically linked with the Revolution of 1642. Hampden, Milton, and Cromwell—these are the only names that occur in the *Elegy*—were originally Cato, Tully, and Caesar in the Eton Manuscript. The revision is crucial, for it poses the issue of heroic presence in immediate historical terms, and in the process it complicates the political (and ethical) associations that are linked to this theme. Cato and Cicero betoken republican virtue, and Caesar the beginnings of empire, and so with the Roman names there would have been something of a binary opposition between liberty and tyranny. With the shift to an English frame of reference, however, the implication that Cromwell was guilty of his country's blood—and Milton, of course, was Cromwell's Latin secretary—suggests that the stanza cannot be understood in terms of such simple political counters.

Like other stanzas in the *Elegy,* stanza 15 is constructed on a base of anaphoric symmetry, with each of the repeated elements corresponding to one of the three compound subjects of the sentence. But what is remarkable is the way the predicate, "here may rest," balances the stanza from within the middle term of the sequence—a Virgilian effect that is intensified by the falling of the caesura after the seventh syllable, which is rare in the English pentameter line in general and in Gray's practice in particular. The first subject, which is attached to a relative clause, extends over two lines; the second occupies half a line; and the third, a single line. Again, within the context of anaphoric symmetry, there is a good deal of syntactical variation.

In the context of the problem of unfulfilled potential that has been developed since stanza 12, the effect of the phrase modifying Cromwell—or rather the Cromwell who might have been—is extremely ironical, of course, and it signifies yet another shift of perspective in the poem's aim at inclusivity. In the previous stanzas, absence had been to presence as a negative to a positive, but now, quite abruptly, we are forced to become aware of a new problematic that looms on the horizon—though one that will not actually be developed until stanzas 17–18 and that we may therefore bracket for the moment.

GRAY'S ANTITHETICAL RELATIONSHIP TO THE HEROIC

The naming of three figures who played a crucial role in English history—and Milton and Cromwell are what Hegel would have called "world-historical" figures—is an indication that the *Elegy* should be considered not merely in relation to the elegiac tradition, but also—albeit antithetically—in relation to a tradition of "heroic" poetry. In this regard, it is important to note that Gray's four-line stanza of alternating rhymes, which came to be regarded as the "elegiac stanza" in the eighteenth century (partly, no doubt, as a result of the *Elegy* itself), was often referred to as the "heroic stanza" during the seventeenth. Criticism, however, has tended to view the poem rather narrowly in the context of the elegies of James Hammond and William Shenstone, both of whom employ the four-line alternating stanza and work in the decadent pastoral mode of the period. Hammond's *Love Elegies*, which Dr. Johnson dismissed as "worthless,"[43] are mainly imitations of Tibullus; they were published in 1743 and were probably known to Gray.[44] Shenstone, who was influenced by Hammond—he refers to the four-line alternating stanza as "Hammond's meter"—published his elegies in 1764, but they had circulated in manuscript for some twenty years and thus may have been seen by Gray before the completion of the *Elegy*.[45] It is unlikely, however, that Gray would have been influenced in any important way by either poet. Hammond is never mentioned in Gray's correspondence; Shenstone receives praise for *The Schoolmistress*, which is pronounced "excellent in its kind,"[46] but all other references to his poetry are disparaging. In the "Prefatory Essay on Elegy" that Shenstone added to the volumes he published in 1764, he observed that "it is in particular the task and merit of elegy to shew the innocense and simplicity of rural life to advantage."[47] Shenstone's notion can be seen as applicable to Gray's *Elegy* only if one conceives of the latter in sentimental terms. Writing to Warton, Gray remarks: "But then there is Mr. Shenstone, who trusts to nature and simple sentiment, why does he do no better? he goes hopping along his own gravel-walks and never deviates from the beaten paths for fear of being lost."[48]

FROM THE HEROIC TO THE ELEGIAC STANZA

In the "Observations on English Metre" that Gray collected in his commonplace book during the period (1752–58) when he and Mason were planning a history of English poetry, neither Hammond nor Shenstone is cited under the section on stanzas of four lines with alternating rhymes. Mention is made of poems by Wyatt, Surrey, Spenser, and Gascoigne, but the most interesting entry, from our point of view, is Dryden's *Annus Mirabilis*.[49] Dryden's poem epitomizes the seventeenth-century heroic (but nonepic) mode, and in his Preface, Dryden indicates that his choice of meter was a concomitant of this mode: "I have call'd my Poem *Historical*, not *Epick*, though both the Actions and Actors are as much Heroick, as any Poem can contain. . . . I have chosen to write my Poem in *Quatrains* or *Stanza's* of four in alternate rhyme, because I have ever judg'd them more noble, and of greater dignity, both for the sound and number, then any other Verse in use amongst us."[50] Later on in the Preface, moreover, Dryden refers to Sir William Davenant, who, in the Preface to *Gondibert*, defends his use of the same meter in similar terms.[51]

Gray, of course, was profoundly influenced by Dryden, to whom he pays ample tribute in both *The Progress of Poesy* and the *Stanza's to Mr. Bentley*. "If there was in his own numbers any thing that deserved approbation," he told James Beattie, "he had learned it all from Dryden."[52] Nor would the influence of Dryden have been merely stylistic. Although Dryden is sometimes thought of as a "reactionary" because of his association with the Royalist cause, he was, as Earl Miner observes, "a historical progressivist with great faith in what man might achieve in time."[53] Dryden's belief in progress is very much in evidence in *Annus Mirabilis*, and this is one of the factors that connects the poem (however antithetically) to the *Elegy* as well as to the more overtly Drydenesque *Alliance of Education and Government*.

Consequently, it is not surprising that in spite of the temperamental differences between the two poets, there is an intimate connection between the rhetorical eloquence of Dryden's heroic verse and the effects for which Gray was striving in the *Elegy*. In the following extraordinary stanza from *Annus Mirabilis*, for example,

Go, Mortals, now, and vex yourselves in vain
    For wealth, which so uncertainly must come:
When what was brought so far, and with such pain,
    Was onely kept to lose it neerer home,[54]

the adverb "when" creates the same kind of grammatical condensation that, as we have seen, Gray uses to such effect in the *Elegy*.[55]

Ian Jack calls attention to Gray's reference to *Annus Mirabilis* in the commonplace book; however, in Jack's view, Dryden comes closest to Gray's use of the meter not in *Annus Mirabilis* but in the *Heroick Stanza's* to the memory of Cromwell.[56] This point is interesting in light of the ironic reference to Cromwell in line 60, although Jack does not explicitly make this connection. Moreover, since the *Heroick Stanza's* constitute an elegy on an heroic figure, the poem marks a convergence of the seventeenth- and eighteenth-century conceptions of the meter. From a stylistic viewpoint, however, the differences between *Annus Mirabilis* and the *Heroick Stanza's* are negligible, and therefore it would seem that Jack's argument is based on a priori generic assumptions about the *Elegy*. If the genre is taken as a fixed category with rigid boundaries, then it would seem farfetched to connect Gray's poem to *Annus Mirabilis*; but, in fact, the elegiac genre was considered an especially fluid one by the eighteenth century. The question of whether, and in what sense, the *Elegy* is *an* elegy is a problematic one that we shall have to confront later on—most especially since the poem itself manifests an awareness of the problem.

In the meantime, if we set aside our generic assumptions, it becomes clear that the formal connection between Gray and Dryden has rather complex thematic and, indeed, generic ramifications. The crucial point to be discerned, however, is simply this: Whereas Dryden's heroic poems celebrate actors and actions that have an immediate bearing on the *public* stage of history, the *Elegy* poses the issue of the heroic from the standpoint of those who have been denied access to this public stage. The heroic quatrain of the seventeenth century becomes the elegiac quatrain of the eighteenth, essentially because of the *disappearance* of the heroic as a viable mode; the *Elegy* maintains contact with the heroic, but only from the standpoint of loss. Thus, whereas in Dryden's *Heroick Stanza's* the heroic and elegiac strains converge from the standpoint of the heroic, in the *Elegy* it is the loss of the heroic itself that is lamented.

This loss of the heroic, which in a certain sense is tantamount to the alienation of poetry from itself, thrusts itself up *athematically,* as it were, from within the overt thematic problem of social alienation predicated on class divisions. The condition of *poverty,* as a result of which the Forefathers were "buried" during their lives, is somehow experienced (both by Gray and by the reader) as contiguous with the conditions situating *poetry;* and the converse of this is also true. Nor is this a loose association whose consequence is the sentimental insertion of the poet "into a poem about people very different from himself," as Winters argued.[57] An examination of the social basis for poetry at the time at which Gray wrote would yield ample evidence of the fact that the poet is increasingly *marginal* to society. Gray's consciousness of this process—his consciousness of a lost center—is more profound than that of any of his contemporaries because it exists not only at the level of content but at the level of form; indeed, it is responsible for transforming the very basis for poetry, as the *Elegy* demonstrates. To a writer such as Johnson, the awareness of the tenuousness of the poet's relationship to society—as in the remarkable *Life of Savage,* for example, or the well-known lines in *The Vanity of Human Wishes:* "There mark what Ills the Scholar's Life assail, / Toil, Envy, Want, the Patron, and the Jail" (159–60)—does not coincide with an awareness of a lost center, does not manifest itself at the deepest levels of form. This is Johnson's strength, and this is perhaps why we tend to view him as central to the age. Ironically, however, it may be that Gray's vision of a lost center is closer to the period's actual center of consciousness.

One measure of the increasing marginalization of the poet and poetry that occurs in the generations separating Pope from Gray (born in 1688 and 1717 respectively) is the simple poetic function of *naming.* There is probably no poet in English who

names his contemporaries more frequently than Pope; yet, ironi-
cally, this simple gesture of naming one's contemporaries,
which for Pope is entirely normal and seemingly unburdened
by complications, is, for Gray, at least in his serious poetry—
and in spite of the palpable influence that Pope exerted upon
him—virtually impossible. The names that occur in Gray's po-
etry are all distanced either by history or by literature, and, as
with the three names that occur in stanza 15 of the *Elegy*, they
only serve to intensify our sense of the separation of the poet
from the public sphere. Not that the theme of anonymity pervad-
ing the *Elegy* is entirely absent from Pope's work, by the way:
it occurs most notably in the *Elegy to an Unfortunate Lady*,
where the lady being memorialized is unnamed. Indeed, in the
conclusion of Pope's elegy, not only the lady but the poet, and
perhaps poetry itself, is enfolded by that *forgetting* which is
attendant upon death:

> Poets themselves must fall, like those they sung;
> Deaf the prais'd ear, and mute the tuneful tongue.
> Ev'n he, whose soul now melts in mournful lays,
> Shall shortly want the gen'rous tear he pays;
> Then from his closing eyes thy form shall part,
> And the last pang shall tear thee from his heart,
> Life's idle business at one gasp be o'er,
> The Muse forgot, and thou belov'd no more![58]

In the *Elegy to an Unfortunate Lady*, however, the poet himself
knows who the lady was, and we are subtly given to understand
that if he does not divulge her name, this is for reasons of
discretion:

> So peaceful rests, without a stone, a name,
> What once had beauty, titles, wealth, and fame.
>
> (69–70)

The oblivion that enfolds both lady and poet in the concluding
passage is simply a product of time's ravages and thus generic
to the species as a whole; the theme of anonymity is, as it
were, accidental and not predicated on a chain of socioeconomic
circumstances.

By contrast, when we arrive at Gray's *Elegy*, we sense that the problem of anonymity is not merely a theme to be taken up or put down as the poet wills but a condition that is somehow implicated in situating the poetic process itself, so that poetry has become, as it were, contiguous with poverty.

"Some Mute Inglorious Milton": A Point of Tropological Convergence

This relationship between poetry and poverty makes itself felt most succinctly in the "mute inglorious Milton" of line 59, a figure whose implications are extremely various. On the most obvious level, the figure is an oxymoron—for to be mute and inglorious is clearly to be no Milton at all. However, if we think of the figure as a *poeta ignotus*, which is one of the several possible interpretations stemming from the potentiality-actuality relationship developed in the previous stanzas, we are thinking of him basically in terms of metonymy—Puttenham's "misnamer" in *The Arte of English Poesie*.[59] (Kenneth Burke, in his essay "Four Master Tropes," views metonymy as a figure of *reduction*,[60] and one could say that a "mute inglorious Milton" reduces the field of possible *poetae ignoti*.) But there is also a sense in which metaphor (which Burke sees in terms of *perspective*) is operating here, since the fame of a Milton provides the perspective against which to measure anonymity. From yet another point of view, however, the figure is a representation of what cannot literally be represented, a name for that which is nameless, and (in the context of the paradox of the One and the Many) a part for the whole—hence a synecdoche. (Burke views synecdoche in terms of *representation*.) As such, however, the figure straddles both ends of the absence-presence dialectic and thus is being galvanized by irony—although, as Burke suggests, it may be that irony is less a trope than the dramatic interaction of tropes. A "mute inglorious Milton" is a representation of what cannot be represented, but the actual Milton is himself a "representative poet" (in the Emersonian sense), and the Poet, considered in the abstract, has a representative function for humanity as a whole. The synecdoche is polarized by its ironical context in the absence-presence dialectic; each of these poles has manifold implications, and each is dependent upon the other pole.

If Gray's "mute inglorious Milton" marks an extreme point of tropological convergence in the poem, this is because the figure not only epitomizes the absence-presence dialectic that has been developed up to this point, but, in doing so, refocuses this dialectic in terms of the poetic process itself, where the salient contrast is no longer between the rich and the poor as such but between the poet of achieved presence and his "mute inglorious" antitype. Here one is reminded of Matthew Arnold's comment that Gray "never spoke out."[61] One should beware of interpreting Gray's figure wholly in autobiographical terms—and Arnold's perspective on Gray is extremely simplistic, as we saw in chapter 1—but there is clearly a self-reflexive aspect to Gray's vision that reverberates with his existential situation.

It is worth noting, therefore, that had it not been for a particular stroke of sheer good luck, it is highly unlikely that Gray would have developed into the great poet and scholar he was to become, the figure who in his later years had the reputation of being the most erudite man in Europe. Gray's parents were people of fairly small means: his father was a scrivener and his mother kept a millinery shop with her sister. Moreover, Gray's father was completely unwilling to contribute to his gifted son's education. However, two of Gray's uncles on his mother's side, Robert and William Antrobus, were assistant masters at Eton College, and these men arranged for Gray to be admitted to the school in 1725, when he was eight years old, and to receive a small scholarship as well. It would be a mistake to identify Gray with the "rude Forefathers" and hence with the "mute inglorious Milton" of the *Elegy*; but, clearly, he must have had a keen awareness that "there but for fortune go I."[62]

From a purely abstract standpoint, however, there is a certain logic—apart from all biographical or historical contingencies—in the fact that the fame-anonymity dialectic of the *Elegy* should turn in upon itself to foreground the poetic process. In the first place, one of the most important aspects of the poetic process

is its *memorializing function*. It is not for nothing that the
Muses are the daughters of Memory. But if we turn the equation
around to regard the memorializing function as primary—since
without it civilization could hardly have developed—then the
poetic process must be seen in its origins as a subsumed aspect
and the primary vehicle of this function. As Eric Havelock ar-
gues in *A Preface to Plato*, without the prosodic and lexical
recurrences of verse it would have been impossible for a preliter-
ate society such as Homer's to transmit crucial cultural informa-
tion from generation to generation.[63]

The implicit paradox in all this, however, is that what the
poetic process memorializes, in addition to some content, is
precisely *itself*. At the point at which society becomes capable
of transmitting information in written form, poetry becomes
less and less the vehicle of an independent content and more
and more the transcendental embodiment of what we can only
term the sacred, since it is cherished for itself rather than for
the utilitarian value of what it contains. At this point, the poem
not only *encloses* what the culture wishes to preserve but is its
own object of preservation.

There is thus a logical connection between the issue of pres-
ence that Gray is raising from a social point of view and the
very nature of the poetic process; and, as a matter of fact, this
connection is implicit in the pastoral tradition. But the existence
of such a connection in the abstract gives us no understanding
of how or why it is manifested from the standpoint of absence
or poverty in the *Elegy* and foregrounded as a subject for poetry
itself. The question that confronts us, then, is how the self-
reflexivity that enters the tradition with Gray's *Elegy* is related
to the previous tradition.

LYCIDAS AND THE PASTORAL ELEGY

The presence of Milton in stanza 15 is a sign of the direc-
tion our investigation must take, and the crucial text in this re-
gard is, of course, *Lycidas*, which, as we noted in chapter 2, has
often been regarded as the "model" for the *Elegy*, even by critics
whose interpretations of Gray's poem are in other respects dia-

metrically opposed.[64] The salient connection between the *Elegy* and *Lycidas* has to do with the fact that Milton's poem is a pastoral elegy and indeed the culmination of that genre in European literature; concomitantly, however, to assume that the *Elegy* is modeled upon *Lycidas* is to fail to take the generic significance of the pastoral elegy into account. For much as the pastoral elegy is addressed to the death of the poet, so Gray's *Elegy* is addressed to the death of those who lacked the conditions to attain to poetry in the first place. Lycidas is a fictional name for an aspiring poet whose actual name (Edward King) is known to us; Gray's "mute inglorious Milton" is a name for the unknown many who cannot be named. Thus, it is clear that the metaphysical basis for the pastoral elegy is inverted in Gray's *Elegy*.

The metaphysical basis for the pastoral, as I shall argue more closely in chapter 4, is a utopian reconciliation between Nature and History, such that civilization appears as an unmediated extension of Nature itself. Given this utopian conception—and given the synthesis of the aristocracy and the peasantry that is also implicit in the form—it is not surprising that the poet himself will be foregrounded through the figure of the shepherd. For it is the poet, after all, who is envisioning a world in which such a reconciliation has already been effected, and since the pastoral *is* this vision, it is logical that it should be peopled by poets. Consequently, there is a correspondence between the *inside* of the pastoral—where, through the image of the poet-as-shepherd, the vision of an already attained harmony is projected—and the *outside* through which this vision is engendered—that is, the poet's *desire* for such a world.

The pastoral elegy builds upon this metaphysics by addressing the problem of death from the standpoint of the Orphic myth. For just as Orpheus gave voice to Nature, humanizing it, in effect, so the death of the poet threatens to tear the unity of the pastoral world asunder, threatens to point up its fictionality, as it were. Thus, addressing the dead poet, Milton writes:

> But O the heavy change, now thou art gone,
> Now thou art gone, and never must return!
> Thee Shepherd, thee the Woods, and desert Caves,
> With wild Thyme and the gadding Vine o'ergrown,

And all their echoes mourn.
The Willow and the Hazel copses green
Shall now no more be seen,
Fanning their joyous leaves to thy soft lays.
As killing as the Canker to the Rose,
Or Taint-worm to the weanling Herds that graze,
Or Frost to Flowers, that their gay wardrobe wear,
When first the White-thorn blows;
Such, *Lycidas*, thy loss to Shepherd's ear.

(37–49)

Yet within the closed world of the pastoral, a world that excludes the tragic, there is never any serious danger of this actually happening; indeed, the reestablishment of an organic relationship between man and Nature is an a priori condition of the form. It would seem that death is introduced only for the purpose of being transcended, and in *Lycidas* this is essentially the consolation that Milton's "uncouth Swain" offers us in the poem's magnificent denouement.

Weep no more, woeful Shepherds weep no more,
For *Lycidas* your sorrow is not dead,
Sunk though he be beneath the wat'ry floor,
So sinks the day-star in the Ocean bed,
And yet anon repairs his drooping head,
And tricks his beams, and with new-spangled Ore,
Flames in the forehead of the morning sky:
So *Lycidas*, sunk low, but mounted high,
Through the dear might of him that walk'd the waves,
Where other groves, and other streams along,
With *Nectar* pure his oozy locks he laves,
And hears the unexpressive nuptial Song,
In the blest Kingdoms meek of joy and love.
There entertain him all the Saints above,
In solemn troops, and sweet Societies
That sing, and singing in their glory move,
And wipe the tears for ever from his eyes.
Now *Lycidas*, the Shepherds weep no more;
Henceforth thou art the Genius of the shore,
In thy large recompense, and shalt be good
To all that wander in the perilous flood.

(165–86)

Dr. Johnson was repelled by Milton's "irreverend combinations"; the "trifling fictions" of the pastoral, he felt, ought not to be mingled with "the most awful and sacred truths."[65] But from an aesthetic point of view, there can be no doubt that Milton's synthesis of the two strains is perfectly seamless. Death is ultimately a foreign element to the organic harmony of the pastoral world, and therefore Lycidas *"is not dead,* / Sunk though he be beneath the wat'ry floor" (my italics). Similarly, "Through the dear might of him that walked the waves," the soul is eternal, and so Lycidas "sunk low, [is] mounted high."

It is worth noting, in this regard, that there is no logical transition to this the poem's denouement. After the "pilot of the *Galilean* lake" has given the parable of the good and bad shepherds (lines 113–31), the river Alpheus is invoked:

> Return *Alpheus,* the dread voice is past
> That shrunk thy streams; . . .
>
> (132–33)

There is no explanation for why the "dread voice," which connects the death of a man to the death of Nature, has disturbed the harmony of the pastoral world, and no explanation for why this harmony is restored. Nor could there be, for in the context of the pastoral world, whose "Ivy [is] never sere" (line 2), death can be incorporated only insofar as its existential meaning has been factored out from the outset.

We return from *Lycidas* to the *Elegy,* conscious, as Harold Bloom would say, of the *belatedness* of Gray's vision. Gray, of course, was thoroughly conscious of his belatedness in regard to the heroic tradition, and this consciousness, paradoxically, is one of the indices of his originality. It is expressed most explicitly in *The Progress of Poesy,* where the poet represents himself obliquely as coming in the wake of Milton, at a time when the "Lyre divine" is heard no more (lines 107–13). Not that Milton himself was unconscious of the problem of belatedness in his handling of the ancient genres, for in *Lycidas* the "uncouth Swain" through whom Milton speaks, though an archetypal fixture of the timeless pastoral world, tells us in the poem's opening lines that he has come "Yet once more" to take up his appointed laurels. But, as in the opening lines of *Paradise Lost*, this is Milton's announcement that he can accept the challenge posed by time and continue to fulfill—*without irony*—the role of the heroic poet. The only ironical thing about *Lycidas*, indeed, is that it is a poem from which irony—the "dread voice" telling us of death and of the unabsorbed residues of History—has been entirely expunged. This is not surprising, for irony, as Vico and Northrop Frye remind us, belongs not to the Golden Age but to the low mimetic age that bears its name.

The unabsorbed residues of History seep down through the succeeding century until they crystallize in Gray's *Elegy*, which is the poem of irony par excellence. In the *Elegy*, it is not so much that the heroic tradition is deconstructed by irony as that it makes its return via irony. Where in *Lycidas* irony is banished, in the *Elegy* it is the heroic—and, in a certain sense, poetry itself—that is in exile. The polarities have been inverted, and yet they remain constant. Moreover, although in the *Elegy* the heroic is reduced to the zero degree, this occurs without loss of poetic power. Indeed, although the poem would seem to occupy a position of *poverty* vis-à-vis the previous tradition, there is a sense in which its scope is greater and its pathos more resonant than what has come before—so that it obliges us to reinterpret the tradition in its own terms, as if that which had come before was an abstract and a too-early vision of what has finally been rendered concrete. In that sense, Gray's "mute inglorious Milton" might be viewed, in Harold Bloom's phrase, as a "transumption" of its illustrious precursor.

Stanzas 16–18

Th'applause of list'ning senates to command,
The threats of pain and ruin to despise,
To scatter plenty o'er a smiling land,
And read their hist'ry in a nation's eyes

Their lot forbad: nor circumscrib'd alone
Their growing virtues, but their crimes confin'd;
Forbad to wade through slaughter to a throne,
And shut the gates of mercy on mankind,

The struggling pangs of conscious truth to hide,
To quench the blushes of ingenuous shame,
Or heap the shrine of Luxury and Pride
With incense kindled at the Muse's flame.

As the problem of unfulfilled potential has been developed in
stanzas 12 to 15, absence has been to presence as a negative to
a positive. This is to say that Value has been submerged in Being
or has been viewed as an extension of it. But in line 60, with the
implication of the actual Cromwell's guilt, we are forced to
become aware of the narrowness of this metaphysical scheme.
To be sure, the phrase "guiltless of his country's blood" seems
to have come almost as a spontaneous afterthought, as if from
the necessity of finding a rhyme for "withstood," and the heavy
syntactical parallelism of stanza 15 makes us read the line at
first from the standpoint of the problem of unfulfilled potential.
But in the end, the phrase has the effect of rupturing the meta-
physical fabric of stanzas 12 to 15 and of opening it up to a new
problematic.[66]

THE PROBLEM OF EVIL

In stanzas 16 to 18, then, the problem of unfulfilled poten-
tial is brought into alignment with the problem of evil. The
connection between the arrogance of power and evil was already
implicit in stanzas 8 to 11, but the shift of perspective that
occurs between stanzas 17 and 18 is nevertheless a radical one—
and it is interesting that this transition is the only one in the
poem that is marked by a full enjambment between stanzas.
(Twenty-six of the poem's thirty-two stanzas conclude in a full
stop, an indication of how completely the quatrain form has
been absorbed as the basic unit of progression.) The enjambment
is produced by the suspension of the main clause from stanza
16 to 17; and this suspension, in turn, is thematically occasioned
by the fact that although line 60 ("Some Cromwell guiltless of
his country's blood") had shifted the discourse in an ethical
direction, the new perspective is not really established until the
turn in stanza 17.

Other things being equal, the analogues of power and presence in stanza 16 are positively valenced, or at least neutral, because in secular terms they betoken fulfillment. Stanza 16 is very much in transition, and we are being pulled in several directions at once, but for the most part we are still on the side of the "virtues."[67] It is true that criminals as well as virtuous men may command applause or despise threats, but line 63 acts as a kind of ethical magnet for the other terms in the sequence because "To scatter plenty o'er a smiling land" is clearly to be virtuous; and it is important to note that Gray's polemic in stanzas 17 and 18 will not be directed against power as such, since the latter can have good as well as evil consequences, but rather against power that is sought for its own sake and wielded in the interests of evil. The parallelism operating in stanza 16, which associates three ethically neutral analogues of power with a positive one, thus represents a kind of coda to the absence-presence dialectic of stanzas 12 to 15 while at the same time begging the ethical question.

Line 64 ("And read their hist'ry in a nation's eyes") deserves special attention because in this line the absence-presence dialectic is recapitulated and essentialized through the linking of History to the paradox of the One and the Many. The personal history of the "historical individual" becomes, by synecdoche, part and parcel of his nation's history. "Read," as Lonsdale points out, has the primary meaning of "discern";[68] the individual is aware of his impact on History and thereby experiences what in secular terms is the apex of personal fulfillment. But the literal meaning of the verb supplies the line with its force and metaphorical richness. The individual who has "gone down" in History does not, of course, read but is read about, but in Gray's metaphorical reversal, the act of reading (about) oneself is tantamount to a triumph over death.

The vicious consequences of power sought for its own sake are adumbrated in stanzas 17 and 18 with a directness and economy that requires little commentary. In stanza 17, the focus is on the violence and cruelty that result from the unbridled ruthlessness of the quest for power, and in stanza 18 it is on the deceit and corruption that result therefrom. The imagery of lines

66 to 67, as Lonsdale indicates, is typically Shakespearean,[69] but the power of these lines stems from Gray's ability to revitalize old metaphors by giving them a subtle twist. Where "wade through blood" would have been a cliché, Gray has restored the strength of the verb by linking it to the abstraction that the metaphor had originally concretized ("slaughter"). The "gates of mercy" is a formula of the popular literature of devotion, but in the bitterly ironic context of Gray's line, and as linked to "on mankind," its effect is very powerful. As it might in Bunyan, the formula has a kind of distanced pathos because its naiveté is comprehended and set against the subtle snares of the sophisticated world.

Stanzas 17 and 18 flow together with the accumulated momentum of Gray's polemic, and in them the motivic strains of stanzas 12 to 15 are taken up in retrograde, as it were. The poet and the political leader had been juxtaposed in stanzas 12 to 15 from the standpoint of potential virtue (although at this point the ethical dimension had not yet fully emerged), and now they are again set in tandem, but this time from the standpoint of potential crime. We noted earlier that in Gray's treatment of the metaphysics of presence, poetry itself is foregrounded because it is simultaneously the vehicle of Memory and that which is to be remembered. In stanza 18, however, poetry—indeed, art in general—is seen as what it all too often is: the vehicle of corruption and ideology. Moreover, implicit in lines 72–74 is the notion that poetry, when in the service of Luxury and Pride, not only facilitates and partakes of evil but is itself a kind of *idol worship*. The "shrine of Luxury and Pride" is linked motivically to the "storied urn and animated bust" of stanza 11—those "Trophies" which, from the perspective of stanza 18, we might say were raised as *fetishes* to call the soul back to the body. That which links poetry to the symbolic triumph over death is what can make it a diabolical instrument of superstition and hubris— and hence the Old Testament flavor of these lines.

The vision of evil contained in stanzas 17 and 18 thus casts the emphasis on self-realization and fulfillment in stanzas 12 to 15 into question and in the process obliges us to reconsider the political implications of the poem. Since the potential for vice

is balanced against the potential for virtue, it could be argued
that Gray is espousing a kind of pessimistic quietism, as a result
of which one would not be inclined to alter the situation of the
poor. Empson, we recall, had claimed that Gray in the "Full
many a gem" stanza is comparing the social arrangement to
Nature in order to make it seem inevitable, and Brooks had
argued that death is the matter on which Gray's irony exerts its
force. But, in fact, there are really *two* principles that Gray is
asserting, and he is asserting them both separately and in terms
of the contradiction between them; for neither of these princi-
ples can be factored out or harmonized with the other, since
both have a separate, albeit one-sided, claim to truth. On the
one hand, as we have seen in stanzas 12 to 15, Gray maintains
the belief, as enunciated by Aristotle in the *Nicomachean Eth-
ics*, that a fully human existence requires the harmonious devel-
opment of the faculties. On the other hand, now in stanzas 17
and 18, Gray asserts the Platonic claim, as derived from the
Republic, that the potential for vice is equal to the potential for
virtue, and that both depend on education, opportunity, and so
forth. There is no attempt on Gray's part to sentimentalize the
situation, but neither does the problem of evil lead him to
assume an attitude of quietism. On the contrary, as our earlier
discussion of *The Alliance of Education and Government* indi-
cated, Gray advocated the transformation of social institutions
and particularly those relating to education.

The *Alliance* is a Platonic tract, and, as Lonsdale notes, during
the period in which Gray was at work on both the *Alliance* and
the *Elegy* he took extensive notes on Book VI of the *Republic*,
where Plato deals with the philosopher's contribution to the
state.[70] Lonsdale quite rightly links the following passage from
Gray's Commonplace book, in which Gray summarizes one of
Plato's arguments, to both the *Alliance* and the *Elegy:*

> Those Excellences & Endowments required to form a Mind
> susceptible of true Philosophy; as a quick & retentive Under-
> standing, high Spirit, & a natural Greatness, & Simplicity of
> Soul (more particularly, if attended with what the World calls
> Blessings; Opulence, Birth, & Beauty of Person) are the most

likely to draw off the Youth that possesses them, from that
very Pursuit they were design'd for: and lighting (as he ex-
presses it) in an improper Soil, that is corrupted by a bad
Education, & ill-regulated Government become the readier
instruments of Mischief to Mankind, by so much more, as
Nature meant them for their Good. for every extraordinary
Wickedness, every action superlatively unjust is the Product
of a vigorous Spirit ill-nurtured; weak Minds are alike incapa-
ble of anything greatly good, or greatly ill.[71]

It is obvious, then, that for Gray (as for Plato) the problem
of evil stems not from education or knowledge, as Brooks's
argument would suggest, but from *bad* education. (Indeed,
Plato's purpose in writing the *Republic* was, among other things,
to transform Greek educational practice.) Given a corrupt soci-
ety, and the corrupt morals and educational system that go along
with it, Gray would argue that vice is as likely to result from
strong capabilities as virtue—and so the poor are at least spared
the possibility of committing great crimes. This does not, how-
ever, make their poverty a good thing. In other words, stanzas
17 and 18 do not cancel out the perspective of stanzas 12 to 15;
they broaden it. What we have, then, is an ethical vision that is
at once tragic, in that it comprehends the problem of evil, and
utopian, in that it sees the possibility and necessity for the
eradication of evil. The crucial nexus between the tragic and
utopian strains in this ethical vision is History. The tragic, for
Gray, is located not only in what is intrinsic to the human
condition but also in what is conditioned by a given set of
cultural forces. Thus, the metaphysics of presence, as developed
in stanzas 12 to 15, is framed by both the problem of death
(stanzas 8–11) and the problem of evil (stanzas 17–18), but it is
by no means canceled out by them.

Stanza 19

Far from the madding crowd's ignoble strife,
Their sober wishes never learn'd to stray;
Along the cool sequester'd vale of life
They kept the noiseless tenor of their way.

In the Eton Manuscript (appendix B), the four stanzas that Gray eventually rejected appear after line 72, and as we saw in chapter 2, some scholars have tended to prefer the "version" of the poem that concludes with those stanzas.[72] But having come so far in tracing the thematic progression of the *Elegy*, we can safely say that if the poem had indeed concluded with the four rejected stanzas, its closure would have been too abrupt and its structure inadequate to the demands of its development. This can be demonstrated through a brief summary of the poem's progression through stanza 18. First comes the description of the landscape (stanzas 1–3), which eventually focuses on the graves of the Forefathers (stanza 4). This leads to the evocation of the lives of the Forefathers (stanzas 5–7) and then to the attack on Ambition and Grandeur, in the context of which the contrast between the rich and the poor is posed against the universality of death (stanzas 8–11). From here the poem takes up the problem of unfulfilled potential, first in itself (stanzas 12–16) and then in relation to the problem of evil (stanzas 17–18). What is revealed by even so bald a summary as this is that the *Elegy* would not have been "rounded off," so to speak, if it had not returned to focus on the actual images presented by the graves of the Forefathers, which, curiously, have not really been described at all up to this point. We see this with the benefit of the standard version, of course, but if Gray had not resituated his meditation in terms of the images themselves, the poem's various thematic threads would have been left hanging and its attempt to arrive at an "organic" terminus would have been unrealized. Moreover, had the poem concluded with the four rejected stanzas after line 72, we would have been left with a denouement of pessimistic withdrawal from the world, and this would have constituted a retreat from the *Elegy*'s humanistic concerns—its attempt to recuperate a sense of the meaningfulness of human strivings even in the face of evil and death. Such a retreat, vitiating the poem's thematic complexity, would, however, have been in keeping with the interpretations of Gray's more conservative critics—which accounts for their preference for the "version" in the Eton Manuscript.

THE OPPOSITION BETWEEN TOWN AND COUNTRY AS A DIVISION BETWEEN CLASSES

What immediately determines the renewed focus on the destiny of the Forefathers in stanza 19 is that the vision of evil of stanzas 17 and 18 is so clearly connected to those who occupy the *center* of society, a center from which the Forefathers are removed both in actual fact and as if by a metaphysical barrier. As Gray interprets the situation, if the virtues of the Forefathers were *circumscribed* by the conditions of their existence, those virtues were nevertheless solid ones; for by remaining aloof from the struggle for wealth and power (though not necessarily by choice), the Forefathers were at least able to maintain their hold on a certain basic integrity—which cannot be said of those consumed by the "madding crowd's ignoble strife." Thus, in stanza 19 the contrast between the rich and the poor confronts us simultaneously as an opposition between Town and Country and as a division between "classes" (if we may tentatively employ this term). The first of the oppositions is the traditional pastoral formulation; the second, however, is actually antithetical to the pastoral ethos.

When we first encountered Ambition and Grandeur in stanza 8, we noted that these figures are metonymically linked to the "upper classes," and clearly this is a fair, if somewhat vague, assumption. But the metaphor of social class, being predicated on the emergence of sociology, is not really part of the vocabulary that Gray has at his disposal. As a matter of fact, when we try to pin Ambition, Grandeur, and their affines down to a particular social formation, we find that there is a sense in which their referentiality is blurred—as if they belonged to a sequence of indefinitely deferred metonymies. Interestingly, the same holds true for those buried in the country churchyard. In line 16, they are referred to as "the rude Forefathers of the hamlet," and in stanza 8 they are associated with poverty and obscurity, but from then on in the poem they are always referred to by the third-person pronoun.

Nevertheless, although Gray does not employ the metaphor

of social class (and it was through Marx, of course, that the latter
became part of the intellectual vocabulary), the metaphor of the
center and its peripheries, which he does employ, and which is
part of the classical apparatus of the pastoral, seems to verge in
stanza 19 on something akin to a class conception *avant la
lettre*. For where in the pastoral the dichotomy between Town
and Country served to delineate a moral conception but not a
social one—since it was precisely this distinction between the
classes that the pastoral sought to suppress—in the *Elegy* the
social distinction is emphasized and buttressed by the moral
one. Gray is able to make use of the *lateral* metaphor of the
center and its peripheries because the *Elegy*, after all, is ad-
dressed to those buried in a *country* churchyard, but his use of
the metaphor corresponds to a *hierarchical* distinction between
social classes.

   Throughout the *Elegy*, as has been suggested, the problem of
Value is implicitly being raised in a number of different forms
and from a number of different perspectives. There are two
dimensions to Gray's concern with the problem of Value, how-
ever. In the tradition of classical ethics, Gray is concerned with
the question of what constitutes a virtuous, good, or full life—
that is, with spiritual values that have a bearing on humanity
in general. But because this concern with universal value is
mediated by the poem's contrast between the rich and the poor,
Gray must also address the values of two distinct "classes."
Thus, the concern with Value in its older, transcendental formu-
lation comes into contact with historical contingencies.

NOBILITY AND *THE* NOBILITY

   Now, in stanza 19, because the moral and social opposi-
tion between the two classes has been fully developed, the two
dimensions of Gray's concern with Value come into direct con-
tact with each other—and this occurs around the question of
nobility. We have seen that in formal and thematic terms the
Elegy bears an antithetical relationship to the "heroic" tradition

of English poetry, but in stanza 19 the ethical and social implica-
tions of this issue are foregrounded. Linguistically, "nobility"
as a virtue and "*the* nobility" as a social formation or class are
homologously linked—and from a Nietzschean point of view,
the former must always be understood as an outgrowth of the
latter. Indeed, in *The Genealogy of Morals*, Nietzsche goes so
far as to argue that "a concept denoting political superiority
always resolves itself into a concept denoting superiority of
soul."[73] Nietzsche is hardly an unbiased witness, but even if his
hypothesis were correct, the fact of the matter is that over
the course of time the two formulations of nobility become
independent of each other—a process that Nietzsche would ar-
gue is a result of the "slave morality" of Christianity. Prior to
the *Elegy*, however, the discrepancy between the two formula-
tions of nobility is not really experienced as such—and, as I shall
argue in chapter 4, this is the result of the accumulated inertia
of the pastoral tradition. Indeed, in the pastoral, the idealized
ethos of *noblesse oblige* is maintained precisely through the
projection of civilized, aristocratic values onto an agrarian land-
scape. But in the *Elegy*, this discrepancy between the two formu-
lations is felt as an outright contradiction, a rift that can never
again be healed. Not only is there no correspondence between
nobility and *the* nobility in the poem—and the latter is presum-
ably the class to which Ambition, Grandeur, and their affines
in the sequence of deferred metonymies would belong—but
there is even a sense in which this spiritual value devolves upon
the Forefathers (i.e., upon the poor or the peasantry).

Insofar as such a reversal takes hold in the *Elegy*, it corre-
sponds to the pattern adumbrated by Hegel in the crucial "Lord-
ship and Bondage" section of *The Phenomenology of Mind*. In
Hegel's dialectic, the Servant, by dint of his servitude, develops
qualities and capabilities originally associated with the Master,
but which the Master, himself limited by his domination of the
Servant, has been able to develop only in a more circumscribed
form.[74] From this Hegelian perspective, the ironies accruing to
the terms *crowd* and *ignoble* in line 73 are extremely complex.
That which is "ignoble" is, on the one hand, of common or

plebeian origin and, on the other, characterized by baseness or meanness.[75] But the "madding crowd's ignoble strife," which is in apposition to the vision of evil of stanzas 17 and 18, is situated at a metaphysical center that is presumably occupied by the nobility—again, insofar as Ambition, Grandeur, and their affines are linked to that class. Although the theme of unfulfilled potential, as developed in stanzas 12 to 15, had suggested that the full emergence of the individual is a process allotted only to the *few* who are at the metaphysical center of the society, this center now turns out to be occupied by an undifferentiated *crowd* of lost souls who are as anonymous in their way as the Forefathers, but in a malignant rather than in a pathetic sense. Against this grim perspective (which anticipates modern visions of society as a *wasteland*), the virtues of the Forefathers—sobriety, integrity, and so forth—stand out in shining relief. Indeed, there is even a sense in which these "homely" virtues begin to subsume the aristocratic ones of heroism and nobility, for a positive conception of Value has passed from the center to the margins of society.

But if such a metaphysical reversal takes hold in stanza 19, it does so only to a limited extent and only by process of elimination, as it were. To identify nobility with the Forefathers would be to indulge in a kind of sentimentality that Gray himself eschews when he tells us that their virtues were *circumscribed* by the conditions of their existence (lines 65–66). And by the same token, it is only provisionally that we can view Ambition and Grandeur as being linked to *the* nobility. If these figures are considered in relation to a social matrix, we have something like a tenor-vehicle situation (in the context of metonymy rather than metaphor), in which the tenor is *indefinitely postponed* throughout the sequence. The reason for this is that since nobility can no longer be seen as homologous with *the* nobility, there literally is no tenor. The nobility has, in a sense, disappeared, and the center is now occupied by an unnamed and invisible class. The "madding crowd's" struggle for power is unequivocally "ignoble," but there is no negation of the negation that would ground a positive conception of nobility in social practice. Thus, the concept of the noble, like the concept of the heroic in

literary terms, though it continues to be of the utmost meaning-
fulness, is entirely unhinged as far as a social matrix is con-
cerned. It corresponds to a lost center and can only be broached
from the standpoint of nostalgia.

It goes without saying that the decentering of aristocratic
values from their putative social matrix, which Gray, however
unconsciously, is representing in the *Elegy*, corresponds to the
bourgeois transformation of economic and social relations. On
numerous occasions, Marx makes the point that the bourgeois
transformation strips away the idyllic fictions of feudal society
to reveal power relationships in their most naked form. In the
context of the bourgeois transformation, both the aristocracy
and the peasantry as such (but they only exist "as such" under
the aegis of rigid feudal hierarchies which are themselves largely
fictional) are seen as disappearing classes. Thus, in the *Elegy*,
the center is occupied by an ignoble crowd; and in *The Deserted
Village* (1768–70), Goldsmith's greatest poem, the disappear-
ance of the peasantry itself is depicted:

> Ill fares the land, to hastening ills a prey,
> Where wealth accumulates, and men decay;
> Princes and lords may flourish, or may fade;
> A breath can make them, as a breath has made.
> But a bold peasantry, their country's pride,
> When once destroyed, can never be supplied.[76]

Goldsmith's vision is a conservative one (which is not to
detract from the beauty of the lines quoted above) because the
loss of the peasantry is mourned unambivalently as the loss of
an anterior plenitude. In the case of the *Elegy*, however, the
situation is far more complex because the desire for self-realiza-
tion and the desire for purity are in conflict with each other.
The peasantry has the aura of purity for Gray, as it does for
Goldsmith and later for Wordsworth, but for Gray it also beto-
kens limitation. Given actual historical circumstances, neither
of the two conflicting desires can be factored out or subsumed
by the other; therefore, the dilemma remains intractable. Conse-
quently, for Gray in the *Elegy*, there can be no *theoretical* solu-
tion to the problem of how to live: what is required in practice

is a continual balancing of one perspective against the other.

Stanza 20

Yet ev'n these bones from insult to protect
Some frail memorial still erected nigh,
With uncouth rhimes and shapeless sculpture deck'd,
Implores the passing tribute of a sigh.

In stanza 20, the *Elegy* returns us to the point in stanza 4 at which the meditation on the Forefathers was begun, and this is indicated by the demonstrative pronoun in line 77. The transition to the theme of unfulfilled potential in stanza 12 was also, we noted, marked by the demonstrative;[77] but by stanza 20, what we may call the poem's speculative trajectory has been completed, and as a result the meditation has turned to a deepened consideration of the actual images presented by the graves. Certain themes that had previously been developed will now, in stanzas 20 to 24, be taken up once again, but this time in retrograde; for where the pathos of "death-in-life" had initially emerged from the pathos of death, the situation is now reversed. The reason for this, as we shall see, is that the framing contrast between the rich and the poor has now been left behind. Having been brought to a climax in stanza 19, the socioeconomic dialectic has now given way to a confrontation with the human condition in its universality.

THE PATHOS OF THE UNIVERSAL

Stanza 20 is clearly in apposition to stanzas 10 and 11, where the memorialization theme had initially been posed. But where the desire of the rich and powerful to perpetuate themselves through tangible memorials had been attacked as a form of *hubris*, the same motivation on the part of the poor is now comprehended from the standpoint of its essential *pathos.* This pathos, however, is much more complex than it would appear on the surface. On the one hand, the poor are seen as pathetic in their feeble—and almost laughable—attempts to memorialize themselves (Gray's adjectives "frail," "uncouth," and "shape-less" come close to replicating the *disdainful smiles* of Ambi-tion and Grandeur in stanza 8, though without actually doing so, of course). But on the other hand, and much more impor-tantly, since the desire to be remembered is now seen as *univer-sal* to the species ("Yet ev'n these bones"), humanity as a whole is now comprehended as pathetic in its relationship to death. What has emerged, in other words—and this is absolutely cru-cial to our understanding of the poem—is the *pathos of the universal.*

It is in stanza 20, then, that the anagogical dimension of the *Elegy* is finally foregrounded, for it is from the standpoint of the universal that the metonymic conjunction of poverty and death ultimately derives its meaning. To be sure, Gray delineates only the negative side to this dialectic, but the pathos of the universal clearly has a positive and even a *redemptive* aspect as well, which manifests itself in both existential and transcendental terms. From an existential point of view, it is what enables us to enter fully into our potential as human beings: such, in any event, is the emphasis on *authenticity* that Christianity extends in various directions, up to and including such thinkers as Hei-degger and Sartre. But there is also a transcendental and even a utopian resonance in the fact that poverty is the vehicle of the principle of universality in the poem, for this recalls the Christian injunction that the meek shall inherit the earth, and, of course, in this respect the Marxist eschatology is merely a logical extension of the Christian.

The foregrounding of the *Elegy*'s anagogical dimension is thus concomitant with the submergence of its socioeconomic dialec-tic. But it is also true that if the socioeconomic dialectic had not previously been developed, the universal would have come *too soon* and would, in consequence, have been merely sentimental. Similarly, if the *Elegy* had failed altogether to take hold of the universal—in other words, if it had concluded with the four rejected stanzas—the poem's structure would have remained unresolved; for the meaningfulness of the socioeconomic dialec-tic is ultimately dependent on the anagogical dimension. From a spatial point of view, just as the problems of poverty and death are metonymically conjoined, so the socioeconomic dialectic and the principle of universality are dependent on each other and hence always present in the poem. But as far as the poem's temporal unfolding is concerned, we might say that the universal had to remain submerged until the socioeconomic dialectic had been fully developed because it lies both *beneath* and *beyond* that dialectic.

Stanza 21

Their name, their years, spelt by th'unletter'd muse,
The place of fame and elegy supply:
And many a holy text around she strews,
That teach the rustic moralist to die.

THE HERMENEUTIC CIRCLE

In Heidegger's concept of the hermeneutic circle, understanding begins as the intuition, or foreknowledge, of a totality that can never be fully grasped because, as Paul de Man notes, "the implicit foreknowledge is always temporally ahead of the explicit interpretative statement that tries to catch up with it."[78] De Man points out that when the concept of the hermeneutic circle is applied to the act of critical interpretation, the intuited totality in question is the poetic text itself; but he adds that the concept is also applicable to the poetic act as well, for *both* are essentially acts of interpretation.[79] This last insight of de Man's is particularly original (it coincides with his critique of the "organicist" poetics of the New Criticism)[80] and therefore deserves to be cited at some length:

> Only when understanding has been achieved does the circle seem to close and only then is the foreknowing structure of the act of interpretation fully revealed. True understanding always implies a certain degree of totality; without it, no contact could be established with a foreknowledge that it can never reach, but of which it can be more or less lucidly aware. The fact that poetic language, unlike ordinary language, pos-

sesses what we call "form" indicates that it has reached
this point. In interpreting poetic language, and especially in
revealing its "form," the critic is therefore dealing with a
privileged language: a language engaged in its highest intent
and tending toward the fullest possible self-understanding.
The critical interpretation is oriented toward a consciousness
which is itself engaged in an act of total interpretation [my
italics]. The relationship between author and critic does not
designate a difference in the type of activity involved, since
no fundamental discontinuity exists between two acts that
both aim at full understanding; the difference is primarily
temporal in kind. Poetry is the foreknowledge of criticism.
Far from changing or distorting it, criticism merely discloses
poetry for what it is.

Literary "form" is the result of the dialectic interplay be-
tween the prefigurative structure of the foreknowledge and
the intent at totality of the interpretative process.[81]

De Man's formulation of the hermeneutic circle is particu-
larly relevant to the point in the *Elegy* that we have now reached;
for as the contrast between the rich and poor recedes into the
background, the poem is thrust back upon its *origins*—which
are nothing more or less than Gray's attempt to grasp hold of
the elusive totality that is his poem. As we noted in the context
of stanza 20, this process of "circling back" manifests itself, in
representational terms, in the belated description of the graves
of the Forefathers and, in anagogical terms, in the foregrounding
of the pathos of the universal. But in stanza 21 it manifests itself
also in the foregrounding of the poetic process itself—not merely
in the abstract, as was the case in stanzas 12 to 15, but from the
self-reflexive standpoint of the poem's own process of composi-
tion. Here, then, is the point at which the tendency of Gray's
language to achieve "the fullest possible self-understanding"
makes itself felt most concretely.

The Principle of Poetry Assimilated
to the Principle of Anonymity

The names and years on the graves of the Forefathers are,
in a sense, like the bones of the dead in stanza 20: there is

nothing to "flesh them out," as it were, and so this is a naming that is *merely nominal* and therefore tantamount to anonymity—indeed, that brings the pathos of anonymity into the sharpest possible focus. These names and years have the significance of traces that lead nowhere; consequently, to say that they supply the place of fame and elegy is to say that they accomplish the very opposite.

But the pathos of anonymity reaches beyond the Forefathers to focus in upon the "unletter'd muse" of line 81. Since the "existence" of the "unletter'd muse"—like that of the Forefathers themselves—can only be inferred by traces which she herself has inscribed, she is both constitutive of the principle of anonymity and herself constituted by that principle.[82] But since the "unletter'd muse" is also, however paradoxically, a muse in her own right, the principle of poetry is assimilated to that of anonymity. In other words, what the metaphor concretizes is a reversal of the contiguous relationship between poetry and Memory that has previously obtained in the poem.

The "unletter'd muse" is clearly one of the lesser (if not orphaned) daughters of Memory, for not only is she nameless and unknown but, being capable only of "uncouth rhymes," she is entirely unable to confer fame. Yet, ironically, it is she who has been allotted the task of strewing holy texts around the graves of the poor—texts whose value, the implication is clear, is vastly superior to that of texts which are merely "poetic" (i.e., texts inscribed in a secular "canon"). Thus, there is a sense in which the "unletter'd muse" not only puts the category of poetry into question but, by doing so, assimilates it to herself anagogically, thereby transcending what at first would appear to be the merely contradictory nature of her own figural identity. For in contrast to stanza 18, where poetry was castigated as an ideological extension of wealth and power, its value is not so much being challenged, in the present context, as affirmed from a standpoint in which its secular dimension has been negated. Indeed, in stanza 21 there is a sense in which poetry and Christianity are reconciled at the very point at which they are most sharply dichotomized. From this point of view, however, poetry emerges as a transcendental principle that is remote from and resistant to all secular appropriation.[83]

It may be noted that the "unletter'd muse" bears a striking resemblance to the "mute inglorious Milton" of stanza 15, not only because both figures can be interpreted in both a negative and a positive light but also because both reflect upon the poetic process itself, and in a manner that is truly uncanny. Gray's "mute inglorious Milton" is the antitype of the real Milton, and so we are strangely drawn by the figure into literary history. Similarly, the relationship of the "unletter'd muse" to the Forefathers ironically replicates Gray's own relationship to his subject matter. In stanza 21, however, the question of self-reflexivity is raised not only by the figure of the "unletter'd muse" but also by an additional uncanny gesture—the actual utterance of the word "elegy" in line 82.

SELF-REFLEXIVITY: THE QUESTION OF GENRE

The effect of the word "elegy" in the stanza is to create an ironical tension between the poem and its title. On the discursive level, what is being implied is simply that no elegies can be addressed to the Forefathers because of their failure to imprint themselves as individuals on their time. This theme has already been thoroughly developed in the poem. However, since the *Elegy* is itself addressed to the Forefathers, line 82 seems to be informing us, from beneath the referential surface, that the poem as a whole is *not* an elegy and that its title is therefore a misnomer. From this point of view, the term "elegy" would be a metonymy—Puttenham's "misnamer"—standing in for a nameless genre that had never previously existed and whose existence is, in a sense, impossible![84]

Our concern here is not, of course, with the academic question of whether *the Elegy* should be considered *an* elegy, since it goes without saying that this category is merely a label that can be used to encompass a range of diverse thematic material. The genre is obviously not limited to the *funeral elegy*, and the eighteenth century was certainly well aware of this. Nevertheless, there is a tendency during the period to regard the funeral elegy as having a kind of primary status within the genre as a whole. We see this, for instance, in Joseph Trapp's *Lectures on Poetry* of 1742. "Under the Title of Elegy," Trapp observes, "is generally and primarily understood a mournful Poem, bewailing the Loss of some Person lately dead; and sometimes has any other melancholy plaintive Circumstance for its Subject."[85] In a similar vein, Trapp notes: "Among our modern Poems, we have few entitled Elegies; those only that are made on Funeral Occasions: But we have many that may be call'd so, in the larger Sense of the Word, as it was used by the Ancients."[86]

Gray's *Elegy* is obviously an elegy in this larger sense of the word. But since the term "elegy" appears in both the title and stanza 21, we are confronted with an apparent contradiction. On the one hand, the title leaves open the possibility that the poem is a funeral elegy, and, on the other, the stanza itself leaves open the possibility that it is not an elegy at all. That Gray himself was fully conscious of these ironies—indeed, that he deliberately encoded them—is indicated by the fact that "elegy" appears neither in the title nor in the text of the earlier version of the poem in the Eton Manuscript.[87] There is no real contradiction in the standard version, however, for the generic marker is actually being used in two different senses in the title and stanza 21. Nevertheless, the ironical tension that is created by the ambiguity alerts us to the fact that the *Elegy* is an elegy precisely insofar as it is *not* a funeral elegy—or at least, not a funeral elegy in the restricted sense of Trapp's definition. That is to say, it is addressed to those who, because they are anonymous, cannot be addressed in a funeral elegy; yet, since this is precisely what the *Elegy* laments, the generic marker remains crucial.

Gray's letter to Walpole of February 11, 1751, in which he asks Walpole to arrange for the *Elegy* to be printed, deserves to be considered in this connection because of the psychological light it sheds on these matters. Walpole had sent the manuscript of the poem to various persons and had thus been instrumental in disseminating it more widely than Gray would have wished.

"As you have brought me into a little Sort of Distress," Gray writes,

> you must assist me, I believe, to get out of it, as well as I can.
> yesterday I had the Misfortune of receiving a Letter from
> certain Gentlemen (as their Bookseller expresses it) who have
> taken the *Magazine of Magazines* into their Hands. they tell
> me, that an *ingenious* Poem, call'd *Reflections* in a Country
> Churchyard, has been communicated to them, wch they are
> printing forthwith: that they were inform'd, that the *excel-
> lent* Author of it is I by name, & that they beg not only his
> *Indulgence,* but the *Honour of his Correspondence,* &c: as I
> am not at all disposed to be either so indulgent or so corre-
> spondent, as they desire; I have but one Way left to escape
> the Honour they would inflict upon me. & therefore am
> obliged to desire you would make Dodsley print it immedi-
> ately (wch may be done in less than a Week's time) from your
> Copy, *but without my Name . . . & the Title must be, Elegy
> wrote in a Country Churchyard* [my italics]. if he would add
> a line or two to say it came into his Hands by Accident, I
> should like it better.[88]

We see, then, that Gray's insistence on having "Elegy" in the
title and his desire to remain anonymous (or at least to *appear*
to desire to remain anonymous) are linked. No doubt he took
pleasure in the fame that the *Elegy* achieved, but it is interesting,
nonetheless, that he should have wished to play out in life the
thematic burden of his poem—as if to disappear inside it.

But whatever Gray's attitude to these matters may have been,
it is clear from the reflexive tensions of stanza 21 that the
problem of anonymity is not simply confined to the referential
surface of the poem. The reason for this, ultimately, is that by
stanza 21 the problem of anonymity (like that of poverty) no
longer confronts us merely as a condition that is associated with
the Forefathers in isolation: it is now a *metaphor* for the human
condition as a whole. Concomitantly, the poetic process itself,
in the profundity of its relationship to the human condition, is
now characterized by its essential *namelessness.* This nameless-
ness no longer has a merely negative meaning, however, for from
the standpoint of the poem's anagogical dimension, it is the

correlative of a vision in which the category of *identity* is itself
transcended.

Stanza 22

For who to dumb Forgetfulness a prey,
This pleasing anxious being e'er resign'd,
Left the warm precincts of the chearful day,
Nor cast one longing ling'ring look behind?

CHRISTIANITY VERSUS HUMANISM

The *Elegy* is, of course, a profoundly religious poem, if
the term "religious" is writ large; but, as we have seen, its
relationship to Christianity is complicated by its attempt to
develop a humanist perspective. Under the aegis of the Christian
mythos, the problems of poverty and anonymity lose their exis-
tential significance as problems and instead take on a positive
coloration as virtues or as signposts along the path to Christ. It
is significant, therefore, that the "holy texts" inscribed on the
graves of the Forefathers do not come into focus until stanza 21
and then only as the result of the sublation of the socioeconomic
dialectic, for if the poem had adopted an explicitly Christian
formulation from the outset, its thematic development would
have been aborted. For the same reason, moreover, the "Chris-
tian perspective" of stanza 21 should be regarded not as the
perspective of the poem as a whole but rather as an approxima-
tion of an as yet unarticulated vision for which Christianity
can nevertheless provide the transcendental symbols. From the
standpoint of stanza 21, to be sure, it would seem that the
principle of anonymity—and hence the Christian renunciation
of self—is being valorized, not only with respect to the Forefa-
thers but, beneath the poem's referential surface, with respect
to the poetic process itself. However, such a valorization of
anonymity poses serious ethical and even aesthetic dangers of
which Gray is by no means unaware. Indeed, insofar as Chris-
tianity aims at the total negation of the self, it may lead to a
form of hubris whose consequences are even more insidious

than the secular hubris of Ambition and Grandeur. To renounce the self is to place oneself above the common limitations of humanity and hence to make oneself a god; consequently, whether the motivation takes a purely religious or a derived artistic form, it constitutes a kind of *Faustian bargain* in reverse and, as such, is compromised from the outset by its insincerity.

The Forefathers, however, would not have been likely to valorize poverty and anonymity, for the simple reason that this was their lot in life. Consequently, much as they had earlier provided the perspective against which to measure the secular hubris of Ambition and Grandeur, so now they provide the perspective for gauging a spiritual hubris which, though never overtly represented in the poem, is clearly a latent tendency in the *Elegy* as a whole and perhaps in Gray himself. Stanza 22 is thus an affirmation—or reaffirmation—of the poem's essential humanism and, as such, is in direct contrast to stanza 11 in particular. This contrast makes itself felt in the fact that in both stanzas (and nowhere else in the *Elegy*) Gray has made use of the rhetorical question as a way of asserting fundamental truths. For where in stanza 11 the universality of death had been invoked as an admonition against Ambition and Grandeur, so now in stanza 22 the desire to hold onto life and to leave a trace of oneself after death is posed as a universal desire whose meaningfulness to a humanist perspective must be insisted upon, since, as a defining characteristic of the human, it cannot be abrogated without bad faith.[89]

THE FIGURE OF "DUMB FORGETFULNESS"

The central figure of stanza 22 is, of course, "dumb Forgetfulness," and this figure is clearly antithetical to that of Memory in stanza 10. In the context of that stanza, we noted that Memory is unable to remember those who are not in some sense *already* remembered by their society—which is to say, those who have failed to leave an imprint upon it during their lives. A similar condensation of the active and passive voices is contained—but even more interestingly—in the figure of "dumb Forgetfulness" in line 85. "Dumb Forgetfulness" yields *forgetting* and *being forgotten*, which reduces further to *death* and being forgotten, for the souls who drink of the waters of Lethe (of which "dumb Forgetfulness" might be taken as the genius loci) forget all that has happened to them on earth. Consequently, in the figure of "dumb Forgetfulness," the two major problematics in the *Elegy*—death and "death-in-life" (whose ramifications, as we have seen, are so many and various)—are assimilated to each other. This assimilation occurs from the standpoint of the universal, for all human beings are a prey to dumb Forgetfulness in both of the senses we have delineated. Nevertheless, in the context in which it occurs, the figure is sufficiently nuanced to retain virtually all the distinctions that Gray has previously entertained. Thus, while all human beings are to some extent a prey to dumb Forgetfulness in both senses, and while all are always and to the same extent a prey to *forgetting* (i.e., death), all are not to the same extent a prey to *being forgotten*, for here the specificity of the socioeconomic dialectic comes into play. We move in the direction of the universal, of the ontological, but without forfeiting the specificity of the historical; and this, of course, is at the heart of Gray's accomplishment in the *Elegy*.

If the figure of "dumb Forgetfulness" is thus a kind of microcosm of Gray's dialectic, it is an indication that the poem has now begun to close the circle on itself. The evocation of a "chearful day" that must be left behind returns us to the pathos of stanzas 5 to 7, in which the "pastoral" description of the lives of the Forefathers had set the ground for the ensuing philosophical meditation. We are thus once again in the realm of description, but what is now being described is grounded in a psychological realism that is very different from the picturesque idealism of those earlier stanzas. Indeed, through the rhetorical question of stanza 22, the existential situation of the individual in confronting the human condition is evoked, and thus the terrain of the meditation shifts from the metaphysical to the psychological. The confrontation with death as an actual *lived* experience had not previously been evoked in the poem in an explicit way, but clearly this confrontation is at the heart of the *Elegy*. It could not previously have been evoked because as long as the Forefathers—whose existence, after all, is nothing more than a series of hypothetical images in the poet's mind—occupied the referential center of the poem, all access to the phenomenology of this experience *as* an experience was blocked. As we have seen, however, the *Elegy* is not simply a poem about the Forefathers as a particular class: on the contrary, the Forefathers provide the perspective against which the human condition can be measured. In stanza 20, Gray begins to grasp hold of the human condition in metaphysical terms; but the psychological aspect of this confrontation is also crucial, and the rhetorical question of stanza 22 provides the bridge from the metaphysical to the psychological.

The ambiguities surrounding the word "resigned" emphasize the individual's dilemma in confronting death—and hence also the poet's dilemma in rendering that experience meaningful from a humanist perspective. Analysis again yields a synchronicity of the active and passive voices of the verb, but this time the two meanings are in contradiction to each other. For all individuals must *resign*—that is, leave or give up—"this pleasing anxious being"; but since none has ever done so without casting "some longing ling'ring look behind" (this is the force of the rhetorical question), it can be said that no one is ever really *resigned* to death. The paradox is that it is human nature to be unable to accept Nature. And here we might again quote the passage from *Paradise Lost* (2.146–51) that Gray is echoing in stanza 22:

> for who would lose,
> Though full of pain, this intellectual being,
> Those thoughts that wander through Eternity,
> To perish rather, swallowed up and lost
> In the wide womb of uncreated night,
> Devoid of sense and motion?[90]

Belial's rhetorical question is, one might say, domesticated in the *Elegy*; for there is no question of rebelling against what is obviously an inexorable fact of nature; yet, neither can the individual "go gently into that good night." Each individual is

a microcosm of Milton's cosmic allegory; thus, the problem for
humanism is to balance conflicting values and perspectives so
as to forfeit nothing that is essential to the dignity and meaning-
fulness of life.

Stanza 23

On some fond breast the parting soul relies,
Some pious drops the closing eye requires;
Ev'n fron the tomb the voice of Nature cries,
Ev'n in our Ashes live their wonted Fires.

THE "PARTING SOUL":
THE CLOSING OF THE CIRCLE

Beginning with stanza 20, the dominant thematic empha-
sis has been on the desire of the individual (as represented
through the Forefathers) to be remembered after death, but in
stanza 22, through the figure of "dumb Forgetfulness," the vari-
ous issues relating to memory and those relating to death as an
actual experience that the individual must undergo are merged
in such a way as to shift the thematic emphasis from the former
to the latter. Consequently, what has been uncovered for stanza
23 is the existential situation of the "parting soul." The the-
matic significance of memory continues in effect, however; for
in the calculus of human need that Gray is delineating, just as
the individual desires to be remembered *after* death, so too
the dying individual requires to be "remembered" by someone
whose life will be diminished by his passing. The two needs
exist on the continuum of what is "natural" to the species
and find their common denominator in the need for human
relatedness generally: thus, "Ev'n from the tomb the voice of
Nature cries."

The experience of the "parting soul" is, of course, the deepest
of all the mysteries, for it is simultaneously one that is lived
and one that culminates in a complete rupture with life. This
theme—if one can refer to it as such, for since the experience

is ineffable it can only be named but not penetrated—finally emerges in stanza 23, but it is clearly at the root of the *Elegy* as a whole, as indicated by the fact that the adjective "parting" occurs in the very first line of the poem: "The Curfew tolls the knell of parting day." For a poem whose thematic material undergoes so many complex permutations, it should be noted that the *Elegy* contains remarkably little lexical redundancy, and the fact that the word "parting" is now being repeated is interesting not only for semantic reasons but as an indication that the poem is now in the process of closing the circle on itself. In fact, however, the figural significance of "parting" in line 89 is the opposite of what it had been in line 1. In the earlier context, what was literally being evoked was the onset of evening, and thus the implication of death was metaphorical both in respect to the description itself and to the fact that this description was being endowed with human significance. However, since Nature in the opening stanzas was conceived as a cyclical—and hence "undying"—process, the adjective "parting" represented an appropriate muting of the concept of death. The ambiguous intersection of Nature and human consciousness resulted in a metaphor that pulled in opposite directions.[91]

In stanza 23, however, the "parting soul" is *literally* a dying soul, and thus the adjective has here a metonymic significance, for Death is being viewed not as something other than what it is but—simultaneously (and oxymoronically)—as a process of separation or discontinuity (i.e., a *partition*) and as a process of transition or continuity (i.e., a *departure*). Thus, the "parting soul" of stanza 23 is in one sense a consonant and in another a dissonant echo of the cyclical conception of Nature that was given in the opening stanzas.

This is only one side to the issue, however, for the ambiguities in the concept of Death that we have noted are themselves mirrored by a similar set of ambiguities in the concept of Nature; thus, the metaphysical ratio is a continuously shifting one. Nature as a cyclical process—what we might call the Wordsworthian or Whitmanian conception of Nature—is consonant with the notion of Death as transition, but in this case the concept of Death *as such* loses its salience—and, of course,

Death is salient only for human beings, who are conscious of discontinuity. From another point of view, however, since Death is an aspect of Nature, the principle of discontinuity is implicit in Nature itself. It will be noticed that although these conceptions of the relationship between Death and Nature have opposing emphases, they are tautological in the sense that the concept of Death is subsumed by that of Nature in both cases. However, Nature can also be conceived—as it often was in the eighteenth century—as a life force (or élan vital) and hence as opposed to Death from within the terms of a simple dualism. Indeed, this is clearly how it is being conceived in stanza 23 ("Ev'n from the tomb the voice of Nature cries"), which is the only point in the poem at which the word "Nature" actually occurs. In stanza 23, "Nature" thus occurs in a context in which its meaning is aligned with *human nature* and opposed to both the cyclical and the nihilistic conceptions of Nature. Both of the latter conceptions are to some extent adumbrated in the *Elegy*; but, by what we may call a metalepsis, we read the "parting soul" of line 89 back into the "parting day" of line 1, so that the earlier representation of Nature, which had seemed to subsume and negate human strivings, is itself humanized.

The human subject—Gray's "parting soul"—is faced with precisely the dilemma that the poet in his poem is faced with: the dilemma not so much of justifying the ways of God to men (for this is beyond its capabilities), as of formulating a relationship to Nature (and hence to Society) that is ethical in the fullest sense and balanced between the extremes of delusion, on the one hand, and cynical resignation, on the other. Gray's humanism thus stands midway between Satan's ultimately sterile rebellion against Nature and the Romantic counter-sublime of Wordsworth or Whitman, in which Nature threatens to overwhelm the individual entirely. Encompassing both extremes, Gray accedes to neither but continually searches for what is ultimately an elusive classical balance. The process is an endless one because—as in Keats's "Vale of Soul-Making"[92]—the "parting soul" is always in the position of having to shape its soul and hence its relationship to what is human.

Stanzas 24–29

For thee, who mindful of th'unhonour'd Dead
Dost in these lines their artless tale relate;
If chance, by lonely contemplation led,
Some kindred Spirit shall inquire thy fate,

Haply some hoary-headed Swain may say,
'Oft have we seen him at the peep of dawn
'Brushing with hasty steps the dews away
'To meet the sun upon the upland lawn.

'There at the foot of yonder nodding beech
'That wreathes its old fantastic roots so high,
'His listless length at noontide wou'd he stretch,
'And pore upon the brook that babbles by.

'Hard by yon wood, now smiling as in scorn,
'Mutt'ring his wayward fancies he wou'd rove,
'Now drooping, woeful wan, like one forlorn,
'Or craz'd with care, or cross'd in hopeless love.

'One morn I miss'd him on the custom'd hill,
'Along the heath and near his fav'rite tree;
'Another came; nor yet beside the rill,
'Nor up the lawn, nor at the wood was he.

'The next with dirges due in sad array
'Slow thro' the church-way path we saw him born[e].
'Approach and read (for thou can'st read) the lay,
'Grav'd on the stone beneath yon aged thorn.'

With the apostrophe of stanza 24, we have arrived at the point at which the problem of structure and meaning that was presented in chapter 2 has again come into focus. Having traced the poem's thematic development thus far, however, we can now see that the point at which the formal problem of interpretation comes into focus is also the point at which the poem's thematic development reaches a *climax*. Since this climax stems from the evocation of the "parting soul" in stanza 23, everything that follows may in a certain sense be regarded as an attempt by dramatic means to impose closure on a meditation that has come full circle but is essentially open-ended. Nevertheless, although the remaining stanzas do not extend the poem's philosophical trajectory, in these final thirty-six lines the implicit eschatological premises of the *Elegy* are concretized in a way that was not previously possible.

The Grammatical Problem

In order to bring the formal issues raised by stanza 24 into alignment with the poem's thematic development, we should first review the grammatical problem posed by the poem, which in chapter 2 we found to be intractable from a strictly formalist standpoint.[93] In essence, this is simply that the prepositional phrase "For thee" is either grammatically redundant (and therefore stylistically awkward) or part of the predicate of a missing clause. For if we regard "For thee" as the object of "inquire," then, as the following transposition makes clear,

> If chance, by lonely contemplation led,
> Some kindred Spirit shall inquire thy fate,
> For thee,

"thy fate" and "For thee" replicate each other very awkwardly. Since "And thou" in the *Stanza's* poses no problem, it is difficult to see why Gray, with his exquisite mastery over syntax, would have committed what is apparently a solecism. Most critics have assumed that Gray changed the case of the pronoun in order to distance the reference; but, as we observed in chapter 2, the reference was already distanced by the second-person pronoun in the *Stanza's*, and there is no reason why a shift from the vocative to the accusative should have this effect.

But if we allow "For thee" to "dangle," for the moment, giving it the dramatic emphasis it requires by pausing significantly after the comma, we shall see that Gray's revision is not only a masterful stroke from a stylistic point of view but a key to the poem as a whole. In order to understand this, however, we have to return to our thematic analysis.

DONNE'S SEVENTEENTH MEDITATION:
THE PRINCIPLE OF UNIVERSALITY

We have seen that the poet's attempt to grasp hold of the universal, beginning in stanza 20, was already latent in the opening stanza of the *Elegy*, although it could not make itself known explicitly until the socioeconomic dialectic had been thoroughly explored. And if we now return to the very first line of the poem—as we also were obliged to do by the echo of "parting" in stanza 23—we find that the grammatical problem of stanza 24, the problem of identifying the "thee" of line 93, and indeed the larger issues of structure and meaning are simultaneously brought into focus:

> The Curfew tolls the knell of parting day . . .
> *For thee.*

To ask whom the "thee" represents is, in effect, to *send to know for whom the bell tolls!* The reverberating passage we are led to, of course, is from the seventeenth Meditation of John Donne's *Devotions upon Emergent Occasions* (1624). The text is here quoted almost in its entirety (with Donne's italics) because of its importance to the *Elegy:*

> Perchance hee for whom this *Bell* tolls, may be so ill, as that he knowes not it tolls for him; And perchance I may thinke my selfe so much better than I am, as that they who are about mee, and see my state, may have caused it to toll for mee, and I know not that. The Church is *Catholike, universall,* so are all her *Actions; All* that she does, belongs to *all.* When she *baptizes a child,* that action concernes mee; for that child is thereby connected to that *Head* which is my *Head* too, and engraffed into that *body,* whereof I am a *member.* And when she *buries a Man,* that action concernes me: All *mankinde* is of one *Author,* and is one *volume;* when one Man dies, one *Chapter* is not *torne* out of the *booke,* but *translated* into a better *language;* and every *Chapter* must be so *translated;* God emploies several *translators;* some peeces are translated by *age,* some by *sicknesse,* some by *warre,* some by *justice;* but Gods hand is in every *translation;* and his hand shall binde up all our scattered leaves againe, for that *Librairie*

where every *booke* shall lie open to one another: As therefore the *Bell* that rings to a *Sermon*, calls not upon the *Preacher* onely, but upon the *Congregation* to come; so this *Bell* calls us all: but how much more mee, who am brought so near the *doore* by this *sicknesse*. There was a *contention* as far as a *suite*, (in which both *pietie* and *dignitie, religion*, and *estimation*, were mingled) which of the religious *Orders* should ring to *praiers* first in the *Morning;* and it was *determined*, that *they should ring first that rose earliest*. If we understand aright the *dignitie* of this *Bell* that tolls for our *evening prayer*, we would bee glad to make it ours, by rising early, in that *application*, that it might bee ours, as wel as his, whose indeed it is. The *Bell* doth toll for him that *thinkes* it doth; and though it *intermit* again, yet from that *minute* that that occasion wrought upon him, hee is united to God. Who casts not up his *Eye* to the *Sunne* when it rises? but who takes off his *Eye* from a *Comet* when that breakes out? Who bends not his *eare* to any *bell*, which upon any occasion rings? but who can remove it from that *bell*, which is passing a *peece of himself* out of this *world?* No man is an *Iland*, intire of it selfe; every man is a peece of the *Continent*, a part of the *maine;* if a Clod bee washed away by the *Sea, Europe* is the lesse, as well as if a *Promontorie* were, as well as if a *Mannor* of thy *friends* or of *thine owne* were; any mans *death* diminishes *me*, because I am involvde in *Mankinde;* And therefore never send to know for whom the *bell* tolls; It tolls for *thee*.[94]

The marvelous irony in all this—which is as if Gray had anticipated the attempts of formalist criticism to fix the reference for the "thee" of line 93—is that we are not to send to know for whom the bells tolls in the *Elegy* because no man is an island entire of itself! The "thee" can be none other than humanity in general (or, as Hegel would say, man considered as a species-being), and as the link to the Donne Meditation shows, this conception of the universal is grounded in the *Elegy* from the outset.

The phrase "For thee" signals the climax of both the Donne Meditation and the *Elegy*, but critics have been unaware of the influence of Donne's text on Gray's poem because in the *Elegy* the phrase is separated from the trope of the passing bell by 92

lines. It is difficult to imagine that Gray was not fully aware of
the ramifications of the Donne text in his poem, at least at the
point at which he made the substitution of "For thee" for "And
thou" in his revision of the *Stanza's*, but it is possible that he was
not conscious of Donne's influence when he began the poem. He
acknowledged to Norton Nicholls, as we noted earlier, that the
opening lines of the *Elegy* were imitated from the *Purgatorio*;
but the Donne Meditation, whose influence is far more impor-
tant, is never mentioned in Gray's correspondence. The connec-
tion of Dante's concern with the universal to Donne's is obvious,
but the Donne Meditation is so palpably impressed on the *struc-
ture* of the *Elegy* that, if Gray had been fully conscious of
Donne's influence from the outset, it might have been impossi-
ble for him to develop his material beyond what for the eigh-
teenth century would have been a mere devotional truism. What
makes the *Elegy* so profoundly original a poem is the manner in
which the principle of universality it locates is mediated by a
complex historical dialectic. For Donne, the principle of univer-
sality is immanently grounded in the institution of the Church:
"The *Church* is *Catholike, universall*, so are all her *Actions*;
All that she does belongs to *All*." Gray begins with the same
anagogical premises, and his absorption of them is at least partly
mediated by the resonance of the Donne text; but immediately
he encounters a series of historical ironies that must be pursued
on their own account and that render Donne's predicates—cath-
olicity, universality, and belongingness—problematic, not so
much in themselves as in their actual connection to social prac-
tice. These ironies must therefore be fully developed before the
principle of universality can be allowed to emerge in its own
right. It is for this reason that the evidence of Donne's influence
is deferred from its point of contact for 93 lines.

    With regard to the formal problem, then, the fact that the
influence of the Donne's Meditation manifests itself at the
poem's *origins* (i.e., it goes back to line 1) indicates that we
cannot refer the "thee" of line 93 to Gray himself—except inso-
far as he too is "a peece of the *Continent*, a part of the *maine*."
It is not sufficient to say, as Bertrand Bronson does, that the

reference is essentially autobiographical but that the decorum of the poem is nevertheless maintained by a distancing technique. As we noted in chapter 2, Bronson, like other formalist critics, takes the principle of univocity for granted. And yet his insight, that "it is *our* voice which has been speaking our own train of thought all the while,"[95] implicitly allows for a non-univocal solution to the formalist impasse that is corroborated by the relationship of the Donne Meditation to the *Elegy*. To Bronson, the phenomenological experience of the reader is, in effect, a poetic illusion that does not really alter the autobiographical nature of the reference. Yet if we extend his insight farther than he himself was willing to do, we might say that *this* phenomenological experience is really what is primary and that the formal constituents of the text must be understood from *this* point of view. What it means is that if the reader is *moved* by the poem, as we say, then the "me" of line 4 ("And leaves the world to darkness and to me") is *already* felt to be his own. This would mean that the "me" is not merely exchanged for the "thee," through a factitious attempt to avoid personal reference, but—as in Buber's conception of the I-Thou relationship—is already implicitly a "thee" from the outset.

The Lyric- or Suffering-I: A New Model of the Lyric

Hegel remarks in the *Aesthetics* that "however intimately the insights and feelings which the poet describes as his own belong to him as a single individual, they must nevertheless possess a universal validity."[96] We have already seen the importance of the principle of universality to the *Elegy* from a thematic point of view, but the same principle enables us to construct a provisional model of the lyric poem in general, notwithstanding the notorious difficulties involved with this category. The basic principle of such a model would be simply that the reader incorporates—and thereby actualizes—what we might call the *lyric-* or *suffering-I* as his own. Since the case of the *Elegy* is obviously problematic, a more typical example of the lyric, such as Words-worth's "I wandered lonely as a cloud," will better serve to illus-trate the point. If the reader is *moved* by this poem, this is clearly not, in the first place, because of Wordsworth's loneliness but be-cause of his own. In actuality, however, it is not simply the read-er's subjectivity in an isolated sense that is engaged; for just as the poet's experience takes on the allegorical lineaments of Ev-eryman's by being shaped in terms of the "lyric-I," so with the reader's experience a similar process occurs.

This conception of the "lyric-I" does not necessarily have to coincide with an actual pronominal reference, but in the case of the *Elegy* it would correspond to the "me" of line 4. This "me" would then have to be distinguished from the poet, who is *actively shaping* the poem (and hence the "lyric-I") from the outside, and whose presence manifests itself solely through the *intentionality* of this shaping process.[97] Failing to make this distinction, we would have to assume, in the manner of nine-teenth-century criticism, that the *Elegy* actually *was* written in a country churchyard.

But the "lyric-I" also enables us to avoid hypostatizing a "speaker," and thus to avoid conflating purely lyric forms with forms such as the dramatic monologue or soliloquy. In the latter forms, to be sure, speech is imitated; but in the lyric, there is no discernible mediating link between the poet and his poem, and so the category of the "speaker" or "persona" is misapplied. The lyric poet, in the process of composing the poem, is neither speaking the poem, for this would mean that the poem exists prior to its composition, nor inventing a speaker as a separate consciousness, for this would mean that there is an ironic dis-tance between the poet and the poem, which is not the case with lyric poetry in the sense in which I am employing the term. Thus, insofar as a speaker enters into the process, this could only be the *reader* (or reciter) of the poem. The reader, however, in the process of rehearsing the poem, actualizes and incorpo-rates *two* experiences simultaneously: the experience of the "lyric-I" (which is already, as we have suggested, a "thee") and the experience of the poet's activity of shaping the poem. The

first, we may say, is primarily emotional; the second, primarily
intellectual: together they form what in the case of great poetry
we experience as a seamless gestalt.

The heuristic value of our metaphor, then, is that it enables
us to avoid the antinomies of logocentric models of the poetic
process in which meaning is referred either to the poet himself
or to the "speaker" of the poem. Of course, since the "lyric-I"
corresponds neither to an actual entity nor to a structure, the
concept ultimately resists formalization. At the same time,
however, it points to the sense in which the poetic process itself,
being allegorical, resists formalization.

As the generic principle underlying the lyric, the principle of
universality pertains not only to the level of *voicing* (which has
been a particular preoccupation of Anglo-American criticism)
but, more broadly, to the relationship of the lyric poet to society.
"The most sublime lyric works," wrote Theodor W. Adorno in
"Lyric Poetry and Society," "are those in which the subject,
without a trace of his material being, intones in language until
the voice of language itself is heard. The *subject*'s forgetting
himself, his abandoning himself to language as if devoting him-
self completely to an object—this and the direct immediacy and
spontaneity of his *expression* are the same."[98] The great paradox
that Adorno's essay uncovers is that "from a condition of unre-
strained individualism, the lyric work strives for, awaits the
realm of the general. ... The generality of the lyric poem's
content is ... essentially social in nature. Only he understands
what the poem says who perceives in its solitude the voice of
humanity."[99] As a Marxist, Adorno views lyric poetry as "the
subjective expression of a social antagonism,"[100] and his concep-
tion of the poet as a "concrete universal" (to employ Hegel's
term in the *Aesthetics*) has an interesting bearing on an aspect
of Gray's dialectic in the *Elegy* that emerged particularly in
stanzas 12 to 15:

> The lyric subject is set apart from the whole in that it owes
> its existence to special privilege: only the fewest individuals,
> given the pressures of the necessities of life, are ever allowed
> to grasp the general truth or shape of things in self-immer-
> sion—few, indeed, have been allowed simply to develop
> themselves as independent individuals, in control of the free

expression of their own subjectivities. The others, however, those who not only stand as strangers before the ill-at-ease poet, as if they were only objects—indeed, they have in the most literal sense been reduced to objects, i.e. victims, of the historical process—these others have the same or greater right to grope for the sounds in which suffering and dream are wed. This inalienable right has asserted itself again and again, in ways however impure, deformed, fragmentary, intermittent—in the only ways possible for those who must bear burdens. All individual lyric poetry is indeed grounded in a collective substratum. If poetry in fact invokes the whole, and not merely that part of luxury, refinement, and tenderness belonging to those who can afford to be tender, then the substantiality even of individual poems derives to a significant degree from their participation in this substratum; in all likelihood it is this substratum that first makes of language the medium in which the subject becomes more than just a subject.[101]

We may note in passing that Adorno's eloquent defense of lyric poetry as "the voice of humanity" (though originating in solitude and under conditions of social antagonism) is currently extremely unfashionable, to say the least. The bent of most contemporary Marxist and feminist criticism is to view the "conditions of authorship" through which the literary work is generated as primary and hence to reject any claim for the universality of the lyric as an idealist illusion. Such criticism is perhaps not without its moment of truth, but what it also reflects is a crisis of poetry that is certainly characteristic of our contemporary situation. As our model of the lyric would suggest, the poetic process ultimately resists formalization: it is easy to assail the principle of universality as an idealistic (or religious) illusion, but it is on that principle that the tradition of lyric poetry rests.

The Theme of Anonymity:
The Blurring of Persons and Pronouns

Clearly, insofar as the *Elegy* corresponds to the model of the lyric that we have adumbrated, it is only through the first twenty-three stanzas. But paradoxically—and hence the relevance of the model nonetheless—the point at which the *Elegy* ceases to be a purely lyric poem is the point at which the *generic principle* underlying the lyric (i.e., the principle of universality) is *thematized* in the poem. This point, of course, is marked by the apostrophe to the "thee" in stanza 24, which simultaneously brings the lyric stage of the poem's development to a close and opens the poem to new generic possibilities.

In spite of the fact that the "thee" is presented in quasi-authorial terms, the apostrophe of stanza 24 and the monologue of the "hoary-headed Swain" have a poetic effect that is very far from leading us back to Gray the man in an isolated sense. On the contrary, their effect is to "shatter the boundaries" of the text, as it were, so that instead of an "omnipotent" poet contemplating the "unhonour'd Dead" from the outside, we are presented with a series of *relationships* (the sense of the verb "relate" in line 94 is crucial) in which what is being related enfolds the individual—or rather, the figure—who is relating it. As a result, the subject-object distinctions that normally characterize the work of art in formal terms seem to break down. The "thee" is presented as relating an "artless tale"; but no sooner is he addressed than—without even the normal full stop after the stanza break—he himself is enfolded by the general theme as the subject of a similarly artless tale that is putatively related by the Swain to a "kindred Spirit," who himself is then addressed as "thou" by the Swain in lines 115–116:

> 'Approach and read (for thou can'st read) the lay
> 'Grav'd on the stone beneath yon aged thorn.'

The "thee" and the "thou" are *kindred* to each other, semiotically as well as thematically, for both are under the sign of the universal, and the Swain's address to the "kindred Spirit" is itself, of course, enfolded by the apostrophe to the "thee."

We saw earlier that Gray would not allow his name to appear under the *Elegy* when he authorized its publication;[102] and as a matter of fact, the result of the blurring of persons and pronouns that occurs in stanzas 24 to 29—in which the second-person pronoun corresponds to the relater of the tale, to what is being

related itself, and even to the reader or interpreter of the tale—
is to make us lose touch with the poet qua poet and hence to
create the illusion that the *Elegy* is an *anonymous* creation.
This, of course, is an aesthetic illusion that Gray is shaping from
the outside. But this illusion is itself in the service of combatting
what to Gray is a serious *ethical* illusion: namely, that the poet
is a kind of god who is indemnified from the common lot of
mankind. We have already seen that in Gray's treatment of the
evil effects of power, the poet has not been accorded a privileged
status. In stanza 24, however, the self-reflexivity of Gray's en-
terprise reaches a climax by actually rupturing the poem's
structure.

"All *mankinde* is of one *Author*, and is one *volume*," writes
Donne. Unlike the topos of the passing bell, Donne's topos of
the universe as a Book is not directly echoed in the *Elegy*, but
we can see how it is related to the moral conception that Gray
is developing. God being the "one *Author*" (and "God, we might
note, is the final word of the *Elegy*), there can be no other
authorial presence that is not enfolded in the general theme.
The logocentric implications of Gray's conception are precisely
rendered by the diction of lines 93–94:

> For thee, who mindful of th'unhonour'd Dead
> Dost in these lines their artless tale relate.

The tale is an *artless* one because the "short and simple annals
of the poor" would seem to leave no room for art or artifice; but
the adjective applies also to the manner in which the "thee" is
imagined to be relating the tale, and this gives a Romantic
emphasis of sincerity and spontaneity to the conception. More-
over, it is important that this is a *tale* that is *related:* the implica-
tion that it is spoken aloud, as in an anonymous oral tradition,
suggests that the "thee" is merely the *vehicle* of the process
rather than its author. We have commented at length on the
Platonic strain in Gray's thought and poetic practice, and the
notion that the poet is the vehicle of the poetic process is, of
course, developed by Plato in the *Ion*. It goes without saying
that the *Elegy* itself is very far from being an "artless tale," or

one that has issued forth in "profuse strains of unpremeditated art," but since "these lines" are referred to in a way that would make them seem equivalent to the "uncouth rhimes" on the graves of the Forefathers, our attention is turned away from Gray's artistry. Ellis, as we saw in chapter 2, took this metaphoric effect literally, and thus for him "these lines" are *actually* the "uncouth rhimes" on the graves—an interpretation that made it necessary for him to hypostatize a "rustic Stonecutter" to whom the apostrophe would then be addressed. From a univocal standpoint, it would be more reasonable, as Sutherland argued, to link "these lines" to the *Elegy* itself.[103] But to assign a fixed reference either to the "thee" or to "these lines" is to miss the point of the structural conception that is being developed here: their meaning is poetic rather than logical (in the Aristotelian sense) and is a function of the blurring of the boundaries of the text.

THE UTOPIAN VISION OF *COMMUNITAS*

Nevertheless, although the "thee" cannot be referred to Gray himself, the fact that it clearly reflects upon his situation as a poet—as indeed upon the situation of poetry in the mideighteenth century generally—is of crucial importance. Through its relationship to the Donne Meditation, we have seen that the "thee" signifies the principle of universality; but since the "thee" is also "mindful of th'unhonour'd Dead," and since that *mindfulness* is what distinguishes the poet as a "representative man," the "thee" is not merely passively subsumed in the universal but is itself the *active signifier* of this principle. The significance of the poet's "lonely contemplation," his spiritual withdrawal from the World in general and from the social class to which he belongs, is that it enables him to see things with greater clarity and in a larger perspective. Consequently, the apostrophized "thee" as a figure of the poet enables Gray not only to recall the poem's dialectic up to this point but, by reflecting upon the process that has engendered the poem, to concretize, in a more explicit way than was previously possible, the poem's underlying eschatological—and, indeed, *utopian*—

vision: its vision of *communitas*, in short, in which the artificial
distinctions that separate human beings have been annulled.
What is especially ironical about the formalist attempt to re-
solve the pronominal ambiguities, then, is that the blurring of
the pronouns coincides with a blurring of class distinctions that
is in the service of this vision.

The Swain's Monologue: A Pastoral Scenario

Thus, in stanzas 25 to 29, the "boundary conditions" that
have marked the *Elegy* as a lyric poem up until this point are
turned inside out, as it were, so that instead of an "impersonal"
meditation on the lives of deceased peasants—that is, in which
the "lyric-I" is a disembodied presence—we are now presented
with a hypothetical scenario in which a stylized pastoral figure
is imagined to be describing the fate of the now deceased "thee"
to a "kindred Spirit." The relationship of the Swain's monologue
to pastoral tradition is immediately evident: not only does the
"hoary-headed Swain" echo the "uncouth Swain" of Milton's
Lycidas (an echo which, in turn, recalls the "uncouth rhimes"
on the graves of the Forefathers), but, as described by the Swain,
the "thee" is clearly a kind of *poeta ignotus* or "melancholy
Jacques" figure. Thus, where in the first twenty-three stanzas
(stanza 24 being transitional), the mimetic basis of Gray's dis-
course was realistic but the dominant grammatical mood sub-
junctive—since the poet was addressing himself to the lives of
real peasants, whose existence, however, was hidden to him—
in the Swain's monologue (although it is presented as hypotheti-
cal and is thus enfolded by the subjunctive frame of Gray's
realism), the discourse is constituted by the literary conventions
of the pastoral, but the grammatical mood is indicative. These
rhetorical and grammatical crossings make the Swain's mono-
logue a kind of obverse reflection of the discourse of the first
twenty-three stanzas—in which, however, the monologue is
embedded. However, the reason that the grammatical mood of
the Swain's monologue is indicative is that the literary conven-

tions of the pastoral enable the poet to represent *as fiction* what could not be represented as reality. That which could not be represented as reality but can be represented as fiction is precisely the vision of classlessness that governs the pronominal ambiguities of stanza 24. Only in the context of the pastoral can the poet and the peasant inhabit the same metaphysical plane, for the pastoral is constituted precisely by this utopian vision, and hence the pastoral content of the Swain's monologue.

But here we come upon a crucial problem—or *aporia*—that has to do with the status of the pastoral conventions that Gray has made use of in the monologue. This problem has less to do with the surface issues of structure and meaning that concerned the formalist critics than with the deeper question of the poem's style-content dialectic. Given the vision of *communitas* at the heart of the poem, the structural necessity for the pastoral scenario is abundantly clear. The real problem, however, is that in order to represent both the vision of classlessness and the consciousness that this vision remains to be achieved, Gray has had to make use of the very fictional mode whose historical specificity and meaningfulness have been transcended by the *Elegy* itself. The problems of poverty, obscurity, and alienation—themes that cannot be encompassed in the pastoral— assume importance for the first time in the *Elegy*, and it is for this reason that the poem represents what I have termed the "dissolution" of the pastoral. However, since Gray has had no other resources for representing his utopian vision than through the very pastoral conventions that the *Elegy* has itself superannuated—and this is because there simply are no other resources available—there is a sense in which the Swain's monologue must, by the nature of the case, be poetically inferior to the reflections that have preceded it. Though beautifully composed, the monologue, when considered in isolation, lacks both the originality and the resonance of the earlier stanzas, and there is a sense in which it verges on sentimentality. This is not because Gray's vision of *communitas* is sentimental, but because the means that he has at his disposal to represent it—and there are no other means—have been undermined by the poem itself.

Stanzas 30–32

The EPITAPH

Here rests his head upon the lap of Earth
A Youth to Fortune and to Fame unknown,
Fair Science frown'd not on his humble birth,
And Melancholy mark'd him for her own.

Large was his bounty, and his soul sincere,
Heav'n did a recompence as largely send:
He gave to Mis'ry all he had, a tear,
He gain'd from Heav'n ('twas all he wish'd) a friend.

No farther seek his merits to disclose,
Or draw his frailties from their dread abode,
(There they alike in trembling hope repose)
The bosom of his Father and his God.

THE EPITAPH IN THE CHURCHYARD AND "THE EPITAPH" IN THE *Elegy*

And so we come at last to the "Epitaph," which has been pointed out to us by the "hoary-headed Swain":

'Approach and read (for thou can'st read) the lay
'Grav'd on the stone beneath yon aged thorn.'

The difficulty in *reading* the "Epitaph," however, is that we have to approach it in two ways simultaneously: first, as an extension of Gray's reflections on the Forefathers in the initial twenty-three stanzas—and hence as "actually" (or already) *present* in the country churchyard (i.e., to the "lyric-I"); and secondly, through the mediation of the "kindred Spirit" in the monologue spoken by the Swain—and hence from the standpoint of a hypothetical *future* that may "chance" (line 95) to occur after the imagined death of the "thee." The second of our two alternatives is logically the more probable one because, although the "Epitaph" is situated in the present by the demonstrative adverb "here," its "presentness" is enfolded by the Swain's monologue and by the hypothetical future that is broached in stanza 24. However, because of the uncanny way in

which it is set off from and framed against the rest of the poem—
and also because of the way in which it takes up the poem's
various thematic burdens in reprise—the "Epitaph" presents
itself as a kind of mirror image or microcosm of the *Elegy* as a
whole. In other words, we are given the illusion that *this* epitaph
"actually" exists within the churchyard and hence that *the*
"Epitaph" is coextensive with the representational realism of
the initial twenty-three stanzas. As with the pastoral orientation
of the Swain's monologue, however, this illusion is ultimately
in the service of the poem's vision of classlessness.

Another way of expressing the difficulty of approaching the
"Epitaph"—but this was already implicit in our discussion of
the problem of univocity with respect to stanzas 24 to 29—is
that the poem successfully resists any attempt to identify the
"Youth to Fortune and to Fame unknown" either with a specific
person or (what amounts to the same thing, though for rather
more complex reasons) with a specific class. If we identify him
with the Forefathers—as in Ellis's "rustic Stonecutter" read-
ing—we are confounded by the assertion that "Fair Science
frown'd not on his humble birth" (line 119). Faced with this
discrepancy, Ellis argued that "Fair Science" refers to something
like native intelligence in this context; but as Sutherland
pointed out in rebuttal, "science" to the eighteenth century
generally means knowledge gained from education and does so
on every other occasion in which it occurs in Gray's work.[104]
On the other hand, if we identify the Youth with Gray himself,
with an undifferentiated narrator, or with someone like Richard
West—as in Shepard's reading—we are confounded by the obvi-
ous thematic and figural resemblances between the description
of the Youth and the earlier reflections on the Forefathers.

CONVERGENCE OF THE HISTORICAL AND
THE ESCHATOLOGICAL

If it is impossible to classify the "Youth to Fortune and
to Fame unknown" in social terms, this has to do with the sense
in which he is an allegorical embodiment not merely of the

poeta ignotus figure as such but of the *poet* as such, and not merely of the poet but of the poet's desire for realization, insofar as that desire is simultaneously projected into the future and sprung back upon the historical ground of present loss. All of this remains to be demonstrated, of course, but from a theoretical point of view, there is no necessary contradiction in the fact that the Youth should be represented as a poet and that it should nevertheless be impossible to identify him with a specific person or class. To be sure, Gray's representation of the Youth has a realistic basis in the social history of his time: Chatterton, as we observed earlier, came from the rural proletariat, and Gray himself was of relatively "humble birth." But Gray's depiction of the Youth is not essentially governed by realism: on the contrary, it is aimed at a future for which there are no images. The Youth of the "Epitaph" is *literally* a "Youth to Fortune and to Fame unknown" because what he concretizes is the "problem of history." If he is represented as a poet, this is because, in Gray's implicit eschatology, the poet is the bearer of the principle of universality and hence classless.

In examining the "Epitaph," therefore, we have to focus on both the resemblances and the discrepancies between the description of the Youth and the earlier reflections on the Forefathers. And it is interesting, in this regard, that the opening lines of stanza 30 reverberate against what is perhaps the central figure of the potentiality-actuality dialectic of stanzas 12 to 15:

> Here rests his head upon the lap of Earth
> A Youth to Fortune and to Fame unknown.
>   (117–118)

> Some mute inglorious Milton here may rest.
>   (59)

The tense distinction is important here, but what underlies it does not become clear until the description of the Youth is examined against the background of stanza 13:

> Fair Science frown'd not on his humble birth,
> And Melancholy mark'd him for her own.
>   (119–120)

> But Knowledge to their eyes her ample page
> Rich with the spoils of time did ne'er unroll;
> Chill Penury repress'd their noble rage,
> And froze the genial current of the soul.
>
> (49–52)

The major break in the chain of resemblances between the Youth and the Forefathers is, as we noted, in regard to knowledge, but the question of knowledge is implicitly connected to that of poetry in the "Epitaph." If we relate the Youth back to the "thee" of lines 93–94,

> For thee, who mindful of th'unhonour'd Dead
> Dost in these lines their artless tale relate,

and by the echo of "here rests" to the "mute inglorious Milton," the connection comes into focus. However, if the Youth thus fits the description of a *poeta ignotus*, this has a more *positive* implication than it did earlier: he is not merely one who *might have* attained to poetry under other conditions but is apparently one who in some measure at least possessed the capabilities to do so. To be sure, this possibility was latent in the potentiality-actuality dialectic of the earlier reflections, but in that context it was strongly countered by the lines on knowledge quoted above from stanza 13.

This brings us to the significance of the second of the personifications in stanza 30: the figure of Melancholy. The latter, of course, is an intrinsically *ambivalent* projection, and it may be that the history of English poetry is bound up with this ambivalence.[105] Brooks, however, interprets the figure in a wholly negative light, contending that the Youth (whom he identifies with the "narrator") "had the knowledge requisite for entering into the competition for fame, *but he was incapacitated* by Melancholy" (my italics).[106] As Lonsdale points out, this argument substitutes a "but" for the "and" of line 120, although the conjunction Gray employs indicates that "Melancholy" is being given a positive meaning in tandem with "Fair Science."[107] Indeed, Gray invokes Melancholy in a spirit that is similar to how Milton, for whom she is the presiding deity of poets and solitary thinkers, invokes her in *Il Penseroso:*

But hail thou Goddess, sage and holy,
Hail, divinest Melancholy.

(11–12)

This is not to deny the ambivalence of the "Epitaph" as a whole. Melancholy, we said, is intrinsically ambivalent, and in the line on "Fair Science" Gray has used a negative assertion to yield a positive result. But if the description of the Youth remains ambivalent, this is because the poet's vision of *realization* has been superimposed upon a ground of historical loss. In the earlier reflections on the Forefathers, the possibility of realization was kept at an antithetical distance from the poet's realism by the subjunctive; in the "Epitaph," however, these two modalities are brought into alignment with each other.

Perhaps the most glaring discrepancy in the chain of resemblances that connect the Youth to the Forefathers is not any particular quality with which he is associated but the very fact that he is the subject of an epitaph at all. At the point in the poem at which Gray had been reflecting on the actual images presented by the graves, we had the following very important lines:

Their name, their years, spelt by th'unletter'd muse,
The place of fame and elegy supply.

(81–82)

In the Eton Manuscript, as we noted, Gray had originally written "Epitaph" instead of "elegy" but made the change around the time he also changed the title from "Stanza's" to "Elegy." As we noted, the obscurity of the Forefathers during their lives precluded the possibility of their being memorialized in an elegy, and thus the appearance of their names and years on the stones had the effect of intensifying the feeling of anonymity associated with them. In the "Epitaph," however, this ratio is reversed; for here we are presented with a generic Youth who is *literally* anonymous—and whose merits and frailties we are to seek no farther (much as we are not to send to know for whom the bell tolls) because in any event the poet has no intention of disclosing them. But this generic Youth is nevertheless the subject of an epitaph—which again suggests that *the* "Epitaph" is partly in contradiction with the earlier reflections.

What is clear, in any event, is that the "Epitaph" combines aspects of the *might have been* that Gray envisions beyond the graves with the *is* or *was* that he visualizes immediately in connection with the graves. (This is to speak hypothetically, of course, because the entire process may be considered as grounded in the imagination.) Thus, the "Epitaph," as a construct, symbolically reconciles the spheres of presence and absence that in the earlier reflections had been delineated grammatically and, from a thematic point of view, in terms of distinct social classes. The question, however, is what meaning this symbolic reconciliation, or synthesis, holds in store for the poem as a whole.

"Trembling Hope"

The issue ultimately hinges on the nature of the "trembling hope" in the penultimate line, for that is the point at which the poem's implicit eschatology finally emerges from its elegiac vision of loss. There can be no doubt, of course, that the "trembling hope" of line 127 is explicitly rooted in the Christian belief in an afterlife. But in the context of the symbolic reconciliation that occurs in the "Epitaph," this hope also aims at a *historical future* in which the Earthly Paradise invoked by the angel Michael will have been achieved:

> for then the Earth
> Shall all be Paradise, far happier place
> Than this of *Eden*, and far happier days.
> (12.463–65)

To be sure, *this* hope is only implicit; and given the historical juncture at which Gray writes, it can only be evoked through the vocabulary of Christian millennialism. Moreover, whereas for Milton, because he is working fully within the Christian mythos, it can be expressed as a possibility on the same horizon as the salvation of the individual soul, for Gray, because of the (new) historical realism of the tapestry on which he is working, it can be intuited only from the antithetical standpoint of present loss. And yet it is implicit in the *Elegy* all the same.

We might say, moreover, that the *sleep* of the Forefathers— that metaphorical sleep by which (as we saw in the context of the opening stanzas) the problem of death is circumvented—is ultimately predicated on this "trembling hope" for the future. In the meantime, however, the "Youth to Fortune and to Fame unknown" *rests* "upon the lap of [Mother] Earth" and *reposes* in "the bosom of his Father and his God." And here the poet also rests. For though his poem has taken him beyond the pastoral and the limits of Christian stoicism, he has nowhere else to go.

Chapter 4

Gray's *Elegy* and the Dissolution of the Pastoral

LIKE ALL poems that are central to their time, and hence to the historical matrix, the *Elegy* is embedded in a tradition (or series of traditions) that it simultaneously subverts. In chapter 3 we saw this to be the case with respect to the heroic, elegiac, and pastoral traditions (although these overlapping categories should not be construed as being more than heuristic devices for the organization of diverse historical particulars). In the case of the pastoral, however, because of its intimate connection to the "problem of history," we are confronted with a series of issues that require fuller theoretical elaboration than could be offered in the context of the sequential reading of chapter 3. For if the problem of history (in the sense of task or telos) is to overcome the problem of history (in the sense of deprivation), then the pastoral is that form which, at a certain stage of historical development, is entrusted with this crucial theme.

In the Introduction to this study, I suggested that the pastoral is primarily constituted by the problem of history and only secondarily, or contingently, by the figure of the shepherd. Even if we concede that there was something "natural" in the choice of the shepherd, if Theocritus had made some other figure the focal point of his *Idylls* and if his imitators had followed suit, then, although the genre would have adopted a different name, nothing essential would have been changed. And even if we choose to adopt Pope's minimal definition of the pastoral, as a form involving the "imitation of the action of a shepherd, or one considered under that character,"[1] still, this leaves us with the problem of penetrating beneath the surface of the form to understand the nature of the representation involved, since clearly the lives of shepherds in and of themselves are not what is really at issue but only a pretext for getting at something else.[2]

What is salient to the pastoral, in any event, is not merely the figure of the shepherd per se but the figure of the *poet-as-shepherd*, a figure that involves a synthesis, under the aegis of poetry itself (since it is in and through poetry that this synthesis is effected), of the upper and lower classes (the aristocracy and the peasantry). The figure of the poet-as-shepherd is informed, in the first place, by the myth of the Golden Age, according to which the original condition of mankind was characterized by harmony and natural sufficiency, without the necessity of either labor or law. Here, for instance, is Ovid's account of the Golden Age myth in the *Metamorphoses* (in Arthur Golding's Elizabethan translation):

> Then sprang up first the golden Age, which of itself maintainde,
> The truth and right of every thing unforst and unconstrainde.
> There was no fear of punishment, there was no threatning lawe
> In brazen tables nayled up, to keep the folke in awe.
> There was no man would crouch or creepe to Judge with cap in hand,
> They lived safe without a Judge in every Realme and Lande.
> The loftie Pyntree was not hewen from mountaines where it stood,
> In seeking straunge and forren landes to rove upon the flood.
> Men knew none other countries yet, than were themselves did keepe:
> There was no towne enclosed yet, with walles and ditches deepe.
> No horne nor trumpet was in use, no sword nor helmet worne.
> The worlde was suche as souldiers helpe might easly be forsworne.
> The fertile earth as yet was free, untoucht of spade or plough,
> And yet it yeelded of itselfe of every things inough.[3]

At the heart of the pastoral, then, is nostalgia—nostalgia not so much for the past as for a mode of life that never existed but that the poet locates in the dim confines of the past.[4] For this reason, however, as W. W. Greg pointed out in his landmark study of the pastoral early in the century, there has often been a good deal of confusion as to the origins of the form:

> We are often, for instance, told that it is the earliest of all forms of poetry, that it characterizes primitive people and permeates ancient literature. Song is, indeed, as old as human language, and in a sense no doubt the poetry of the pastoral age may be said to have been pastoral. It does not, however, follow that it bears any essential resemblance to that which subsequent ages have designated by the name.[5]

The distinction between the pastoral and the poetry of the "pastoral age" is crucial because, as Greg observes, "a constant element in the pastoral is the recognition of a contrast, implicit or expressed, between pastoral life and some more complex type of civilization."[6] Other writers have emphasized the same point. Frank Kermode, for example, notes that "the first condition of pastoral is that it is an urban product,"[7] and Renato Poggioli, that the pastoral originated not in Hellenic but in Hellenistic times, "with the decline of the ancient *polis* and . . . the appearance of a quasi-modern metropolis."[8] To this one must add, however, that as an urban product, the pastoral is obliged to camouflage its origins, and that this is intrinsic to the transcendental or utopian basis of the form. Here we arrive at the essence of the pastoral: by superimposing the values of a civilized upper class onto a fictional agrarian landscape, the pastoral projects the vision of a reconciliation between Nature and History, such that civilization appears as an *unmediated* extension of Nature itself.

As Greg remarks, the importance of the pastoral as a form lies in the fact that it is "the expression of instincts and impulses deep-rooted in the nature of humanity."[9] But from a Marxist perspective, it might be observed that these instincts and impulses are conditioned by the division of labor and the attendant alienation resulting from the formation of social classes—in short, by the problem of history, which is at once a product and the origin of cultural development. From this point of view, the pastoral is a utopian form insofar as it projects a vision in which the highest attainments of civilization—including poetry itself—are possessed *without the necessity of history*.[10] The utopian synthesis implicit in the pastoral involves a kind of telescoping of the problem of history, with the result that the actual process of history is submerged and circumscribed, as it were. Yet at the same time, the pastoral points to the final mastery of man over Nature—to the *end* of history, both in the sense of its practical conclusion and also of its telos.

The pastoral is thus insulated from history and hence from the problem of history in its negative aspect. As Poggioli beautifully remarks, the desire on the part of the pastoral to *forget history*, which is what links it to the Golden Age myth (whether or not the latter is explicitly foregrounded), is, in a sense, true of poetry as a whole—and this is perhaps why there are so many different "versions" of pastoral:

> In a certain sense, and in its purest form, the pastoral represents ideally the Golden Age of poetry. Poetry, however, is not only the child of fancy, but also the daughter of memory; and this makes her the sister of history. It is when she tries to forget her sister, and yearns after a dreamland outside of time, that poetry becomes idyllic, if not in form at least in content.[11]

This yearning for a dreamland outside of time must, however, be concretized in temporal terms; thus, since the future is a mere abstraction and since the poverty of the present is what has occasioned the yearning in the first place, the pastoral turns for its images to the past—or rather to a past of its own devising.

The attempt on the part of the pastoral to "forget history" has often been regarded as mere escapism, especially by the Marxist tradition, but this is inaccurate or at least insufficiently nuanced. Under certain circumstances, the pastoral can become mere escapism; but in itself, and insofar as it is capable of producing great works of art, the pastoral impulse is a utopian response to the same problem of history that will later emerge explicitly in the *Elegy*. In the pastoral, however, the problem of history is represented only from the standpoint of a kind of abstract idealism, as if the *problem* posed by history had been factored out from the outset and the Earthly Paradise already attained. In the world of historical relationships, the art of poetry, requiring leisure and knowledge in the highest degree, is the product of a social surplus and thus the province not of shepherds but of a privileged upper class; yet what the poet-as-shepherd motif concretizes is precisely a situation in which the aristocrat and the shepherd are not isolated by social differences but, under the transcendental aegis of poetry, can exist as one.

The pastoral thus involves a negation of social differences, but there are two perspectives from which this can be interpreted. On the one hand, following the tendency of at least one strain of Marxism, we can reduce the pastoral to a mere ideological formation: we can say that the "organic" society posited by the pastoral is nothing more than an attempt on the part of a ruling elite (whether aristocratic or bourgeois) to deny the existence of social inequality and to present the illusion of social harmony.[12] On the other hand, accepting the idealism of the pastoral as sincere, we can maintain that its utopian dream is a "necessary fiction" that, in presenting us with the vision of *un*alienated man, serves to create the conditions in which that vision can eventually be realized. From this point of view, the very idealism of the pastoral (as of art in general) is itself a kind of social praxis and not merely the distorted reflection of prevailing social norms.

The two perspectives taken together represent opposing sides of an aesthetic debate that has its roots in the argument between Plato and Plotinus.[13] But both are overly schematic in that they fail to take account of how the aesthetic possibilities afforded by the pastoral are mediated by actual historical circumstances. Whatever our attitude to the pastoral may be in theory, it is clear, in any event, that the pastoral vision of an Earthly Paradise, from its reemergence in the Renaissance to its demise in the eighteenth century, is absolutely central to European art. That is why the form undergoes so many permutations during the period and why its generic possibilities seem virtually endless. In Shakespeare's romantic comedies, for example, not only the stage but the entire theater becomes a vehicle for the creation of an enchanted space in which the upper and lower classes can, if not merge, at least mingle on equal terms. The pastoral ethos of noblesse oblige, binding up all classes into an organic whole, is intended to have a humanizing impact particularly on those in the uppermost ranks of society—so that when Duke Senior and his retinue leave the Forest of Arden, or when Prospero bids farewell to his island and returns to Milan, it is not, presumably, to be guided solely by the Machiavellian pursuit of power.

Such, at any rate, is the social myth perpetuated by the pastoral. But how, then, explain the demise of the transcendental pastoral, a demise which, most commentators would agree, occurred in the eighteenth century? Perhaps we can say that if the negation of social differences inherent in the pastoral is a "necessary fiction" because it presents the vision of *un*alienated man, it ceases to be so at the point at which man becomes capable of eliminating the forms of alienation in practice. When this point is reached—or at least, when it is glimpsed as a real possibility by the intellectual center (as it seems to have been during the Enlightenment)—then the transcendental pastoral forfeits its utopian function and takes on instead the reactionary lineaments of an ideological weapon that is wielded in the narrow interests of those in power rather than in the universal interests of humanity as a whole. At this point, the pastoral becomes a mere husk of itself, denuded of its authentic utopian content, and the utopian impulse passes to a tendency which, having emerged from the pastoral, is realistic and antipastoral in its orientation. Amid the "puerile conceits of the Petit Trianon," in Greg's phrase,[14] where we find Marie Antoinette playing at being a milkmaid, the final image cast by the pastoral is shadowed by the Revolution.

"The modern world," writes Poggioli, "destroyed the conventional and traditional pastoral through four cultural trends that arose together and partly coincided. These were the humanitarian outlook, the idea of material progress, the scientific spirit,

and artistic realism."[15] Ironically, it is precisely the point at
which the belief in material progress takes hold that we see the
demise of the transcendental pastoral, for at that point the old
dream of an Earthly Paradise comes to seem an actual obstacle
to the task at hand. "Till we have built Jerusalem, / In Englands
green & pleasant Land," writes Blake at the close of the eigh-
teenth century,[16] but here the emphasis is no longer on dreaming
but on building and transforming. In *The Communist Mani-
festo*, that document in which the spirit of "scientific" socialism
emerges from its utopian variant, Marx offers the bourgeoisie
what is in effect a backhanded compliment for having "put an
end to all patriarchal, idyllic relations." "For exploitation, veiled
by religious and political illusions," he remarks, "it has substi-
tuted naked, shameless, direct, brutal exploitation."[17] From a
certain point of view, "there is no document of civilization
which is not at the same time a document of barbarism," as
Walter Benjamin observes in one of his "Theses on the Philoso-
phy of History."[18] However that may be, by the middle of the
eighteenth century, the long period in which the old pastoral
conventions had furnished the artist with an enabling fiction,
through which he could represent his deepest hopes and ideals,
has come to an end. To make use of the poet-as-shepherd motif
and the other props of the genre in the old, naive way now comes
to seem an insincere denial of the actual impoverishment of the
rural working class.

If the *Elegy* represents the symbolic dissolution of the pasto-
ral, this is because it is in the *Elegy* that the problem of history—
which, in its sublimated form, had given rise to the pastoral
in the first place—is fully comprehended for the first time.
However, the demise of the old pastoral in English poetry can
be traced to an earlier point in the eighteenth century, when the
transcendental synthesis implicit in the form has begun to break
down but before the *meaning* of this crisis has been fully grasped.
In Pope's "Discourse on Pastoral Poetry" (1717), for example,
we can already sense a certain amount of repressed disquietude
resulting from the cleavage between the pastoral idealization
and actual social conditions. "We must," writes Pope, "use

some illusion to render a Pastoral delightful; and this consists in exposing the best only of a shepherd's life, and in concealing its miseries."[19] The point, once again, is not that poets were previously naive in regard to the illusion underlying pastoral but rather that they had felt no need to justify it. The fact that Pope now begins to speak in terms of the pastoral *illusion* indicates that he is already treading on rather shaky ground.

In light of Pope's "Discourse," it is interesting that the first frontal attack on the transcendental pastoral was mounted three years earlier, in 1714, by his friend John Gay, in a series of six eclogues entitled *The Shepherd's Week*. Gay's attitude in this work warrants close attention, not only because it reflects the collapse of the transcendental pastoral but also because it indicates the degree to which the "antipastoral" tendency that emerges in the wake of the collapse can allow for the venting of a social snobbism that may always have been latent in the older form but that was generally repressed. The negation of social differences that we have seen to be intrinsic to the pastoral is a fundamentally ambiguous phenomenon: it can either express the desire for an Earthly Paradise or it can reflect the camouflaging of social inequities. There are, however, possibly as many versions of antipastoral as there are of pastoral.

Written as a burlesque imitation of Spenser's *Shepherd's Calendar*, Gay's poem remains a pastoral in the minimal sense of Pope's definition; but, as the "Proem" to the work makes clear, *The Shepherd's Week* undermines the metaphysical basis of the pastoral by denuding it of its Golden Age myth:

> Other Poet travailing in this plain High-way of Pastoral know I none. Yet, certes, such it behoveth a Pastoral to be, as Nature in the Country affordeth; and the Manners also meetly copied from the rustical Folk therein. In this also my Love to my native Country *Britain* much pricketh me forward, to describe aright the Manners of our own honest and laborious Plough-men, in no wise sure more unworthy a *British* Poet's imitation, than those of *Sicily* or *Arcadie*; albeit, not ignorant I am, what a Rout and Rabblement of Critical Gallimawfy hath been made of late Days by certain young Men of insipid Delicacy, concerning, I wist not what, *Golden Age*, and other outrageous Conceits, to which they

would confine Pastoral. Whereof, I avow, I account not at all, knowing no Age so justly to be stiled *Golden*, as this of *our Soveraign Lady Queen ANNE.*

This idle trumpery (only fit for Schools and Schoolboys) unto that ancient *Dorick* Shepherd *Theocritus*, or his Mates, was never known; he rightly, throughout his fifth *Idyll*, maketh his Louts give foul Language, and behold their Goats at Rut in all Simplicity.[20]

The Shepherd's Week is superficially an attempt to demystify the pastoral, but the argument could be made that in actuality it is more mystified than the transcendental pastoral itself because it has simply lost touch with the historical problematic that is submerged in the older form. Gay's shepherds are mere country bumpkins, and thus the idealistic vision of the transcendental pastoral is reduced to farce in his work. Gay's attitude betrays a fundamental ambivalence: on the one hand, by attacking the Golden Age myth he places himself on the side of the Moderns (in the still raging Battle of the Ancient and Moderns), and this, of course, allows him to engage in patriotic flattery of a rather fulsome kind; but on the other hand, affecting an antique "pastoral" style, he claims that he is returning to "the true ancient guise of Theocritus." The utopian pastoral had made use of archaism as a way of distancing itself from the present, but in Gay's contradictory gestures we can see that the old tropes and conventions have been reduced to the status of a mere entertainment.

In the eclogues themselves, Gay's archaism is the vehicle of bathos and serves to heighten the discrepancy between the eclogue form and the coarseness of rural manners. Dr. Johnson, we know, hated pastoral; but it is difficult to credit his comment, that "the effect of reality and truth became conspicuous, even when the intention was to shew [Gay's shepherds] groveling and degraded. These Pastorals became popular and were read with delight, as just representations of rural manners and occupations."[21] On the contrary, the net effect of Gay's satire is not realism but, as the following passage indicates (in which the voice of Ambition and Grandeur is heard behind that of the Maid), one long, drawn-out Augustan sneer (carefully modulated, it is true) at the old-fashioned literary form it espouses and at the "quaintness" of country life in general:

> Ah! didst thou know what Proffers I withstood,
> When late I met the *Squire* in yonder Wood!
> To me he sped, regardless of his Game,
> While all my Cheek was glowing red with Shame;
> My Lip he kiss'd, and prais'd my healthful Look,
> Then from his Purse of Silk a *Guinea* took,
> Into my Hand he forc'd the tempting Gold,
> While I with modest struggling broke his Hold.
> He swore that *Dick* in Liv'ry strip'd with Lace,
> Should wed me soon to keep me from Disgrace;
> But I no Footman priz'd nor golden Fee,
> For what is Lace or Gold compar'd to thee?[22]

The demise of the old pastoral coincides with a number of new forms or tendencies that are all in their own ways dominated by the spirit of realism (or pseudo-realism) that emerges in the eighteenth century. The relationship of these newly emergent forms, both to actual social conditions, on the one hand, and to the vision of *communitas* stemming from the Golden Age myth, on the other, is quite different from that of the old pastoral. Although they are sometimes grouped together under the "anti-pastoral" rubric, if the latter is seen in monolithic terms it can be as distorting as the "pastoral" label itself. For instance, *The Shepherd's Week* is clearly antipastoral in the sense that Gay is attacking the transcendental vision embodied in the old pastoral; but on the other hand, Gay maintains the props of the old pastoral, which thus becomes the husk of itself in his hands. From a social standpoint, there is no difference essentially between the Tory spirit motivating Gay's and Pope's pastorals, even though Pope remains formally within the context of the old pastoral while Gay does not. Although the breakdown of the old pastoral occurs under the aegis of the new realism, Gay's rustics have no more intrinsic reality than Spenser's (but Spenser, we must remember, was not striving for realism), and it is clear that they are merely grist for his satiric, but not very serious, mill.

The case is very different with George Crabbe's poem *The*

Village (1783), a poem of the utmost seriousness, which comes in the wake both of the Industrial Revolution and, we immediately feel, of Gray's *Elegy. The Village* opens with a series of chastened and chastening "Remarks upon Pastoral Poetry" (as the poet himself refers to them), in which the conventions of the old pastoral are explicitly viewed as an ideological subterfuge:

> Fled are those times, when, in harmonious strains,
> The rustic poet praised his native plains:
> No shepherds now, in smooth alternate verse,
> Their country's beauty or their nymphs' rehearse;
> Yet still for these we frame the tender strain,
> Still in our lays fond Corydons complain,
> And shepherds' boys their amorous pains reveal,
> The only pains, alas! they never feel.
>   On Mincio's banks, in Caesar's bounteous reign,
> If Tityrus found the Golden Age again,
> Must sleepy bards the flattering dream prolong,
> Mechanic echoes of the Mantuan song?
> From Truth and Nature shall we widely stray,
> Where Virgil, not where Fancy, leads the way?
>   Yes, thus the Muses sing of happy swains,
> Because the Muses never knew their pains:
> They boast their peasants' pipes; but peasants now
> Resign their pipes and plod behind the plough;
> And few, amid the rural-tribe, have time
> To number syllables, and play with rhyme;
> Save honest Duck, what son of verse could share
> The poet's rapture and the peasant's care?[23]

Oddly enough, although Crabbe polemicizes against the pastoral fiction, he does not wholly dispense with it, as his suggestion that in former times "the rustic poet praised his native plains" indicates. To us it goes without saying that shepherds have always been poor and that those privileged enough to become poets have never been shepherds; apparently, however, the pastoral myth could still be maintained even after the pastoral conventions had been abandoned. Crabbe writes as one who regards those conventions as being now in bad taste because they contrast so markedly with existing social conditions; at the same time, he implicitly invokes a past in which the pastoral mirrored reality.

In *The Village*, which was published in 1783, the antipastoral tendency is fully manifest, but in *The Deserted Village*, which appeared thirteen years earlier, what is lamented is precisely the loss of the "pastoral" way of life. The social changes lamented by Goldsmith are clearly connected to the demise of the transcendental pastoral (and for the reasons that Crabbe enunciates); but, interestingly, as the two poems taken together indicate, the demise of the transcendental pastoral is synonymous with the advent of a new form, one that might be termed the demotic pastoral. Where the transcendental or utopian pastoral superimposed the values of the aristocracy upon an imaginary rural landscape, synthesizing the nobleman and the shepherd in the poet-as-shepherd motif (because it was under the aegis of poetry that this transcendental synthesis was effected), the demotic pastoral involves at least the attempt (though one that is sometimes distorted and insincere) at realism in its depiction of the peasantry. Similarly, where the transcendental pastoral had insulated itself from history, the demotic pastoral involves an engagement with precisely those historical factors that led to the loss of the "pastoral" way of life and the loss of the transcendental pastoral itself—though often this engagement with history is so fraught with bourgeois sentimentalism as to be entirely unhistorical in its net effect.

Both tendencies are very much in evidence in *The Deserted Village*. On the one hand, Goldsmith is as realistic as Marx himself in his understanding of how the Enclosure Acts and the incursions of capitalism have changed the face of the countryside:

> Ye friends to truth, ye statesmen who survey
> The rich man's joys increase, the poor's decay,
> 'Tis yours to judge, how wide the limits stand
> Between a splendid and a happy land.
> Proud swells the tide with loads of freighted ore,
> And shouting Folly hails them from her shore;
> Hoards, even beyond the miser's wish abound,
> And rich men flock from all the world around.
> Yet count our gains. This wealth is but a name
> That leaves our useful products still the same.
> Not so the loss. The man of wealth and pride,

Takes up a space that many poor supplied;
Space for his lake, his park's extended bounds,
Space for his horses, equipage, and hounds;
The robe that wraps his limbs in silken sloth,
Has robbed the neighbouring field of half their growth;
His seat, where solitary sports are seen,
Indignant spurns the cottage from the green;
Around the world each needful product flies,
For all the luxuries the world supplies.
While thus the land adorned for pleasure all
In barren splendour feebly waits the fall.[24]

On the other hand, where Marx is unsparing in his analysis of
how the bourgeoisie has "rescued a considerable part of the
population from the idiocy of rural life,"[25] Goldsmith depicts
the life of the vanished peasantry essentially as an idyll in which
"health and plenty cheered the labouring swain" (2).

Gray's hypothetical description of the lives of the Forefathers,
in stanzas 5–7 of the *Elegy*, is similarly idyllic; moreover, as we
noted in chapter 3, the sense of loss evoked by these stanzas is
not merely in relation to individuals who are "no more" but, as
in *The Deserted Village*, to a way of life and an entire class.
However, where in Goldsmith's poem this is the sole perspec-
tive that is adumbrated, in the *Elegy* it is countered by the
development of a thematic strain that is at odds *both* with
the transcendental pastoral and with the as yet unarticulated
demotic pastoral: the theme of unfulfilled potential (or "death-
in-life")—which is to say, the "problem of history."

In relation to the pastoral, then, Gray can be seen as coming
both at the end of a long tradition and at the beginning of a
new one—and here we should remember that the poem was
published almost at the exact midpoint of the century, at the
point historians have traditionally marked as the onset of the
Industrial Revolution and, with it, the Modern era. Gray's rein-
terpretation of the idealistic pastoral tendency from the stand-
point of the realistic georgic tendency allows for a balancing
of thematic and generic possibilities that gives the poem an
extraordinary resonance and richness of scope. The *Elegy* thus
stands at the center of a confluence of forces that will lead to

the emergence of several new forms, including the antipastoral tendency of Crabbe and the demotic pastoral tendency that will later culminate in Wordsworth.[26] The emergence of the problem of history in the *Elegy*, together with the contrast between the rich and the poor that is a consequence of this thematic development, is thus connected to the dissolution of the transcendental pastoral; but it is also connected to a new vision that, though only implicit, makes itself felt in the poem as a kind of "trembling hope" for the future. As we saw in chapter 3, the *principle of universality* is latent from the very outset in the figure of the passing bell, which, in resonating throughout the poem, connects us to Donne's "No man is an island" meditation. In the *Elegy*, however, the principle of universality cannot explicitly emerge until the socioeconomic aspect of Gray's dialectic has been fully developed—lest the poem succumb to what for its own time would have been mere devotional cliché. And yet, the suspension of the principle of universality is ultimately what allows the evocation of the universal to be felt with so much force when it finally does emerge. Similarly, although the explicit emergence of the "problem of history" in the *Elegy* is tantamount to the dissolution of the transcendental pastoral, the utopian impulse that had been dominant in the old pastoral is burdened by a deepening melancholia but is not lost.

Chapter 5

Wordsworth and the Reconstitution of the Pastoral

To argue, as I have done, that the "problem of history" emerges in the *Elegy*, and, consequently, that the poem represents an important turning point or watershed in the English poetic tradition is to pose a challenge to a number of received assumptions about literary history and particularly to what might be called the "Wordsworthian version of Romanticism": first, because the symbolic moment I have accorded the *Elegy* has generally been reserved for Wordsworth and, second, because the categories of literary history have themselves been delineated around a conception of the poetic canon as a whole in which Wordsworth occupies precisely this central position.

Literary criticism has always tended to regard Gray and Wordsworth as antithetical figures, and in this it has followed the example of Wordsworth himself, who was at pains to distance himself from Gray. Consequently, given the centrality of Wordsworth in the canon, it is not surprising that Gray has generally been relegated to its peripheries. Of course, from the standpoint of the received categories of literary history, it is difficult to conceive of Gray otherwise than as a "pre-Romantic" or "post-Augustan." But besides the issue of canon formation, there is another reason why we should now turn our attention to Wordsworth's vision and Wordsworth's relationship to Gray, and this is that Gray in the *Elegy* exerted a profound—indeed a formative—influence on Wordsworth, though one that criticism has generally underestimated or failed to recognize.[1]

In the received view of literary history, the Romantics effected a break with Augustan poetic norms by aligning themselves with Milton and by translating the theological premises of *Paradise Lost* into a new kind of humanistic (and interiorized) discourse. Hence the assumption of a "Miltonic-Romantic" tradition. That view, which has tended to promote Wordsworth, in particular, to a position of preeminence because of what has been called his "levelling revolution in diction, and in the location of archetypes in common rather than in heroic life,"[2] obviously contains a great deal of truth; but a problem arises when we attempt to link Wordsworth's demotic poetics and his adherence to Milton both to each other and to the question of ideological content. The fact of the matter is that Wordsworth eventually became a Tory in his politics; therefore, we need to ask whether his "levelling revolution in diction" should be regarded, as it usually is, as a radical extension of his early involvement in the French Revolution or whether it should not rather be seen as the extension of an essentially conservative orientation. Critics have often tended to assume that there is a kind of seamless continuity between Milton and Wordsworth and hence between the Revolution of 1642 and the Romantic movement. Indeed, as a result of the tendency to regard Wordsworth as the revolutionary successor to Milton (a tendency that originates with Wordsworth himself), and because of his later political turn, there has been a corresponding tendency on the part of critics to *depoliticize* Wordsworth's poetry—or rather, to deploy political categories solely in terms of the aesthetic dimension. In this regard, Modernism inherits a series of strategies that have already been well prepared by the Romantics—as a result of which it becomes possible to "have one's cake and eat it too." Thus, despite their reactionary political views, Pound and Eliot continue to be seen as "revolutionary" writers whose stylistic innovations are therefore in some way "progressive."

Related to this tendency to submerge the political in the aesthetic dimension—where, however, it is empty of content— since the Romantics, and beginning perhaps with the publication in 1800 of the Preface to *Lyrical Ballads*, there has also been a tendency to conceive of the poetic tradition as being split into two main "lines." To understand the nature of this dichotomy, one might consider the following passage from *The Visionary Company* (1961), Harold Bloom's study of the Romantics. Bloom's formulation is especially interesting in that it shrewdly (albeit erroneously, in my view) locates the nexus between ideological and aesthetic factors. There are, he suggests,

> at least two main traditions in English poetry, and what distinguishes them are not only aesthetic factors but conscious differences in religion and politics. One line, and it is the central one, is Protestant, radical and Miltonic-Romantic; the other is Catholic, conservative, and by its claims classical. French culture has been divided between those who have accepted the French Revolution and its consequences and those who have sought to resist them. Similarly, but more subtly, English culture has been divided between those who have accepted the Puritan Revolution of the late sixteenth and seventeenth century and those who have fought against it."[3]

The implication of Bloom's remarks seems to be that while the French Revolution has divided the French, the English—owing no doubt to the sluggish nature of their character, as Edmund Burke might say—have remained fixated on the English Revolution, so that only the latter is salient to their situation. This hypostatization, which avoids such inconvenient facts as that Wordsworth and Coleridge both turned against the French Revolution, enables the critic to preserve his dichotomized view of the tradition, in terms of which the central line is "Protestant, radical and Miltonic-Romantic." (Indeed, Bloom includes Auden, who for a time was a Marxist, in the Catholic, conservative camp, and D. H. Lawrence, who for a time flirted with fascism, in the Protestant, radical one.)[4] But what concerns us here is not the inadequacies of Bloom's formulation but rather that this view of the tradition is one which, in its basic outlines, has generally prevailed since the Romantics themselves—and not only among those critics, like Bloom himself, who have been partisans of the Romantics but among those who have tended to oppose them as well. Bloom's argument in *The Visionary Company* was specifically directed against Eliot and the New Critics, but Eliot would have accepted his formulation as far as it went, though of course from an opposing point of view. The two sides disagree with each other about the value of individual poets and individual tendencies but not about the main outlines and categories of literary history.

Given those categories, it is not difficult to understand why the significance of Gray's achievement in the *Elegy* has not been understood. As a poet who was influenced by Milton and Spenser, on the one hand, and by Pope and Dryden, on the other, he firmly occupies a middle ground that is excluded by the artificial polarities of literary history. Of course, the problem of classification that has resulted from those polarities pertains not only to Gray but to all the poets of the second half of the eighteenth century. For a long time, these poets were classified as "post-Augustans" or "pre-Romantics"—as if they came too late or too soon to fit into either of the "two main traditions"; and although they are now generally referred to as "Poets of Sensibility," as a result of Northrop Frye's attempt to define a shift in emphasis during the period from poetic product to poetic process,[5] it may be that the "Sensibility" rubric has not resolved but has actually exacerbated the problem of classification by cordoning off the period from the rest of literary history. No doubt all three of the labels mentioned above describe some of the tendencies of the period; in the case of the *Elegy*, however, they are not only inadequate but even misleading. Significantly, in Frye's essay the *Elegy* is never mentioned, just as it is not mentioned in Earl Wasserman's study of the eighteenth-century use of personification.[6] Thus, the various classification systems have had the effect of excluding what is arguably the greatest poem produced by the eighteenth century.

So much, in any event, may serve as a sketch of the problem that the *Elegy* poses in relation to literary history. In order to come to grips with the problem, we have to examine Wordsworth's poetic vision, both in itself and in relation to Gray.

Wordsworth's Attack on Gray

In considering Wordsworth's relationship to Gray, one naturally begins with the Preface to *Lyrical Ballads* of 1800, with its famous attack on Gray's diction in the "Sonnet on the Death of Richard West." The Preface, of course, has long been regarded as *the* manifesto of the Romantic movement in English poetry, and therefore it would be natural to assume that the thrust of Wordsworth's polemic was directed against the school of Pope and Johnson. But in fact, it is Gray who is Wordsworth's primary antagonist in the Preface. To understand why Wordsworth should have singled out Gray for censure, we have to take account of his professed aims and underlying motives in writing the document.

At the beginning of the Preface, Wordsworth informs the reader that the poems in *Lyrical Ballads* were written according to a theory of poetry and to demonstrate that theory;[7] but of course it was the other way round: poems are never written according to a theory. On the contrary, Wordsworth's real purpose in writing the Preface was to create the conditions in which his own poems would be understood and appreciated, and this involved defending himself against the charge leveled against the first edition that both the style and the subject matter of the *Lyrical Ballads* were too "low" for polite discourse. However, Wordsworth's Preface is much more than just a defense of his own poetry: it is a sweeping polemic against the poetic diction of the eighteenth century and, in a still more radical sense, against the very notion of "poetic diction" itself. The Preface is thus, as it has always been understood to be, a profoundly revolutionary document, though with what ideological implications is by no means clear. Its influence, even unto the present day, is impossible to exaggerate. One measure of this sometimes paradoxical influence is that the very term "poetic diction" has tended to retain the pejorative connotations that Wordsworth gave it. Thus, when the Modernists rejected the poetry of the Romantics, for instance, they did so, ironically, on the very basis of the argument enunciated in Wordsworth's Preface.

Wordsworth's professed purpose in writing the *Lyrical Ballads,* of course, was "to imitate, and, as far as possible, to adopt the very language of men" (1:130). That observation, repeated several times in the Preface, may be regarded as the poet's *minimal* claim for his poems, but actually he is going much further. He is not merely attempting to establish the validity of his procedure, as one possible option among many, he is extrapolating a universal precept from the example of his own poems. This precept, which is likewise repeated several times, is that "there neither is, nor can be, any *essential* difference between the language of prose and metrical composition" (1:135; Wordsworth's emphasis).[8]

All this, of course, is well known. But what criticism has somehow failed to emphasize—and in this it has followed the poet himself—is that in the overall context of his program for poetry, Wordsworth's theoretical perspective had a rather significant inconvenience: it set him apart from Milton and from the Spenserian-Miltonic line generally. It goes without saying that for both Spenser and Milton the language of poetry is at the furthest possible remove from the language of ordinary prose (assuming that there is such a language). Ben Jonson remarked that "for affecting the ancients, Spenser writ no language," and Milton's diction has been under almost continual attack since the seventeenth century from adherents of the "plain style." However—and this also goes without saying—Milton was not only the single greatest influence on Wordsworth but the ever-present model for his highest poetic ambitions. Indeed, since an important aspect of Wordsworth's program was precisely to forge a link between his own poetry and Milton's, it was necessary for him to evade the implications of the precept he had enunciated.

The obvious point that needs to be made is that in the Preface to *Lyrical Ballads,* Wordsworth was caught on the horns of a profound dilemma, one that manifests itself in various guises throughout his poetry as a conflict between his "demotic" commitments, on the one hand, and his "Miltonic" aspirations, on the other. For this reason, having declared that the language of poetry should not differ from that of good prose, Wordsworth immediately adds, with obvious anxiety: "The truth of this assertion might be demonstrated by innumerable passages from almost all the poetical writings, *even of Milton himself*" (1:132; my italics). And then, in the very next sentence, he launches his attack on Gray: "To illustrate the subject in a general manner, I will here adduce a short composition of Gray, who was at the head of those who, by their reasonings, have attempted to widen the space of separation betwixt Prose and Metrical composition, and was more than any other man curiously elaborate in the structure of his own poetic diction" (1:132).

It is unnecessary to rehearse Wordsworth's specific criticisms of the Sonnet, for this would be to mistake the forest for the trees, as in a sense Wordsworth wants us to do, and as criticism has followed him in doing. The "Sonnet on the Death of West," although very highly rated by the generation preceding Wordsworth's, as Stuart Curran notes,[9] is by no means free of the inflated rhetoric that Wordsworth found in it. In any event, as Coleridge suggested in his discussion of the Preface in *Biographia Literaria*, there is no such thing as poetic diction in the abstract, apart from a variety of other formal and generic factors. Thus, if the Sonnet fails, this is not because it contains *poetic diction* but because its diction is *not poetic enough* to make the piece memorable.[10] In the end, the only criterion for poetry is the subjective or intersubjective one of Beauty or poetic excellence, which means that the mediating formalisms must be judged in terms of the success or failure of the work as a whole. Be that as it may, the fact remains that Wordsworth might have chosen a hundred poems by a hundred other poets to illustrate his point. What is significant and what concerns us here is not the substance of his remarks on the Sonnet but rather that he chose to level his attack on Gray.

He did so, first of all, to evade the problem posed by Milton. But the choice of Gray was by no means arbitrary; nor was it merely occasioned by Wordsworth's desire to distance himself from a generation of poets of whom Gray, by all acknowledgments, was the most distinguished figure. Gray's views on po-

etic diction were diametrically opposed to Wordsworth's, and if
Wordsworth had perused Mason's edition of Gray's letters, he
might have come upon the following pronouncement (made in
a letter to Richard West):

> The language of the age is never the language of poetry;
> except among the French, whose verse, where the thought or
> image does not support it, differs in nothing from prose. Our
> poetry, on the contrary, has a language peculiar to itself, to
> which almost every one, that has written, has added some-
> thing by enriching it with foreign idioms.
>
> (*Corresp.* 1:192)

This passage has often been quoted; but as the following addi-
tional statements make clear (which I give because they are
not as well known), Gray, notwithstanding his philosophical
inclinations, saw himself primarily as a lyric poet intent on
creating "music" rather than on reflecting "the very language
of men":

> The true lyric style, with all its flights of fancy, ornaments
> & heightening of expression, & harmony of sound, is in its
> nature superior to every other style.
>
> (*Corresp.* 2:608)

Again:

> There is . . . a *toute ensemble* of sound, as well as of sense,
> in poetical composition always necessary to its perfection.
> What is gone before still dwells upon the ear, and insensibly
> harmonizes with the present line, as in that succession of
> fleeting notes which is called Melody.[11]

And in a letter to Mason, where the criticism might have been
directed against Wordsworth himself, he writes that

> extreme conciseness of expression, yet pure, perspicuous, &
> musical, is one of the grand beauties of lyric poetry. this I
> have always aim'd at, & never could attain. the necessity of
> rhyming is one great obstacle: another & perhaps a stronger
> is that way you have chosen of casting down your first Ideas
> carelessly & at large, and then clipping them here and there
> and forming them at leisure. this method after all possible

pains will leave behind it in some places a *laxity*, & a dif-
fuseness. the frame of a thought (otherwise well invented,
well-turned, & well-placed) is often weaken'd by it.

(*Corresp.* 2.551–52)

Clearly, Gray was the logical choice for an opponent—al-
though in practice Wordsworth and Gray are much closer than
their theoretical positions would suggest. But the curious thing
is that in his attack on Gray, Wordsworth was following the
lead of none other than Dr. Johnson,[12] who, disliking Gray's
style in general, though making an exception of the *Elegy* (as we
saw in chapter 1), had complained: "Gray thought his language
more poetical as it was more remote from common use."[13] John-
son, interestingly, had tempered his enormous enthusiasm for
Milton with a number of adverse comments on Milton's diction
that echo his criticism of Gray:

> Through all his greater works there prevails an uniform pecu-
> liarity of Diction, a mode and cast which bears little resem-
> blance to that of any former writer, and which is so far
> removed from common use, that an unlearned reader, when
> he first opens his book, finds himself surprised by a new
> language. This novelty has been, by those who find nothing
> wrong in Milton, imputed to his laborious endeavours after
> words suitable to the grandeur of his ideas. . . . But the truth
> is, that both in prose and verse, he had formed his style by a
> perverse and pedantick principle. He was desirous to use
> English words with a foreign idiom.[14]

In leveling the same kind of criticism against both Milton and
Gray, Johnson was at least being consistent—more consistent
than Wordsworth could afford to be under the circumstances.
But what is truly fascinating is that the positions of the two
critics should coincide to so remarkable a degree. We generally
think of the Preface to *Lyrical Ballads* as marking a radical break
with the poetic norms of the eighteenth century, and surely this
is true to a certain extent; but on the crucial issue of poetic
diction, at least, here is Wordsworth following the lead of the
eighteenth century's greatest—and in some respects most typi-
cal—critic.[15] All of which suggests that Wordsworth's attack

on Gray, although narrowly accommodated to the sphere of stylistics, has submerged ideological implications.

Before addressing these implications directly, however, we need to delineate what Wordsworth found in Gray that was essential to his own vision—and this means coming to grips with that vision, as well as with its imaginative pairing of Milton and Gray. We have seen that in committing himself to the principle that there is no essential difference between the language of poetry and prose, Wordsworth focuses his attack on Gray in order to evade the problem that this principle poses in his relationship to Milton. But paradoxically, the importance of Gray's influence emerges at precisely those moments at which Wordsworth confronts his relationship to Milton most directly. Indeed, Wordsworth's relationship to Milton is *mediated* by his relationship to Gray, but there is a positive as well as a negative sense in which this occurs.

"Far from the Madding Crowd": Wordsworth's Humanism

The mediating influence of Gray is most readily apparent in the lines "On Man, on Nature, and on Human Life" that Wordsworth published as a "Prospectus" to *The Recluse*, including them in the Preface to the 1814 edition of *The Excursion*. The "Prospectus" is of the highest significance in Wordsworth's oeuvre, not only on its own very considerable account but because it represents a kind of précis of the philosophical epic on which he set his highest hopes as a poet; thus, the fact that Gray's influence should make itself felt in the "Prospectus" is also highly significant. The only section of *The Recluse* proper that Wordsworth managed to write was the "Home at Grasmere" fragment, which was originally intended to form Book I. In one of the extant manuscripts of "Home at Grasmere," Wordsworth appended an earlier version of the lines "On Man, on Nature, and on Human Life" that later became the "Prospectus." The lines may date from as early as 1798 or from several years later.[16]

In any event, the "Prospectus" is both the most purely Miltonic passage in all of Wordsworth's poetry and at the same time the one in which he differentiates himself from Milton most completely. It is an astonishing performance and certainly represents Wordsworth at his most radical. Together with *Tintern Abbey*, a poem it resembles in certain respects and which may indeed have grown out of it, the "Prospectus" is the most concentrated piece of blank verse that Wordsworth ever wrote, and one of the greatest in the entire Miltonic-Romantic tradition. Not only is it an announcement of Wordsworth's intention to render the Miltonic sublime in demotic terms and to reduce its theological "fictions" to what the Enlightenment called "natural philosophy" (Wordsworth actually uses the term "fictions" in line 51, and though the explicit reference is to pagan mythology, the actual implication is clear), but in the power and density of its blank verse, it is perhaps the most triumphant example of that rendering in Wordsworth's entire corpus:

> All strength—all terror, single or in bands
> That ever was put forth in personal form—
> Jehovah—with his thunder, and the choir
> Of shouting Angels, and the empyreal thrones—
> I pass them unalarmed.[17]

For "Jehovah" in these lines, one could as well read "Milton"— but there is no passage in the poem that does not implicitly express the same point:

> Paradise, and groves
> Elysian, Fortunate Fields—like those of old
> Sought in the Atlantic Main—why should they be
> A history only of departed things,
> Or a mere fiction of what never was?
> For the discerning intellect of Man,
> When wedded to this goodly universe
> In love and holy passion, shall find these
> A simple produce of the common day.
>
> (5:47–55)

Wordsworth's ambition in *The Recluse* was clearly to produce a *modern* version of the Miltonic sublime, a radically humanist

version that would forego all mythological input while sacrific-
ing nothing of Milton's power and Milton's grandeur. This,
we may say in passing, is in marked contrast to the versions
attempted by the other Romantics, who, in their efforts to cir-
cumvent Milton—and Genesis, either invent myths of their
own or look to the Greeks for assistance, but in any event are
forced to rely on some form of allegory. This perhaps explains
why Wordsworth was unable to go on with *The Recluse*, at least
as that poem was initially conceived, and why he was forced to
settle for the more diffuse narrative mode of *The Prelude* and
The Excursion. Lacking Milton's enabling fiction, Wordsworth's
only access to the sublime was through his reaction *against*
Milton and through the few humanistic generalizations he was
able to muster. The simple fact of the matter is that in the
107 lines of the "Prospectus," he had essentially exhausted his
material, having said all that he had to say. Nevertheless, there
is no question but that the "Prospectus" constitutes poetry of
the highest order; indeed, there is even a sense in which it is
not a prelude to an unfinished work but *is* that work itself, in
its essence if not its intention. However, in order to understand
Wordsworth's accomplishment in this poem, we have to exam-
ine both the nature of his humanism and, equally important,
his construction of a poetic persona to dramatize it. And here is
where Gray's influence makes itself felt.

Wordsworth's humanism is both epistemological and teleo-
logical. On the one hand, it proclaims the "marriage" between
the external world and the human mind as already given in the
nature of things (this is the aspect of Wordsworth's thought that
may seem most simplistic to us now), but on the other, it seeks
to "win" humanity from its fallen state to "noble raptures."
(There is a contradiction here, perhaps, but it is one that is
implicit in the entire Platonic tradition, and in Wordsworth's
poetry it exerts a fruitful tension.) The two components of
Wordsworth's humanism are articulated more succinctly, if not
more eloquently, in the "Prospectus" than anywhere else in his
poetry; and in the following lines we have what amounts to the
locus classicus for his "high argument":

I, long before the blissful hour arrives,
Would chant in lonely peace the spousal verse
Of this great consummation:—and, by words
Which speak of nothing more than what we are,
Would I arouse the sensual from their sleep
Of Death, and win the vacant and the vain
To noble raptures; while my voice proclaims
How exquisitely the individual Mind
(And the progressive powers perhaps no less
Of the whole species) to the external World
Is fitted:—and how exquisitely too—
Theme this but little heard of among men—
The external World is fitted to the Mind;
And the creation (by no lower name
Can it be called) which they with blended might
Accomplish:—this is our high argument.

                                        (5:56–71)

Blake, as many critics have noted, complained that Words-
worth's philosophy amounted to a kind of violence against the
intellect: "Does not this Fit, & is not Fitting most exquisitely
too—but to what? not to the Mind, but to the Vile Body only &
to its Laws of Good and Evil & its Enmity against Mind."[18]
There is something to be said for this point of view, especially if
one considers the overly diffuse quality of some of Wordsworth's
poetry; but as far as the "Prospectus" itself is concerned, Blake's
inability to make use of this really authentic note in Words-
worth says something about his own limitations, great poet that
he was. In our own time, Wallace Stevens was certainly able to
make use of it:

And out of what one sees and hears and out
Of what one feels, who could have thought to make
So many selves, so many sensuous worlds,
As if the air, the mid-day air, was swarming
With the metaphysical changes that occur
Merely in living as and where we live.[19]

There is nothing in Wordsworth's "high argument" that re-
minds us of the more skeptical Gray, except perhaps, and then
only when other issues have come into focus, the adjectives

"lonely" in line 57 and "noble" in line 62. But while the Words-
worthian version of the sublime is not in itself derived from
Gray, it is mediated by the elegiac pathos that Gray discovered in
the "rude Forefathers of the hamlet." Not only does Wordsworth
absorb this elegiac pathos unto himself, and not only is it impli-
cated in his demotic rendering of the Miltonic sublime, but, by
locating his own existence in the socially marginal terms that
Gray had reserved for an objectively distinct class, and by doing
so, moreover, in a way that represses the socioeconomic side to
Gray's dialectic, Wordsworth is able to construct a new poetic
archetype through which to dramatize his humanistic vision.
This is not merely a case of the "egoistical sublime," in the usual
sense in which that phrase has been applied to Wordsworth: it
is not Wordsworth the man who is singing to us in the "Prospec-
tus," but the Recluse who is doing so—which is to say, an
archetype of the poet as universal man. Thus, through the medi-
ation of Gray, Wordsworth arrives at a poetic standpoint in
which the "lyric-I" has assumed *epic* possibilities—the poetic
standpoint not of Milton, nor of anyone else in the English
tradition, but of Dante.

→ 180

Indeed, the very title of Wordsworth's poem tells much of the
story, recalling as it does an important aspect of Gray's dialectic
in the *Elegy*. For by remaining "far from the madding crowd's
ignoble strife," Wordsworth's Recluse is able to grasp the univer-
sal in human experience in a manner that would not otherwise
be possible. The Romantic paradox (if we may borrow a later
terminology) is that if society is "alienated," then it is necessary
to remove oneself (or alienate oneself) from society in order to
live harmoniously and to achieve an integrated vision. This
paradox is obviously central to Rousseau's thought, and of
course it has deep roots in Christianity; but in Wordsworth's
poetic derivation, the influence of Gray is most salient.

It is immediately after the lines quoted above, in which
Wordsworth had summarized his "high argument," that the
influence of Gray makes itself felt most directly—and it makes
itself felt in the single word *madding*, which for Wordsworth is
weighted not only with the force of his desire to remove himself

from the life of the city but, one might even say, with all that
is negative in his vision. This word, which Gray of course had
made his own in the *Elegy* (it hardly corresponds to the language
of prose), is the only palpable trace of an influence that is not
primarily linguistic in its manifestations, but its existence in
the text is all the more important for that. It occurs at the point
in the "Prospectus" at which the poet confronts his responsibil-
ity to redescend into the maelstrom of alienated human exis-
tence, much in the way that Plato's philosopher in the famous
allegory is obligated to rejoin the unenlightened souls in the
cave:

> —Such grateful haunts foregoing, if I oft
> Must turn elsewhere—to travel near the tribes
> And fellowships of men, and see ill sights
> Of madding passions mutually inflamed;
> Must hear humanity in fields and groves
> Pipe solitary anguish; or must hang
> Brooding above the fierce confederate storm
> Of sorrow, barricadoed evermore
> Within the walls of cities—may these sounds
> Have their authentic comment; that even these
> Hearing, I be not downcast or forlorn!—
>
> (5:72–82)

Then follows the magnificent conclusion to the poem, in which
Wordsworth invokes the "prophetic Spirit that inspir'st / The
human Soul of universal earth, / Dreaming on things to come"
(5:83–85).

We saw in the *Elegy* that the poor are the vehicle of Gray's
evocation of the essential pathos of the human condition be-
cause of their inability to cover their nakedness, as it were.
Wordsworth's involvement in so many of his poems with leech-
gatherers, beggars, and the like testifies to a similar attempt to
penetrate to the core of the human condition via those who
are most marginal to society. Indeed, the keyword "common"
functions in Wordsworth's poetry in much the same way as the
theme of anonymity does in the *Elegy:* both class-specifically
and universally.[20] In the "Prospectus," however, what is salient

is not so much Wordsworth's social sympathies per se as the
way in which his adoption of the Recluse archetype provides
him with access to a universalizing rhetoric and thus enables
him to articulate a new, humanistic version of the Miltonic
sublime. Yet the leech-gatherers and beggars are clearly on a
continuum with the Recluse, and what the echo from Gray
enables us to see is how Wordsworth's internalization of the
condition of marginality has the paradoxical effect of imagina-
tively liberating the "lyric-I" from a world that is empirically
characterized by the social fragmentation of class distinctions,
while at the same time enabling the "lyric-I" to contemplate
that alienated world from the standpoint of its transcendence.
Thus, through the mediating influence of Gray, Wordsworth
arrives at a utopian synthesis that is capable of carrying the
Miltonic sublime beyond its theological predicates and at least
of approaching the epic from the standpoint of the lyric, as had
not been possible since Dante.

Lacking a fully articulated mythos, Wordsworth was ulti-
mately faced with the dilemma of having to choose either lyric
resonance or epic extension, and for this reason he was unable
to go on with *The Recluse* in the form in which the poem was
originally conceived. But in the "Prospectus," this dichotomiza-
tion of his powers had not yet taken hold; thus, as M. H. Abrams
suggests, the "Prospectus" stands as Wordsworth's great poem
of election, the one in which he not only formulates his epic
project but comes into his own as a poet.[21] Wordsworth's con-
frontation with Milton is therefore at its most intense in the
"Prospectus," and by the same token the influence of Gray is
also most crucial there. But "the hermit in the poet's meta-
phors," to quote Wallace Stevens once again (this time from
Notes toward a Supreme Fiction),[22] continues in effect in Words-
worth's poetry, a sign both of the poet himself and of his struggle
to grasp hold of the human condition in its universality, so that
when the figure occurs, it is almost always juxtaposed against an
echo of "the madding crowd's ignoble strife." Thus, in *Tintern
Abbey*, where the possibilities developed in the "Prospectus"
are extended to the terrain of personal experience, Wordsworth

envisions the landscape in its symbolic connection to "some Hermit's cave, where by his fire / The Hermit sits alone" (1:21–22), describing how his memory of it has sustained him "'mid the din / Of towns and cities" (1:25–26). And even in *The Prelude*, where Wordsworth has moved farther along the personal axis of literary experience and correspondingly farther away from the archetypal, the conjunction of Gray and Milton continues in effect, so that in the very opening passage of the poem, the poet's expression of joy at leaving behind the city culminates in a metalepsis on the conclusion of *Paradise Lost:* "The earth is all before me" (1.14). In order to begin where Milton had left off, Wordsworth had to pass through the alembic of Gray's *Elegy.*

Wordsworth's Pastoral Vision

Given the importance of Gray's influence on Wordsworth, both in itself and in mediating his relationship to Milton, the question of why Wordsworth should have focused his attack on Gray in the Preface becomes all the more compelling. Of course, if Wordsworth had simply been responding to a side of Gray's poetry that had nothing to do with the *Elegy*, then the situation would appear less strange; but what Wordsworth rejected in Gray and what he took from him are really two sides of the same coin, and both are a function of his relationship to the *Elegy.* Our original question can therefore be reformulated to ask what it was in the *Elegy* itself that Wordsworth found threatening and impossible to accept. The answer, if so complex an issue can be summed up in a phrase, is Gray's vision of unfulfilled potential—or, more broadly, the "problem of history."

To Wordsworth, as we have seen, the condition of marginality is to be reckoned almost unambivalently as a good, since what it signifies is the human condition in its universality. Wordsworth not only identifies *himself* with the condition of marginality, through the Recluse archetype, but, in so doing, equates the condition of marginality with the purity of Nature (Nature, of course, being his master concept). Wordsworth's outlook, like

Rousseau's, is founded on a binary opposition between Nature and Society, and therefore it is hardly surprising that he should echo the "Far from the madding crowd" stanza from the *Elegy* as often as he does. To Gray, however, as our analysis in chapter 3 has indicated, although the obscurity of the Forefathers has certain positive features—and they are precisely the ones that Wordsworth's poetry will adumbrate—it is also synonymous with real deprivation, not only of a material kind but in the larger sense of Aristotle's concept of *steresis*,[23] and not only with deprivation but therefore with social alienation predicated on class divisions. All of which is to repeat once more that the *Elegy* discovers (or uncovers) the "problem of history" that had been camouflaged (or buried) by the religious or utopian idealism of the pastoral tradition. Thus, although Wordsworth is profoundly influenced by the *Elegy*, he reacts just as profoundly against a crucial aspect of its dialectic. Indeed, by making Nature central once again (as in a sense it had been in the old pastoral), by identifying himself with the condition of marginality and thereby blurring the class distinctions that Gray had entertained—in short, by *suppressing* the "problem of history"— Wordsworth's poetry may be said to represent the reconstitution of the pastoral ethos, though now from an orientation that is neither aristocratic nor utopian but essentially demotic and conservative. Here, then, is where the two poets diverge, and the effects of this fundamental divergence can be traced along a number of different dimensions, from the stylistic to the political.[24]

The pastoral ethos of Wordsworth's poetry should be examined in the context of his political odyssey. It is well known that after his early involvement with the Girondists in France Wordsworth turned increasingly in a conservative direction and, as the "Genius of Burke" passage he included in the 1850 *Prelude* makes clear (7.511–43), that he was eventually reconciled to the author of the *Reflections on the Revolution in France*. As a result, there has been a tendency to assume that Wordsworth's repudiation of the Revolution occurred *after* his greatest poems had been written and that it was at least partly responsible for the deterioration of his later work. Furthermore, as I pointed out earlier, these assumptions have in turn spawned the view that Wordsworth's "revolutionary" or "apocalyptic" poetics are an extension, or perhaps an internalization, of his revolutionary politics. However, as James K. Chandler has recently argued, the tendency to view Wordsworth's "apocalyptic" poetics as an outgrowth of his early involvement with the French Revolution fails to place sufficient weight on the actual political content of his poetry.[25] Chandler demonstrates that already by 1798 or 1799, when Wordsworth was residing at Goslar, Germany, he had come over to Burke's point of view—in spite of having earlier attacked Burke indirectly in the "Letter to the Bishop of Llandaff" of 1793. What this means, of course, is that even in the poems of his "great decade" (1798–1808) Wordsworth's ideological perspective is already akin to Burkean conservatism (although, as Chandler hastens to add, he never went so far as to embrace Burke's argument for inherited privilege); and this in turn means that Wordsworth's shift to the right cannot be blamed for whatever loss of poetic power he may have experienced in his later years.

Wordsworth's pastoral ethos is nowhere better illustrated than in the "Home at Grasmere" fragment that he originally intended to form Book I of *The Recluse*, and the conservative aspects of his outlook are immediately clear. In contrast to the vision of "homelessness" permeating the *Elegy*, Wordsworth, upholding the paternal ideals of hearth and home, conveys a sense of optimism about the possibility of creating "A true Community, a genuine frame / Of many into one incorporate" (5:615–16). The language here is not only reminiscent of Burke's vision in the *Reflections* but also of medieval conceptions of the "organic" community. In the following passage, Wordsworth distances himself, once again, from "the vast Metropolis," which, borrowing Plato's metaphor, he likens to a cave. The Hermit puts in yet another appearance, and there is once again an echo of the "Far from the madding crowd" stanza:

> he truly is alone,
> He of the multitude whose eyes are doomed

To hold a vacant commerce day by day
With objects wanting life, repelling love;
He by the vast Metropolis immured,
Where pity shrinks from unremitting calls,
Where numbers overwhelm humanity,
And neighbourhood serves rather to divide
Than to unite. What sighs more deep than his,
Whose nobler will hath long been sacrificed;
Who must inhabit, under a black sky,
A City where, if indifference to disgust
Yield not, to scorn, or sorrow, living Men
Are ofttimes to their fellow-men no more
Than to the Forest Hermit are the leaves
That hang aloft in myriads—nay, far less,
For they protect his walk from sun and shower,
Swell his devotion with their voice in storms,
And whisper while the stars twinkle among them
His lullaby. From crowded streets remote,
Far from the living and dead wilderness
Of the thronged World, Society is here
A true Community, a genuine frame
Of many into one incorporate.
That must be looked for here, paternal sway,
One household, under God, for high and low,
One family, and one mansion; to themselves
Appropriate, and divided from the world
As if it were a cave, a multitude
Human and brute, possessors undisturbed
Of this Recess, their legislative Hall,
Their Temple, and their glorious Dwelling-place.

                                                (5:592–624)

But what is particularly interesting, as the ensuing verse-paragraph makes clear, is that in the process of developing his pastoral conception, Wordsworth does not merely revert to the older transcendental form. On the contrary, he begins precisely at the point at which Gray had left off—that is, from the standpoint of the *dissolution* of the older pastoral conventions. Indeed, in this passage Wordsworth actually touches in an explicit way on a series of concerns that we examined in chapter 3 but that are only implicit in the *Elegy* itself. He "dismisses" the Golden Age

myth and "all Arcadian dreams," not in order to open up the
"problem of history," but, ironically, because his belief in pure
immanence (i.e., fulfillment within the immediate terms of
Nature itself) is so strong that it amounts to a rejection of the
"problem of history" and hence the necessity for its transcen-
dental resolution via the Golden Age myth:

RUE

> Dismissing, therefore, all Arcadian dreams,
> All golden fancies of the golden Age,
> The bright array of shadowy thoughts from times
> That were before all time, or are to be
> Ere time expire, the pageantry that stirs
> And will be stirring when our eyes are fixed
> On lovely objects, and we wish to part
> With all remembrance of a jarring world,
> —Take we at once this one sufficient hope,
> What need of more? that we shall neither droop,
> Nor pine for want of pleasure in the life
> Scattered about us, nor through dearth of aught
> That keeps in health the insatiable mind;
> That we shall have for knowledge and for love
> Abundance; and that, feeling as we do
> How goodly, how exceeding fair, how pure
> From all reproach is yon ethereal vault,
> And this deep Vale its earthly counterpart,
> By which, and under which, we are enclosed
> To breathe in peace, we shall moreover find
> (If sound, and what we ought to be ourselves,
> If rightly we observe and justly weigh)
> The Inmates not unworthy of their home
> The Dwellers of their Dwelling.
>
> (5:625-48)

In a certain sense, then, Wordsworth is actually *more*, rather
than less, idealistic than the practitioners of the transcendental
pastoral had been. In building on the foundations of the Golden
Age myth, the older poets were intuitively aware that the value
of their "golden fancies" lay precisely in the fact that they were
indeed fancies, beautiful dreams that could not be realized in
terms of actual social relations. Gray remains within the tradi-
tion of these older writers in the sense that he, too, albeit by

negation, is possessed of a vision of "homelessness." In confronting the "problem of history" that for so long had been camouflaged and literally circumscribed by the "golden fancies of the Golden Age," Gray lifts the painted veil, as it were, not in order to profane that which had been consecrated as holy but in order to probe its melancholy origins. Wordsworth, however, is so convinced that the plenitude promised by the Golden Age myth can be realized within the context of Nature itself—either in solitude or sometimes in the company of a "happy band" of enlightened souls—that he is willing to dispense with the myth. If he dismisses "all Arcadian dreams," it is not so much because he sees them as no longer historically viable, as was the case with Crabbe,[26] but because he sees them as essentially *unnecessary*.[27] From this point of view, the Wordsworthian pastoral is actually diametrically opposed to its transcendental counterpart—although, like the old pastoral, the Wordsworthian version remains essentially ahistorical. That is why Wordsworth is both an apocalyptic poet and one whose vision has "conservative" or "quietist" or even "reactionary" political implications. For if it is possible to achieve fulfillment by withdrawing from society and immersing oneself in "Nature," then clearly the necessity for *transforming* society is eliminated. Indeed, from this point of view, the meaningfulness of History is cast into doubt, and not only revolution but any social praxis is seen as an illusion.

In the following passage from *The Excursion*, we can take the measure of Gray's enormous influence on Wordsworth and simultaneously of the profound gulf between the two poets. Once again, Gray's influence makes itself felt in the context of an epic opening because of his role in mediating Wordsworth's relationship to Milton. The passage occurs at the point at which Wordsworth digresses from his narrative to introduce us to his hero, the Wanderer; its theme should by now be familiar to us:

> Oh! many are the Poets that are sown
> By Nature; men endowed with highest gifts,
> The vision and the faculty divine;
> Yet wanting the accomplishment of verse,

(Which in the docile season of their youth,
It was denied them to acquire, through lack
Of culture, and the inspiring aid of books,
Or haply by a temper too severe,
Or a nice backwardness afraid of shame)
Nor having e'er, as life advanced, been led
By circumstance to take unto the height
The measure of themselves, these favoured Beings,
All but a scattered few, live out their time,
Husbanding that which they possess within,
And go to the grave, unthought of. Strongest minds
Are often those of whom the noisy world
Hears least; else surely this Man had not left
His graces unrevealed and unproclaimed.
But, as the mind was filled with inward light,
So not without distinction had he lived,
Beloved and honoured—far as he was known.
And some small portion of his eloquent speech,
And something that may serve to set in view
The feeling pleasures of his loneliness,
His observations, and the thoughts his mind
Had dealt with—I will here record in verse;
Which, if with truth it correspond, and sink
Or rise as venerable Nature leads,
The high and tender Muses shall accept
With gracious smile, deliberately pleased,
And listening Time reward with sacred praise.

(5:1.77–107)

The passage is clearly a gloss on Gray's theme of "the poet
without a name" in the *Elegy*, but Wordsworth's treatment
of the theme is strikingly different from Gray's. First of all,
Wordsworth's use of the organic metaphor in the opening lines
of the passage ("many are the Poets that are sown / by Nature")
returns us to the old pastoral conception in which the creation
of poetry, and hence of the poet himself, is an unmediated
extension of Nature, rather than a historical process determined
by the twin processes of realization and alienation (to make use
of a still indispensable Marxian terminology). It was through
the representation of the Poet as a Shepherd that the old pastoral
had presented the highest attainments of aristocratic civiliza-

tion as an unmediated outgrowth of Nature itself—thereby circumscribing and camouflaging the problem of history. Wordsworth's conception, however, is not an attempt to recuperate the older, transcendental form but rather a reconstitution of the pastoral ethos in demotic terms: the poets he envisions, and the Wanderer himself, are clearly marginal figures who have been denied "the accomplishment of verse ... through lack / Of culture, and the inspiring aid of books." Yet in Wordsworth's conception, these limitations are *incidental and superficial* rather than essential: the figures he invokes are no less poets for the deprivation they have experienced, "men endowed with highest gifts, / The vision and the faculty divine."

Compare this to the twelfth and thirteenth stanzas of the *Elegy* where, as we noted in chapter 3, the somewhat sentimental notion that extraordinary creative capacities can flourish under conditions of deprivation, while the individuals possessing them remain unknown, is immediately countered by historical realism:

> Perhaps in this neglected spot is laid
> Some heart once pregnant with celestial fire,
> Hands, that the rod of empire might have sway'd,
> Or wak'd to extasy the living lyre.
>
> But Knowledge to their eyes her ample page
> Rich with the spoils of time did ne'er unroll;
> Chill Penury repress'd their noble rage,
> And froze the genial current of the soul.

"These favoured Beings," as Wordsworth calls them, "live out their time, / Husbanding that which they possess within, / And go to the grave unthought of." In Wordsworth's conception, the sense of loss is not linked to a failure of development that would have the effect of "freezing" (in Gray's metaphor) innate capacities but only to the circumstance that the individuals "endowed with greatest gifts" have remained unknown. Indeed, Wordsworth goes so far as to *invert* the potentiality-actuality dialectic of the *Elegy*, suggesting that those who have remained unknown are precisely those who have developed the greatest gifts: "Strongest minds / Are often those of whom the noisy world / Hears least," he writes, faintly echoing the "Far from the madding crowd" stanza once again.

Finally, in the conclusion of the passage quoted above, having narrowed and smoothed over the complex sense of loss that went into Gray's dialectic, Wordsworth actually takes it upon himself, as the spokesman for the Wanderer (i.e., for the principle of universality), to make good on all the losses by reconciling the contradictions within his own person. Returning to his protagonist, the Wanderer, whose role is clearly to mediate between the unknown poets that Wordsworth has been conjuring and his own subjective desires, the poet writes: "But, as the mind was filled with inward light, / So not without distinction had he lived, / Beloved and honoured—far as he was known"—lines that serve to erase the previous observation that men of the Wanderer's type "go to the grave, unthought of." Indeed, it turns out after all that the Wanderer will not remain unknown because Wordsworth plans to "record in verse" his thoughts and observations, "the feeling pleasures of his loneliness." All of this is as much to say: "All losses are restored, and sorrow's end." And then, irony of ironies (in a passage whose style is very far from the language of common prose), Wordsworth invokes "the high and tender Muses." He thus manages to have his cake and eat it too. Apparently, his valorization of and identification with the condition of marginality comes with a handsome indemnity; for in the end he is rewarded with an allegorical apotheosis sufficiently pompous to grace the court of Louis XIV.

Indeed, one might almost say that Wordsworth's attempt to invert Gray's metaphysics in the *Elegy*, by giving it an optimistically sentimental turn, is the hidden agenda of *The Excursion*. In Books VI and VII, for example, both of them subtitled "The Churchyard Among the Mountains," Wordsworth's Pastor (another one of his didactic rustics) narrates the histories of those buried in *his* (i.e., Wordsworth's) country churchyard. The tragic irony envisioned by Gray—that is, that the rude Forefathers of the hamlet, never having impressed themselves as individuals upon history, can be perceived only as a generic mass—is thus simply *wished away* by Wordsworth. But the problem with these books of *The Excursion*, as anyone who has wended his way through them must know, is that all the characters presented to the reader—not only the Pastor and his interlocutors, the Solitary and the Wanderer, but also those who lie beneath the stones: a Deaf Man, a Blind Man, a Peasant, and so forth—simply merge into one another as avatars of rural piety. Indeed, they are quite as generic as Gray's rude Forefathers—but with the difference, of course, that Gray's appraisal of the situation is both realistic and imaginatively penetrating, while Wordsworth's presentation of his rustics as discrete individuals is forced and artificial.

This explains why Wordsworth's blank verse in *The Excursion* is as unremittingly tedious as the same instrument in the "Prospectus," in *Tintern Abbey*, and in sections of *The Prelude* is resonant with vitality. However, if we examine Wordsworth's argument in the three *Essays upon Epitaphs*, which were written in 1810, around the same time as Books V, VI, and VII of *The Excursion* (indeed, the first of the *Essays* was appended to *The Excursion*),[28] we might almost say that the dullness of the latter poem is by design. Attacking Pope (and Johnson, who had praised Pope for avoiding commonplaces in his epitaphs), Wordsworth argues in *Essay II:* "Now in fact . . . it is not only no fault but a primary requisite in an Epitaph that it shall contain thoughts and feelings which are in their substance common-place and even trite" (2:78). It is true that great poetry can be composed out of thoughts that are commonplace in themselves, as has been said often enough of the *Elegy*, and it could be argued that Wordsworth is here speaking only of epitaphs and not of poetry in general. But if we examine the *Essays upon Epitaphs* carefully, it becomes apparent that Wordsworth regards the sincerity of grief to be incompatible with poetic language and hence with poetry itself. Like Plato (and the later Tolstoy), Wordsworth upholds Truth over Art and regards Truth as being incompatible with Art, but unlike Plato he does not renounce poetry: he wishes to have his cake and eat it too. Thus, as I suggested was the case with the Preface to *Lyrical Ballads*, Wordsworth's

argument in the *Essays upon Epitaphs* takes on the lineaments
of an attack, not only on poetic diction, but on poetry itself as
traditionally conceived. In *Essay III*, for example, praising an
epitaph that he candidly admits is crudely prosaic, Wordsworth
writes that if the author "had called in the assistance of English
verse the better to convey his thoughts, such sacrifices would,
from various influences, have been made *even by him*, that
though he might have excited admiration in a thousand, he
would have truly moved no one" (2:86). It could be argued that
the tension between Art and Truth, being intrinsic to the very
nature of poetry, is an enabling one for Wordsworth; this may
be true, but at the same time I think we should see that it results
in a kind of duplicity in the poet's thought, whereby Art, having
been exiled, is nevertheless smuggled in the back door.

It has been suggested that Wordsworth writes "the first truly
'sincere' poetry."[29] I would argue, however, that there is a deep
vein of insincerity in such poems as *The Excursion* and that the
theoretical premises of both the Preface and the *Essays upon
Epitaphs* amount to a blueprint for insincerity. (To be fair, it is
much easier for us to see this, from our vantage point in the
twentieth century—the era of the so-called naked poetry—than
it would be if we were immediately confronted, as Wordsworth
was, with the eighteenth-century version of insincerity and fac-
ticity.) In theoretical terms, Wordsworth wishes to negate the
distinction between poetry and prose, or between the language
of poetry and that of common speech; but he nevertheless
wishes to retain his *own* distinction as a poet. Indeed, it often
seems as if he wishes to stand alone in the field. On the level of
content, the same desire to negate crucial distinctions manifests
itself as denial of the tragic consequences of history, conse-
quences that Gray had uncovered in the *Elegy*. For this reason,
as Laurence Lerner has recently suggested, Wordsworth is more
to be trusted on ontological than on ideological grounds.[30] Ideo-
logical factors are constantly "getting in our way" in his poetry,
but there is nothing we can do about the problem because the
ideological dimension simply cannot be separated from what it
is in Wordsworth's vision that makes his poetry so great. (That

was not the case with the old pastoral, where the implicit ideology was sublimated in the transcendental machinery.) Wordsworth's poetry enfolds all antinomies in an overweening synthesis and, consequently, all mere contingencies become grist for his mill. The passages from *The Excursion* that we have been examining are no exception: they are either deeply moving or intensely irritating, depending on one's mood and point of view—and eventually one learns to be moved without entirely losing sight of the quality of duplicity that is sometimes present even in Wordsworth's greatest poems.

Consider the case of *Resolution and Independence*, for example. In this poem, we are confronted with a figure who epitomizes deprivation perhaps to a greater extent than any other character in English poetry. "How is it that you live, and what is it you do?" the poet repeatedly asks the old Leech-gatherer (119). The old man appears "not all alive nor dead" to the poet, and is likened first to a stone and then to a sea-beast (57–64). The poem is an uncanny vision of poverty in which civilization appears in danger of being pulled back into the primordial ooze and in which the social overlaps with the ontological. But what do we make of the banal and self-consoling moral of the final stanza?

> I could have laughed myself to scorn to find
> In that decrepit Man so firm a mind.
> "God," said I, "be my help and stay secure;
> I'll think of the Leech-gatherer on the lonely moor!"
> (137–40)

From being an enormously haunting symbol of deprivation, the Leech-gatherer is reduced to a mere symbol of "resolution and independence," with whom the poet can identify as he strives to achieve personal security. There is something terribly wrong—wrong even from an aesthetic point of view—with a process of identification which, under the guise of the universal, has the effect of negating essential differences. And why did Wordsworth give this poem so ungainly a title rather than simply calling it "The Leech-Gatherer?" Lewis Carroll's parody in

Through the Looking Glass, in which the White Knight sings Alice a song about an Aged Man who lives by searching for haddocks' eyes, points to a process of over-idealization and sentimentalization that is merely the other side of the coin of callousness.[31] What Wordsworth was defending himself against in the title, as well as in the concluding moral, was the phrase "revolution and independence." The poem, great as it is, is literally a reaction-formation against a vision that the poet found too troubling to accept. As such, it is marred not so much by its ideological focus as by its failure to take responsibility for what the imagination has evoked. The dream of a common language, manifested as a denial of *difference*, of irony—in short, of the "problem of history"—is not only facile but underscores a brand of utopianism that in the twentieth century has had totalitarian implications.

But this, of course, is too severe, and one is reluctant to conclude on so sour a note. There is in Wordsworth a refusal of melancholy, an insistence on living in the present rather than in the past or the future, that offers an important corrective to the vision contained in Gray's *Elegy*. We are all transitory beings, as Wordsworth asserts in the "Prospectus," and we are so much the product of an infinitude of historical circumstances that to focus on the issue of unfulfilled potential, as if there were ever the possibility of total realization—as if, in other words, we were gods—may ultimately be beside the point. This is not to accept an attitude of quietism, but it is perhaps to assert—against but also with Gray—the value of Wordsworth's "one sufficient hope," that "all which we behold is full of blessings."

Appendix A   Appendix B

Notes   Bibliography   Index

Appendix A: Elegy Written in a Country Church Yard

The Curfew tolls the knell of parting day,
The lowing herd wind slowly o'er the lea,
The plowman homeward plods his weary way,
And leaves the world to darkness and to me.

Now fades the glimmering landscape on the sight,   5
And all the air a solemn stillness holds,
Save where the beetle wheels his droning flight,
And drowsy tinklings lull the distant folds;

Save that from yonder ivy-mantled tow'r
The mopeing owl does to the moon complain   10
Of such, as wand'ring near her secret bow'r,
Molest her ancient solitary reign.

Beneath those rugged elms, that yew-tree's shade,
Where heaves the turf in many a mould'ring heap,
Each in his narrow cell for ever laid   15
The rude Forefathers of the hamlet sleep.

The breezy call of incense-breathing morn,
The swallow twitt'ring from the straw-built shed,
The cock's shrill clarion, or the ecchoing horn,
No more shall rouse them from their lowly bed.   20

Source: *The Complete Poems of Thomas Gray*, ed. H. W. Starr and J. R. Hendrickson (Oxford: The Clarnedon Press, 1966).

For them no more the blazing hearth shall burn,
Or busy housewife ply her evening care:
No children run to lisp their sire's return,
Or climb his knees the envied kiss to share.

Oft did the harvest to their sickle yield,   25
Their furrow oft the stubborn glebe has broke;
How jocund did they drive their team afield!
How bow'd the woods beneath their sturdy stroke!

Let not Ambition mock their useful toil,
Their homely joys, and destiny obscure;   30
Nor Grandeur hear with a disdainful smile,
The short and simple annals of the poor.

The boast of heraldry, the pomp of pow'r,
And all that beauty, all that wealth e'er gave,
Awaits alike th'inevitable hour.   35
The paths of glory lead but to the grave.

Nor you, ye Proud, impute to These the fault,
If Mem'ry o'er their Tomb no trophies raise,
Where thro' the long-drawn isle and fretted vault
The pealing anthem swells the note of praise.   40

Can storied urn or animated bust
Back to its mansion call the fleeting breath?
Can Honour's voice provoke the silent dust,
Or Flatt'ry sooth the dull cold ear of Death?

Perhaps in this neglected spot is laid   45
Some heart once pregnant with celestial fire,
Hands, that the rod of empire might have sway'd,
Or wak'd to extasy the living lyre.

But Knowledge to their eyes her ample page
Rich with the spoils of time did ne'er unroll;   50
Chill Penury repress'd their noble rage,
And froze the genial current of the soul.

Full many a gem of purest ray serene,
The dark unfathom'd caves of ocean bear:
Full many a flower is born to blush unseen,   55
And waste its sweetness on the desert air.

Some village-Hampden, that with dauntless breast
The little Tyrant of his fields withstood;
Some mute inglorious Milton here may rest,
Some Cromwell guiltless of his country's blood.   60

Th'applause of list'ning senates to command,
The threats of pain and ruin to despise,
To scatter plenty o'er a smiling land,
And read their hist'ry in a nation's eyes

Their lot forbad: nor circumscrib'd alone   65
Their growing virtues, but their crimes confin'd;
Forbad to wade through slaughter to a throne,
And shut the gates of mercy on mankind,

The struggling pangs of conscious truth to hide,
To quench the blushes of ingenuous shame,   70
Or heap the shrine of Luxury and Pride
With incense kindled at the Muse's flame.

Far from the madding crowd's ignoble strife,
Their sober wishes never learn'd to stray;
Along the cool sequester'd vale of life   75
They kept the noiseless tenor of their way.

Yet ev'n these bones from insult to protect
Some frail memorial still erected nigh,
With uncouth rhimes and shapeless sculpture deck'd,
Implores the passing tribute of a sigh.   80

Their name, their years, spelt by th'unletter'd muse,
The place of fame and elegy supply:
And many a holy text around she strews,
That teach the rustic moralist to die.

For who to dumb Forgetfulness a prey,   85
This pleasing anxious being e'er resign'd,
Left the warm precincts of the chearful day,
Nor cast one longing ling'ring look behind?

On some fond breast the parting soul relies,
Some pious drops the closing eye requires;   90
Ev'n from the tomb the voice of Nature cries,
Ev'n in our Ashes live their wonted Fires.

For thee, who mindful of th'unhonour'd Dead
Dost in these lines their artless tale relate;
If chance, by lonely contemplation led,   95
Some kindred Spirit shall inquire thy fate,

Haply some hoary-headed Swain may say,
'Oft have we seen him at the peep of dawn
'Brushing with hasty steps the dews away
'To meet the sun upon the upland lawn.   100

'There at the foot of yonder nodding beech
'That wreathes its old fantastic roots so high,
'His listless length at noontide wou'd he stretch,
'And pore upon the brook that babbles by.

'Hard by yon wood, now smiling as in scorn,   105
'Mutt'ring his wayward fancies he wou'd rove,
'Now drooping, woeful wan, like one forlorn,
'Or craz'd with care, or cross'd in hopeless love.

'One morn I miss'd him on the custom'd hill,
'Along the heath and near his fav'rite tree;   110
'Another came; nor yet beside the rill,
'Nor up the lawn, nor at the wood was he.

'The next with dirges due in sad array
'Slow thro' the church-way path we saw him born[e].
'Approach and read (for thou can'st read) the lay,   115
'Grav'd on the stone beneath yon aged thorn.'

The Epitaph.

Here rests his head upon the lap of Earth
A Youth to Fortune and to Fame unknown,
Fair Science frown'd not on his humble birth,
And Melancholy mark'd him for her own.   120

Large was his bounty, and his soul sincere,
Heav'n did a recompence as largely send:
He gave to Mis'ry all he had, a tear,
He gain'd from Heav'n ('twas all he wish'd) a friend.

No farther seek his merits to disclose,   125
Or draw his frailties from their dread abode,
(There they alike in trembling hope repose)
The bosom of his Father and his God.

Appendix B: Stanza's Wrote in a Country Church-Yard (The Eton Manuscript)

The Curfeu tolls the Knell of parting Day,
The lowing Herd wind slowly o'er the Lea,
The Plowman homeward plods his weary Way,
And leaves the World to Darkness & to me.

Now fades the glimm'ring Landscape on the Sight,
And now the Air a solemn Stillness holds;
Save, where the Beetle wheels his droning Flight,
Or drowsy Tinklings lull the distant Folds.

Save, that from yonder ivy-mantled Tower
The mopeing Owl does to the Moon complain
Of such as wandring[1] near her secret Bower
Molest her ancient[2] solitary Reign.

Beneath those rugged Elms, that Yewtree's Shade,
Where heaves the Turf in many a mould'ring Heap,

Source: From the original manuscript now preserved in the Memorial Buildings at Eton College; reprinted in *Gray & Collins: Poetical Works*, ed. Austin Lane Poole (London: Oxford University Press, 1974), 181–87.

1. stray too *is written above* wandring.
2. & pry into *is written above* Molest her ancient.

Each in his narrow Cell for ever laid
The rude Forefathers of the Hamlet[3] sleep.

For ever sleep, the breezy Call of Morn,
Or Swallow twitt'ring from the strawbuilt Shed,
Or Chaunticleer so shrill or ecchoing Horn,
No more shall rouse them from their lowly Bed.

For them no more the blazing Hearth shall burn,
Or busy Huswife ply her evening Care;
No children run to lisp their Sire's Return,
Nor climb his Knees the coming[4] Kiss to share.

Oft did the harvest to their Sickle yield;
Their Furrow oft the stubborn Glebe has broke;
How jocund did they drive their Team a-field!
How bow'd the Woods beneath their sturdy Stroke!

  Let not Ambition mock their useful[5] Toil,
Their rustic Joys & Destiny obscure:
Nor Grandeur hear with a disdainful Smile,
The short and simple Annals of the Poor.

The Boast of Heraldry the Pomp of Power,
And all, that Beauty, all that Wealth, e'er gave
Awaits alike th'inevitable Hour.
The Paths of Glory lead but to the Grave.

  Forgive, ye Proud, th'involuntary Fault,
If Memory to These no Trophies raise,
Where thro' the long-drawn Ile, & fretted Vault
The pealing Anthem swells the Note of Praise.

3. Village *has been struck out and* Hamlet *written above.*
4. envied *is written above and* doubtful? *is written in margin.*
5. homely *is substituted for* useful *in margin.*

Can storied Urn, or animated Bust,
Back to its Mansion call the fleeting Breath?
Can Honour's voice awake[6] the silent dust,
Or Flattery sooth the dull cold Ear of Death?

I. Perhaps in this neglected Spot is laid
Some Heart, once pregnant with celestial Fire,
Hands, that the Reins of Empire might have sway'd,
Or waked to Ecstasy the living Lyre:

4.   Some Village Cato   [7]with dauthless Breast
The little Tyrant of his Fields withstood;
Some mute inglorious Tully here may rest;
Some Caesar, guiltless of his Country's Blood.

2.   But Knowledge to their eyes her ample Page,
Rich with the Spoils of Time, did ne'er unroll:
Chill Penury had damp'd[8] their noble Rage,
And froze the genial Current of the Soul.

3. Full many a Gem of purest Ray serene
The dark unfathom'd Caves of Ocean bear.
Full many a Flower is born to blush unseen,
And waste its Sweetness on the desert Air.

Th'Applause of listening Senates to command,
The Threats of Pain & Ruin to despise,
To scatter Plenty o'er a smiling Land,
And read their Hist'ry in a Nation's Eyes,

Their Fate[9] forbad: nor circumscribed alone
Their struggling[10] Virtues, but their Crimes confined;
Forbad to wade through Slaughter to a Throne,
And shut the Gates of Mercy on Mankind

The struggleing Pangs of conscious Truth to hide,
To quench the Blushes of ingenuous Shame,

6. provoke *is substituted for* awake *in margin.*
7. *A word is lost through the fraying of the paper at the crease.*
8. depress'd repress'd *written above.*
9. Lot *written above.*
10. growing *written above.*

And at[11] the Shrine of Luxury & Pride
With[12] Incense hallowd in[23] the Muse's Flame.

The thoughtless World to Majesty may bow
Exalt the brave, & idolize Success
But more to Innocence their Safety owe
Than Power & Genius e'er conspired to bless

And thou, who mindful of the unhonour'd Dead
Dost in these Notes their[14] artless Tale relate
By Night & lonely Contemplation led
To linger in the gloomy Walks of Fate

Hark how the sacred Calm, that broods around
Bids ev'ry fierce tumultuous Passion cease
In still small Accents whisp'ring from the Ground
A grateful Earnest of eternal Peace

No more with Reason & thyself at Strife;
Give anxious Cares & endless Wishes room
But thro' the cool sequester'd Vale of Life
Pursue the silent Tenour of thy Doom.

Far from the madding Crowd's ignoble Strife,
Their sober Wishes never knew to stray:
Along the cool sequester'd Vale of Life
They kept the silent[15] Tenour of their Way.

Yet even these Bones from Insult to protect
Some frail Memorial still erected nigh
With[16] uncouth Rhime, & shapeless Sculpture deckt
Implores the passing Tribute of a Sigh.

Their Name, their Years, spelt by th'unletter'd Muse,
The Place of Fame, & Epitaph supply

11. Crown *written above* at.
12. Burn *is struck out and* With *inserted above.*
13. kindled at *written below,* by *instead of* in *written above.*
14. *In* thy *the* y *is struck out and* eir *written above.*
15. noiseless *written above.*
16. With *substituted for another word, perhaps* In, *which has been inked out.*

And many a holy Text around she strews,
That teach the rustic Moralist to die.

For who to dumb Forgetfulness, a Prey,
This pleasing anxious Being e'er resign'd;
Left the warm Precincts of the chearful Day,
Nor cast one longing ling'ring Look behind?

On some fond Breast the parting Soul relies,
Some pious Drops the closing Eye requires:
Even fron the Tomb the Voice of Nature cries,
And buries Ashes glow with Social Fires.

For Thee, who mindful &c: as above.

If chance that e'er some pensive Spirit more,
By sympathetic Musings here delay'd,
With vain, tho' kind, Enquiry shall explore
Thy once-loved Haunt, this long-deserted Shade.

Haply some hoary headed Swain shall say,
Oft have we seen him at the Peep of Dawn
With hasty Footsteps brush the Dews away
On the high Brow of yonder hanging Lawn

Him have we seen the Green-wood Side along
While o'er the Heath we hied, our Labours done,
Oft as the Woodlark piped her farewell Song
With whistful Eyes pursue the setting Sun.

Oft at the Foot of yonder hoary[17] Beech
That wreathes its old fantastic Roots so high
His listless Length at Noontide would he stretch,
And pore upon the Brook that babbles by.

With Gestures quaint now smileing as in Scorn,
Mutt'ring his fond Conceits[18] he would he[19] rove,

17. spreading *is written above*, nodding *in the margin.*
18. wayward fancies *is written above.*
19. wont to *is struck out*, loved *is written above and struck out, finally*
would he *is written above.*

Now drooping, woeful wan,[20] as one forlorn,
Or crazed with Care, or cross'd in hopeless Love.

One Morn we miss'd him on th'customd[21] Hill,
By[22] the Heath[23] and at[24] his fav'rite Tree.
Another came, nor yet beside the Rill,
Nor up the Lawn, not at[25] the Wood was he.

[26]The next with Dirges meet in sad Array
Slow thro[27] the Church-way Path we saw him born
Approach & read, for thou can'st read the Lay
Wrote[28] on the Stone beneath that[29] ancient Thorn:

There scatter'd oft the earliest of ye Year[30]
By Hands unseen are frequent[31] Vi'lets found
The Robin[32] loves to build & warble there
And little Footsteps lightly print the Ground.

Here[33] rests his Head upon the Lap of Earth
A Youth to Fortune & to Fame unknown
Fair Science frown'd not on his humble birth
And Melancholy mark'd him for her own

Large was his Bounty & his Heart sincere;
Heaven did a Recompence as largely send.
He gave to Mis'ry all he had, a Tear.
He gained from Heav'n; twas all he wish'd, a Friend

20. *The line originally stood* Now woeful wan, he droop'd. drooping *is inserted above and* he droop'd *is struck out.*
21. ac[customd] ac *struck out.*
22. Along *written above*
23. side *is written after* Heath *and struck out.*
24. Near *written above* at.
25. By *written above.*
26. *Between these stanzas is written and struck out* There scatter'd oft, the earliest.
27. By *written above.*
28. Graved carved *written above.*
29. yon *written above.*
30. Spring *struck out and* year *written above.*
31. Showers of *written above.*
32. Redbreast *written above.*
33. The Epitaph *is written along the outer margin at right angles to the other stanzas.*

No further seek his Merits to disclose,
Nor seek[34] to draw them from their dread Abode
(His frailties there in trembling Hope repose)
The Bosom of his Father & his God.

34. think *is written above* seek.

Notes

Introduction

1. *Pastoral Poetry and An Essay on Criticism*, ed. E. Audra and Aubrey Williams, vol. 1 of *The Poems of Alexander Pope*. 11 vols. (London and New Haven: Methuen and Yale University Press, 1961), 24.

2. See chap. 3, pp. 56–59.

1. Popularity, Resonance, Originality: The Question of Evaluation

1. Edmund Gosse, *Gray* (London: Macmillan, 1882), 97.

2. Herbert W. Starr, "Introduction," *Twentieth Century Interpretations of Gray's Elegy*, ed. Herbert W. Starr (Englewood Cliffs, N.J.: Prentice-Hall, 1968), 9.

3. Samuel Johnson, *Lives of the English Poets*, ed. G. B. Hill (New York: Octagon Books, 1967), 3:435.

4. *The Prose Works of William Wordsworth*, ed. W. J. B. Owen and J. W. Smyser (Oxford: The Clarendon Press, 1974), 1:130.

5. Amy L. Reed, *The Background of Gray's Elegy: A Study in the Taste for Melancholy Poetry 1700–1751* (New York: Columbia University Press, 1924), 1–2.

6. Matthew Arnold, "Thomas Gray," *English Literature and Irish Politics*, vol. 9 of *The Complete Prose Works of Matthew Arnold*, ed. R. H. Super (Ann Arbor: University of Michigan Press, 1973), 200.

7. See Roger Lonsdale, ed., *The Poems of Gray, Collins and Goldsmith* (London: Longmans Group, 1969), 113.

8. Arnold, 191.

9. I. A. Richards, *Practical Criticism* (New York: Harcourt, Brace & World, 1929), 253.

10. W. K. Wimsatt, "Imitation as Freedom," in *Forms of Lyric: Selected Papers from the English Institute*, ed. Reuben H. Brower (New York: Columbia University Press, 1970), 156; reprinted in *Day of the Leopards* (New Haven and London: Yale University Press, 1976), 124. Wimsatt's statement is oddly in contradiction to a position he had

previously outlined in his essay, "The Structure of the 'Concrete Universal' in Literature": "In each poem there is something (an individual intuition—or a concept) which can never be expressed in other terms" (in *Criticism: The Foundations of Modern Literary Judgment*, ed. Mark Schorer, Josephine Miles, and Gordon McKenzie, rev. ed. [New York: Harcourt, Brace, and World, 1958], 403). One of the hallmarks of the New Criticism was, of course, its stance against the "heresy of paraphrase." (See, for example, Cleanth Brooks, "The Heresy of Paraphrase," *The Well-Wrought Urn* [New York: Harcourt, Brace, and World, 1947], pp. 192–214.)

11. Graham Hough, *The Romantic Poets* (London: Hutchinson's University Library, 1953), 15.

12. *Lives of the Poets*, 3:441–42.

13. In his "Preface to Shakespeare" (1765), for example, Johnson comments as follows: "To works, however, of which the excellence is not absolute and definite, but gradual and comparative; to works not raised upon principles demonstrative and scientific but appealing wholly to observation and experience, no other test can be applied than length of duration and continuance of esteem. What mankind have long possessed they have often examined and compared; and if they persist to value the possession, it is because frequent comparisons have confirmed opinion in its favour." *Johnson on Shakespeare*, vol. 12 of *The Yale Edition of the Works of Samuel Johnson*, ed. Arthur Sherbo (New Haven and London: Yale University Press, 1968), 59–60.

14. Harold Bloom, *The Anxiety of Influence* (New York: Oxford University Press, 1973), 149.

15. Ibid., 150.

16. "[*Lycidas*] is not to be considered as the effusion of real passion; for passion runs not after remote allusions and obscure opinions. Passion plucks no berries from the myrtle and ivy, nor calls upon Arethuse and Mincius, nor tells of rough *satyrs* and *fauns with cloven heel*. Where there is leisure for fiction there is little grief. In this poem there is no nature, for there is no truth; there is no art, for there is nothing new. Its form is that of a pastoral, easy, vulgar, and therefore disgusting: whatever images it can supply, are long ago exhausted; and its inherent improbability always forces dissatisfaction on the mind." *Lives of the Poets*, 1:164.

17. Bloom, *A Map of Misreading* (New York: Oxford University Press, 1975), 4.

18. Through the trope of metalepsis, Bloom argues, "the dead return, by a reversal, to be triumphed over by the living" (*A Map of Misreading*, 74). The problem with the theory, however, is that it provides no concrete basis for determining whether the traces of precursor texts are a sign of strength or weakness; criticism is thus thrust back on its own resources. Therefore, it is simply a matter of personal taste as to whether or not one agrees with Bloom in a given instance; there

is no way of deciding the matter on the basis of the theory alone; but of course, this is always the case with poetic theory.

19. My discussion of Gray's antithetical relationship to the heroic is developed at a number of points in chapter 3, but particularly in relation to stanza 15 of the *Elegy*; see pp. 90–94.

20. Bloom, *Anxiety*, 19–45.

2. Structure and Meaning: The Formal Problem of Interpretation

1. F. W. Bateson, "Gray's *Elegy* Reconsidered," *English Poetry: A Critical Introduction* (London: Longmans, Green, 1950), 181.

2. Frank Brady, "Structure and Meaning in Gray's *Elegy*," in *From Sensibility to Romanticism*, ed. Frederick W. Hilles and Harold Bloom (New York: Oxford University Press, 1965), 177.

3. Lonsdale, 114.

4. *The Complete Works of William Hazlitt*, ed. P. P. Howe (New York: AMS Press, 1967), 5:118.

5. Paul de Man, *Blindness and Insight: Essays in the Rhetoric of Contemporary Criticism*, 2d ed. (Minneapolis: University of Minnesota Press, 1983), 27, 31. De Man argues that in spite of the organicist premises of the New Criticism, which derive from Coleridge, the rejection of the principle of intentionality led to the reification of the poem as a static entity.

6. According to Lonsdale, "It seems clear . . . that, after Gray had transcribed the poem [to the point of the four rejected stanzas], there was a definite interval of time before he added the new ending. In that interval the MS was folded and stained and the paper itself deteriorated slightly" (104).

7. Odell Shepard, " 'A Youth to Fortune and to Fame Unknown,' " *Modern Philology* 20 (1923), 347–73; hereafter cited in the text.

8. The fullest discussion of the debate over the *Elegy*'s origins is provided by Lonsdale, 103–110.

9. Lonsdale, 107.

10. Herbert W. Starr, " 'A Youth to Fortune and to Fame Unknown': A Re-estimation," *Journal of English and German Philology* 48:1 (January, 1949), 97–107; reprinted in *Twentieth Century Interpretations of Gray's Elegy*, 41–50.

11. In arguing that Gray would have been reticent in acknowledging West as the Youth of the "Epitaph," Shepard (365) suggests that West's death from consumption may have been hastened by suspicions that his mother, abetted by a family friend whom she subsequently married, had poisoned his father. Norton Nicholls, in his "Reminiscences of Gray," quoted Gray as saying that West's illness was brought

about by the "fatal discovery which he made of the treachery of a supposed friend, and the viciousness of a mother whom he tenderly loved; this man under the mask of friendship to him and his family intrigued with his mother; and robbed him of his peace of mind, his health and his life" (see *Correspondence of Thomas Gray*, ed. P. Toynbee and L. Whibley [London: Oxford University Press, 1971], 3:1300). R. W. Ketton-Cremer, Gray's biographer, adds that "the friend in question was presumably John Williams, the secretary of West's father" (see *Thomas Gray* [Cambridge: Cambridge University Press, 1955], 55).

12. R. S. Crane, *The Languages of Criticism and the Structure of Poetry* (Toronto: University of Toronto Press, 1953), 176. Crane, as a member of the neo-Aristotelian "Chicago School," derived his category of the imitative lyric from the *Poetics*. But as Käte Hamburger points out, Aristotle explicitly omits a consideration of lyric poetry from the *Poetics* because his central theme in that work is *mimesis*, which he felt pertained to drama and epic but not to lyric. "Aristotle," notes Hamburger, "drew the dividing line between mimetic and elegiac art, where he separated ποιεῖν from λέγειν" (see *The Logic of Literature*, trans. Marilynn J. Rose [Bloomington: Indiana University Press, 1973], 233). The Chicago School was sometimes opposed to the New Critics, and Crane's argument is specifically directed against Cleanth Brooks's interpretation of the *Elegy*; however, both schools tended in practice to view lyric poetry in dramatic terms.

13. Yvor Winters, *Forms of Discovery: Critical and Historical Essays on the Forms of the Short Poem in English* (Denver: Alan Swallow, 1967), 157.

14. Frank Ellis, "Gray's *Elegy*: The Biographical Problem in Literary Criticism," *PMLA* 66 (1951), 971–1008; hereafter cited in the text.

15. W. M. Newman had previously connected the *Elegy* to the trial of the Scottish lords; however, Newman's article is mainly focused on the poem's origins and is not connected to a larger interpretive conception. See W. M. Newman, "When Curfew Tolled the Knell," *The National Review* 127 (September 1946), 244–48; reprinted in *Twentieth-Century Interpretations of Gray's Elegy*, 17–22.

16. Ellis points to the fact that in the line "Dost in these Notes their artless Tale relate" in the Eton Manuscript, Gray had originally written "thy" and then corrected it to "their" (see appendix B). But even if we assume with Ellis that the reference in "thy artless Tale" is to the poet himself, Ellis's conclusion that the speaker is alluding to his own history does not necessarily follow; for the reference may be to the tale of "the unhonour'd Dead" (in the previous line) that he has been telling. By this reasoning, although the essential meaning of the line would not have altered, Gray would have changed the pronoun in order to eliminate an unwarranted ambiguity.

17. The suggestion that "thee" in line 93 refers not to Gray but to a "fictitious village poet who had commemorated the 'unhonour'd

Dead' " had earlier been made by Herbert Starr (see " 'A Youth to Fortune and to Fame Unknown': A Re-estimation," 44). And as Starr points out (44), Shepard had entertained—and rejected—the possibility that the reference is to a *poeta ignotus* (Shepard, 348). It is Ellis who expands this possibility into a full-scale interpretation, however.

18. John H. Sutherland, "The Stonecutter in Gray's 'Elegy,' " in *Twentieth-Century Interpretations of Gray's Elegy*, 80.

19. Sutherland, 80.

20. Morse Peckham, "Gray's 'Epitaph' Revisited," in *Twentieth-Century Interpretations of Gray's Elegy*, 77–78.

21. Peckham, 77.

22. Sutherland, 80.

23. Cleanth Brooks, "Gray's Storied Urn," *The Well-Wrought Urn: Studies in the Structure of Poetry* (New York: Harcourt, Brace & World, 1947), 105–23. In chapter 3, I examine Brooks's discussion of the *Elegy* on a number of different levels: in relation to Gray's use of personification, in relation to the "Death-the-Leveler" topos, and in relation to Gray's sociopolitical attitudes. See chap. 3, pp. 69–74 et passim.

24. Brady, 177–89.

25. Bertrand H. Bronson, "On a Special Decorum in Gray's *Elegy*," in *From Sensibility to Romanticism*, 172; hereafter cited in the text.

3. A Reading of Gray's *Elegy*

1. *Lives of the Poets*, 1:77. Johnson's definition of "local poetry" is made with reference to Denham's poem, *Cooper's Hill*.

2. The importance of perspective in Gray's poetry in general and in the *Elegy* in particular was first emphasized by Frank Brady, "Structure and Meaning in Gray's *Elegy*," 177–89.

3. Ian Jack, "Gray's *Elegy* Revisited," in *From Sensibility to Romanticism*, 160–61. Jack's excellent discussion of Gray's versification in the *Elegy* is the fullest treatment of the subject.

4. Lonsdale, 117.

5. *Corresp.* 3:1297.

6. Ibid.

7. Lonsdale, 117.

8. *Purgatorio*, trans. Allen Mandelbaum (Berkeley: University of California Press, 1982), 8.1–6.

9. *Inferno*, trans. Allen Mandelbaum (Berkeley: University of California Press, 1980), 2.1–6.

10. Dante was not very much admired—or even read—by the Augustans; it was not until after the appearance of H. F. Cary's translation in 1814 that he became popular. (See Werner P. Friedrich, *Dante's Fame Abroad: 1350–1850* [Chapel Hill: University of North Carolina Press, 1960], 212–30.) However, Gray translated the story of Ugolino as early as 1737 or 1738, and his personal affinity to Dante is stronger than that

of any English poet since Milton. Paget Toynbee noted in his *Dante in English Literature* (1909) that with the exception of the scholar Thomas Tyrwhitt, Gray was "more intimately acquainted than any other Englishman of the eighteenth century" with Dante's poetry (cited by Lonsdale, 23).

11. See T. H. Warren, *Essays of Poets and Poetry, Ancient and Modern* (London: John Murray, 1909), 229.

12. Commenting on the grammatical sequencing of Gray's versification in the *Elegy*, Jack (160–61) notes that the poem contains fifteen or more examples of the "balanced adjectival line" (adjective-noun-adjective-noun) of which line 17 provides an example. Jack also suggests that the adjective-noun-verb-adjective-noun pattern of a line such as "Chill Penury repress'd their noble rage" (line 51), of which there are almost a dozen examples in the *Elegy*, may be viewed as the English equivalent of the Latin "golden line," in which two adjectives are followed by a verb and then two substantives.

13. See Lonsdale, 121.

14. Lucretius, *De Rerum Natura (The Way Things Are)*, trans. Rolfe Humphries (Bloomington: Indiana University Press, 1969), 3.902–905. Gray would probably have known this passage in the Dryden translation (see Lonsdale, 121) as well as in the original, but Humphries's modern translation is closer both to the original and to Gray's imitation in stanza 6. The passages from the *Georgics* cited in the text are rendered in a modern version rather than in Dryden's translation for the same reason.

15. See Lonsdale, 121.

16. Jacques Perret, "The *Georgics*," in *Virgil*, ed. Steele Commager (Englewood Cliffs, N.J.: Prentice-Hall, 1966), 34.

17. *Virgil's Georgics*, trans. Smith Palmer Bovie (Chicago: University of Chicago Press, 1956), 4.559–66. Further references to the *Georgics* will hereafter be cited from this edition in the text.

18. Perret, 32–33.

19. L. P. Wilkinson, *The Georgics of Virgil* (Cambridge: Cambridge University Press, 1969), 49–55.

20. Horace, *The Odes and Epodes*, trans. C. E. Bennett (Cambridge, Mass.: Harvard University Press, 1968), 369.

21. See Bertrand H. Bronson, "Personification Reconsidered," *ELH* 14 (1947):163–77.

22. In what is perhaps the best-known treatment of personification in eighteenth-century poetry, Earl Wasserman argues that the use of the figure during the period should be viewed in the context of the empiricist philosophical tradition. It is interesting, therefore, that Gray is never once mentioned in Wasserman's rather lengthy article. See Earl R. Wasserman, "The Inherent Values of 18th-Century Personification," *PMLA* 45 (1950):453–63.

More recently, Gabriele Bernhard Jackson has argued that the eighteenth-century use of personification manifests the relationship to language embedded in the epistemology of John Locke (see "From Essence to Accident: Locke and the Language of Poetry in the Eighteenth Century," *Criticism* 29:1 [Winter 1987], 27–66). Emphasizing the fact that Gray did a paraphrase of Locke's *Essay Concerning Human Understanding* in 1740, Jackson notes that given the Lockean epistemology, "it would seem more accurate to describe a child playing as chasing 'the rolling circle's speed' (choosing two primary qualities: shape and motion), as Gray does in his 'Ode on a Distant Prospect of Eton College,' than to name the inscrutable hoop' " (40–41). She argues, furthermore, that after 1740 there is an increasing tendency in poetry to develop figures that "group physical similarities rather than spiritual qualities together" (42). However, Jackson also observes that another stylistic tendency of the period, sanctioned by Locke, involved mental concepts that " 'have no being but in the Understanding. . . . When we speak of *Justice* or *Gratitude*, we frame to our selves no Imagination of any thing existing . . . but our Thoughts terminate in the abstract Ideas of those Vertues, and not farther' " (*Essay on Understanding* 3.5.5, 3.5.12; cited by Jackson 44). Ironically, although Locke's epistemology is, of course, antithetical to Plato's (as nominalism is to realism in Scholastic philosophy), in practical terms, as far as the question of personification is concerned, the two tendencies intersect.

23. Cited by Wasserman, 440.

24. Brooks, 114.

25. Brooks, 109–10.

26. Brooks, 114. Having suggested that Knowledge is being viewed ironically, Brooks then attempts to distinguish it from "Fair Science" in the "Epitaph" (115). But as several commentators have noted, "knowledge" and "science" are synonymous to the eighteenth century. It will be recalled that in order to preserve his own interpretation Ellis had attempted to read "Fair Science" as "native intelligence"; see chap. 2, p. 34.

27. Brooks, 112–13.

28. *Corresp.* 1.241.

29. Philip Wheelwright, ed., *Aristotle: Selections* (New York: Odyssey Press, 1951), xxxii.

30. Ibid., 333.

31. There is an additional irony in the connection between Chatterton and Gray. Chatterton originally sent his "Rowley Poems" (i.e., the poems he represented as being the work of a fifteenth-century poet, Thomas Rowley) to Horace Walpole, no doubt because of Walpole's interest in antiquities. Walpole was at first receptive to Chatterton, but when he discovered that the poems were a "forgery," he broke off the correspondence. Consequently, Walpole has often been blamed for Chatterton's suicide. He is exonerated, however, by Wilmarth S. Lewis's *Rescuing Horace Walpole* (New Haven: Yale University Press, 1978), 134–41. Chatterton is not mentioned in Gray's correspondence.

32. Brooks, 114.

33. Ellis, 1001.
34. William Empson, *Some Versions of Pastoral* (New York: New Directions, 1974), 4–5.
35. Edmund Burke, *Reflections on the Revolution in France,* ed. Conor Cruise O'Brien (New York: Penguin Books, 1978), 139.
36. See Karl Marx, *Capital,* trans. Samuel Moore and Edward Aveling (New York: International Publishers, 1979), 1:71–83.
37. *The Poems of Edmund Waller,* ed. G. Thorn Drury (New York: Greenwood Press, 1968), 128.
38. Since T. S. Eliot's *Four Quartets* represent a kind of paradigm for the twentieth century of the modern poem of resignation, it is interesting to note that Eliot borrowed rather heavily from the *Elegy.* Indeed, George T. Wright, arguing that the *Quartets* were modeled upon the *Elegy,* provides an extensive list of Eliot's borrowings from Gray (see George T. Wright, "Eliot Written in a Country Churchyard," *ELH* 43 [1976]:227–43). It is likely that Eliot's borrowings were unconscious, however, because his political attitude is antithetical to Gray's. Eliot's relationship to the subjunctive, for example, as in the following lines from "Burnt Norton," is illustrative of the political differences between these two poets (who in other respects are so similar):

What might have been is an abstraction
Remaining a perpetual possibility
Only in a world of speculation.
What might have been and what has been
Point to one end, which is always present.

(*The Complete Poems and Plays of T. S. Eliot: 1909–1950* [New York: Harcourt, Brace & World, 1971], 1–17.
To Eliot, "What might have been is an abstraction" and therefore need not be considered. To Gray in the *Elegy,* however, it is essential to consider what might have been. Eliot's quietism clearly has conservative ideological implications, and although in one sense it could be said that Gray dwells more on loss than Eliot does, this is because Gray has not relinquished his *hope* in this world. From this point of view, Eliot is actually the more melancholy of the two poets.
39. See Lonsdale, 85.
40. There is something almost inevitable about the fact that Gray was unable to complete *The Alliance,* and it is worthwhile commenting on this matter since it has a bearing on the style-content dialectic of Gray's poetry as a whole. In the first place, the Augustan verse-essay mode had been so fully appropriated by Pope that a poet as attuned to the problem of originality as Gray would have found it a quite intractable medium unless he was fully centered in the Augustan aesthetic, which was not the case with Gray. According to both Mason and Walpole, in any event, Gray abandoned *The Alliance* on the grounds that certain of its parts bore too strong a resemblance to the *Dunciad* (see Lonsdale,

87). Gray is a poet of lyric density rather than discursive expansiveness, and in this respect he is a more "modern" poet than the others of his age. Norton Nicholls's "Reminiscences" (*Corresp.* 3.1291) are enlightening on this issue:

> I asked him why he had not continued that beautiful fragment beginning "As sickly plants betray a niggard earth" He said, because he could not; when I expressed surprise at this, he explained himself as follows; That he had been used to write only lyric poetry in which the poems being short, he had accustomed himself, & was able to polish every part; that this having become habit, he could not write otherwise; & that the labour of this method in a long poem would be intolerable; besides which the poem would lose its effect for want of Chiaro-Oscuro; for that to produce effect it was absolutely necessary to have weak parts.— He instanced in Homer, & particularly in Milton, who he said in parts of his poem rolls on in sounding words that have but little meaning.

One is here reminded of Poe's argument that a long poem is a contradiction in terms. But in any event, as Nicholls's "Reminiscences" indicate, the reason that Gray wrote as little as he did seems to have something to do with the nature of his artistry, a kind of artistry—like that of Mallarmé—in which density substitutes for length as such.

41. *Corresp.* 1.310.

42. Empson, 5.

43. *Lives of the Poets,* 2.315.

44. See J. Fisher, "James Hammond and the Quatrain of Gray's *Elegy,*" *MP* 32 (1935): 302.

45. See J. Fisher, "Shenstone, Gray, and the 'Moral Elegy,' " *MP* 34 (1937):273–94.

46. *Corresp.* 1.295.

47. William Shenstone, *Works* (London, 1764), 1.4; cited by Golden, 68.

48. *Corresp.* 2.566.

49. See "Observations on English Metre," in *Gray's Poems, Letters and Essays,* ed. John Drinkwater and Lewis Gibbs (London: Dent, 1966), 338.

50. John Dryden, *Poems: 1649–1680,* ed. Niles Hooker and H. T. Swedenberg, Jr., vol. 1 of *The Works of John Dryden* (Berkeley: University of California Press, 1956), 50–51.

51. Dryden, ibid., 51. See also Sir William Davenant's *Gondibert,* ed. David F. Gladish (Oxford: The Clarendon Press, 1971), 17.

52. Lonsdale, 174.

53. Earl Miner, "Introduction" to *John Dryden: Selected Poetry and Prose* (New York: The Modern Library, 1969), xxvi.

54. Dryden, "Annus Mirabilis," *Poems: 1649–1680,* 125–28.

55. See pp. 68–69.
56. Jack, 154.
57. See chap. 2, p. 28.
58. *The Rape of the Lock and Other Poems*, ed. Geoffrey Tillotson, vol. II of *The Poems of Alexander Pope* (London: Methuen; New Haven: Yale University Press, 1962), 75–82.
59. George Puttenham, *The Arte of English Poesie*, ed. Gladys Doidge Willcock and Alice Walker (Cambridge: Cambridge University Press, 1936; reprinted 1970), 180–81.
60. Kenneth Burke, *A Grammar of Motives and A Rhetoric of Motives* (Cleveland and New York: The World Publishing Company, 1962), 503–17.
61. *The Complete Prose Works of Matthew Arnold*, 9.189.
62. See R. W. Ketton-Cremer, *Thomas Gray* (Cambridge, England: Cambridge University Press, 1955), especially the first two chapters.
63. Eric Havelock, *A Preface to Plato* (Cambridge, Mass.: Harvard University Press, 1963), 36–60 et passim.
64. See chap. 2, pp. 26–27.
65. *Lives of the Poets*, 1.165.
66. It may be noted in passing that the contradiction that Gray confronts in line 60 of the *Elegy* marks the point at which the Aristotelian conception of Value comes into conflict with the Platonic. For Plato, the Good is a transcendental concept, but for Aristotle it is employed variously, according to the context in which it is to be applied. Whitney J. Oates argues, convincingly to my mind, that Aristotle's conception of Value is ultimately contradictory for this reason (see Whitney J. Oates, *Aristotle and the Problem of Value* [Princeton: Princeton University Press, 1963]). The point in the *Elegy* at which the contradiction between the Aristotelian notion of fulfillment or happiness and the Good emerges is thus the point at which the Aristotelian perspective gives way to a Platonic one. This is perhaps overly schematic: Aristotle, of course, remained a Platonist in many crucial respects but, as Oates maintains, not as far as the Being-Value relationship is maintained.
67. But the word "virtues," although contrasted with "crimes," is itself ambiguous because of its Roman, or Renaissance-humanist, connotation of "heroic manliness" (i.e., the Latin *virtus*) appropriate to the political leader.
68. Lonsdale, 129.
69. Ibid.
70. Lonsdale, 89. But it is interesting that those scholars, such as Lonsdale, who have pointed out the influence of Plato on Gray's thought in the *Elegy*, have located this influence only in the negative context of stanza 17. Gray was a Platonist, and he was influenced by Plato's utopianism as well as by Plato's pessimism. That this has not been recognized is another indication of the tendency to view the *Elegy* in a conservative ideological context.

71. Commonplace Book, 1:340; cited by Lonsdale, 89.
72. See chap. 2, pp. 20–21 et passim.
73. Friedrich Nietzsche, *On the Genealogy of Morals*, trans. Walter Kaufmann and R. J. Hollingdale (New York: Random House, 1969), 31.
74. G. W. F. Hegel, *The Phenomenology of Mind*, trans. J. B. Baillie (New York: Harper & Row, 1967), 234–40.
75. See *Webster's Third International Dictionary, Unabridged*, 1967.
76. *Collected Works of Oliver Goldsmith*, ed. Arthur Friedman (London: Oxford University Press, 1966), 4.51–56.
77. See p. 75.
78. De Man, 31.
79. Ibid., 30–31.
80. See chap. 2, p. 18.
81. De Man, 31.
82. If we analyze the "unletter'd muse" in mimetic terms, it is possible to associate her with the "rustic Stonecutter" of Ellis's interpretation (see chap. 2, pp. 32–33), and without necessarily accepting the dramatistic implications of Ellis's argument. It is clear that in an *actual* churchyard, someone along the lines of a "rustic Stonecutter" would have fulfilled the function that Gray ascribes to the "unletter'd muse." However, if we consider the unletter'd muse to be both constitutive of the principle of anonymity and constituted by that principle, then it follows that Ellis's Stonecutter introduces an unnecessary level of mediation while at the same time circumscribing the figural richness of Gray's trope. Nevertheless, as we noted in chapter 2, Ellis's interpretation is one of the few to stress the importance of the fame-anonymity dialectic in the poem.
83. It could be argued, from a Marxist or perhaps a Deconstructionist point of view, that by reaffirming poetry from a Christian perspective, Gray is merely reinstating the ideological dimension against which he had polemicized in stanza 18—in other words, that his desire to make of poetry something "pure" is itself an expression of the material forces from which that desire is in flight. It is difficult to respond to this line of reasoning except to say that insofar as art is reduced to the sphere of ideology, it loses its specificity as art. In any event, it is clear that at least the *desire* to transcend the ideological is reflected in the *Elegy*.
84. In a recent study that intersects at a number of points with my own, Anne Williams argues that after 1700 such genres as the epistle, satire, elegy, pastoral, and tragedy are appropriated by the lyric, which henceforth comes to dominate over poetry as a whole (see Anne Williams, *Prophetic Strain: The Greater Lyric in the Eighteenth Century* [Chicago and London: University of Chicago Press, 1984]). In her chapter on Gray's *Elegy* (93–110), Williams views this process of generic appropriation and transformation specifically in terms of the elegy; her argument is thus immediately relevant to stanza 21.

85. Joseph Trapp, *Lectures on Poetry* (Menston, England: The Scholar Press, 1973), 163.
86. Ibid., 169.
87. See chap. 1, pp. 15–16.
88. *Corresp.* 1.340–41.
89. From the perspective of stanza 22 especially, we can see how profoundly Gray diverges from Swift's notion (in "Thoughts of Various Subjects") that "there is no intrinsic value" in the fact that people desire to be remembered by having inscriptions set on their graves and that this is the case "even among the vulgar." See chap. 1, pp. 14–15.
90. See chap. 1, pp. 13–14.
91. See pp. 45–46.
92. See *Letters of John Keats,* ed. Robert Gittings (London: Oxford University Press, 1970), 249–51.
93. See chap. 2, pp. 36–38.
94. John Donne, *Selected Prose,* ed. Evelyn Simpson (Oxford: Clarendon Press, 1967), 100–101.
95. Bronson, "On a Special Decorum in Gray's *Elegy,*" 176.
96. G. W. F. Hegel, *Aesthetics: Lectures on Fine Art,* trans. T. M. Knox. 2 vols. (Oxford: The Clarendon Press, 1975), 2:1111.
97. I use the term "intentionality" in the sense in which Paul de Man employs it in "Form and Intent in the American New Criticism." In his critique of the New Criticism, de Man argues that the rejection of the principle of intentionality leads to "a hardening of the text into a sheer surface that prevents the stylistic analysis from penetrating beyond the sensory appearances to perceive [the] 'struggle with meaning' of which all criticism, including the criticism of forms, should give an account. For surfaces also remain concealed when they are being artificially separated from the depth that supports them" (p. 24; see chap. 2, p. 18). De Man, of course, does not hold to a naively "Romantic" conception of intentionality, according to which the poetic process is an unmediated extension of the poet's presence. However, in order to maintain a conception of intentionality without falling into the same fallacies that originally led to the rejection of the principle of intentionality by the New Critics, one would have to distinguish in some manner between the poet's shaping process and the "lyric-I" of the poem.
98. Theodor W. Adorno, "Lyric Poetry and Society," trans. Bruce Mayo, *Telos* 20 (Summer 1974), 62.
99. Ibid., 57.
100. Ibid., 63.
101. Ibid., 63–64.
102. See pp. 120–21.
103. See chap. 2, pp. 32–33.
104. See chap. 2, p. 34.
105. In a famous letter to West of 1742, Gray writes: "Mine, you are

to know, is a white Melancholy, or rather leucholy for the most part; which though it seldom laughs or dances, nor ever amounts to what one calls Joy or Pleasure, yet is a good easy sort of state . . . But there is another sort, black indeed, which I have now and then felt, that has somewhat in it like Tertullian's rule of faith, Credo quia impossibile est; for it believes, nay, is sure of every thing that is unlikely, so it be but frightful; and, on the other hand, excludes and shuts its eyes to the most possible hopes, and every thing that is pleasurable; from this the Lord deliver us!" (*Corresp.* 1. 209). Gray's distinction parallels the two Renaissance attitudes toward melancholy that Milton concretizes in *L'Allegro* and *Il Penseroso*. As John Carey and Alastair Fowler note, "the first, originating in Galenic medicine, viewed [melancholy] as a source of stupidity, fearfulness and illusions; the second, originating in Aristotle's *Problemata* and adopted by Ficino in *De Studiosorum Sanitate Tuenda*, stressed that all who have become eminent in philosophy, poetry or the arts have been of melancholy temperament. At the beginning of *L'Allegro* Milton exorcises the Galenic melancholy: in *Il Penseroso* he celebrates the Aristotelian" (*The Poems of John Milton*, ed. John Carey and Alastair Fowler [London: Longmans Group Limited, 1968], 131).

106. Brooks, 109–10.

107. Lonsdale, 139.

4. Gray's *Elegy* and the Dissolution of the Pastoral

1. See Introduction, n. 1.

2. The conclusion arrived at by Paul Alpers, in a recent attempt to define pastoral, replicates Pope's minimal definition. Alpers sees the lives of shepherds as what he calls the "representative anecdote" of pastoral: "To say that shepherds' lives is the representative anecdote of pastoral means that pastoral works are representations of shepherds who are felt to be representative of some other or of all other men" ("What Is Pastoral?" *Critical Inquiry*, 8:3 [Spring 1982], 456). However, Alpers makes no effort to explain the nature of the representation involved, or even why a central literary genre should have focused on the figure of the shepherd in the first place; consequently, since the generic marker itself means "pertaining to shepherds," his attempt at definition is merely tautological.

3. Ovid, *Metamorphoses*, trans. Arthur Golding (1567; New York: Macmillan, 1965), 1:103–16.

4. My discussion of the relationship between pastoral poetry and nostalgia overlaps at a number of points with Laurence Lerner's discus-

sion in *The Uses of Nostalgia: Studies in Pastoral Poetry* (New York: Schocken, 1972).

5. W. W. Greg, *Pastoral Poetry and Pastoral Drama* (1906; New York: Russell and Russell, 1959), 4.

6. Ibid.

7. Frank Kermode, *English Pastoral Poetry* (London: George G. Harrap, 1952), 14.

8. Renato Poggioli, *The Oaten Flute: Essays on Pastoral Poetry and the Pastoral Ideal* (Cambridge, Mass.: Harvard University Press, 1975), 3.

9. Greg, 2.

10. It will be noted that I am using the term "utopian" in a very general sense, as pertaining to the notion of an Earthly Paradise. To the extent that the term connotes an explicit recognition of and struggle against prevailing conditions, it cannot, of course, be applied to the pastoral.

11. Poggioli, 41.

12. The concept of *ideology* and its relationship to art is an extremely vexed issue in Marxist thought and has resulted in a great deal of confusion. When Marx uses the term "ideology" (as in his references to "bourgeois ideology"), he almost always uses it to mean a species of systemic falsehood whose ultimate purpose is to uphold the prevailing social system. Marx's use of the term is thus, emphatically, nonrelativistic: he writes from a "privileged" standpoint as one in possession of truth. Furthermore, on those occasions in which Marx writes about art or literature, he generally refrains even from broaching the concept of ideology, and certainly the tendency of so-called vulgar Marxism to reduce art to ideology is foreign to his own impulse to privilege the work of art. Later Marxists, however, particularly those of the Althusserian school, tend to see all thought as bound by ideological constructs. From this point of view, however (which is certainly foreign to Marx's explicit voluntarism, although perhaps implicit in certain structuralist aspects of his system), the concept of ideology becomes a distinction without a difference.

13. Plato, it will be recalled, sees art essentially as a representation (mimesis) of physical appearances that stands as a representation of the true forms—and thus as one step further removed from Truth than the phenomena themselves. Plotinus, however, while accepting Plato's Doctrine of Ideas, argues (against Plato) that the work of art transcends the phenomenal world by establishing a direct relationship to the forms.

14. Greg, 2.

15. Poggioli, 31.

16. "Preface to *Milton*," *The Poetry and Prose of William Blake*, ed. David V. Erdman (New York: Doubleday, 1970), 15–16.

17. Karl Marx and Friedrich Engels, "Manifesto of the Communist Party," trans. Samuel Moore, in *Marx and Engels: Basic Writings on*

Politics and Philosophy, ed. Lewis S. Feuer (New York: Doubleday, 1959), 9.

18. Walter Benjamin, *Illuminations,* ed. Hannah Arendt (New York: Schocken, 1969), 256.

19. Pope, *Pastoral Poetry and An Essay on Criticism,* 27.

20. *Poetry and Prose of John Gay,* ed. Vinton A. Dearing and Charles E. Beckwith. 2 vols. (Oxford: The Clarendon Press, 1974), 1:90.

21. *Lives of the English Poets,* 2:269; cited by Stuart Curran, *Poetic Form and British Romanticism* (New York: Oxford University Press, 1986), 92.

22. *Poetry and Prose of John Gay,* 1:107.

23. George Crabbe, *Poems,* ed. Adolphus William Ward (Cambridge: Cambridge University Press, 1905), 1:1–28.

24. "The Deserted Village," *Collected Works of Oliver Goldsmith,* ed. Arthur Friedman (London: Oxford University Press, 1966), 4:265–86. Further references to the poem will be given by line number in the text.

25. Marx, "The Communist Manifesto," 11.

26. This is the reason that two such eminent theorists of the pastoral as Poggioli and Erwin Panofsky can speak of the *Elegy* in terms that are precisely antithetical. In his analysis of the *Et in Arcadia ego* motif, Panofsky observes that Virgil was the first poet to align the pastoral with elegiac nostalgia, "opening up the dimension of the past and thus inaugurating the long line of poetry that was to culminate in Thomas Gray" (*Meaning in the Visual Arts* [Garden City, N.Y.: Doubleday, 1955], 301). Conversely, in a discussion of *The Village* Poggioli associates the antipastoral tendency of Crabbe with Gray: "Instead of describing fictitious beings and an imaginary way of life, Crabbe chooses to depict 'the poor laborious natives of the place,' and to sing, like Gray in his *Elegy,* 'the short and simple annals of the poor' " (p. 31).

5. Wordsworth and the Reconstitution of the Pastoral

1. A recent exception is an essay by Wallace Jackson and Paul Yoder, "Wordsworth Reimagines Thomas Gray: Notations on Begetting a Kindred Spirit," *Criticism* 21:3 (Summer 1989), 287–300. Jackson and Yoder argue—much as I do in the present chapter, but without focusing on Milton or on the issues raised by the pastoral—that Gray exerted a mediating influence on Wordsworth's poetry. This influence, they suggest, expresses itself in terms of "the thematics of marginality" as well as "the shaping of a poetic vehicle capable of conveying the self's sense of passage" (294).

2. Northrop Frye, "Introduction," *Romanticism Reconsidered,* ed. Northrop Frye (New York and London: Columbia University Press, 1966), vii.

3. Harold Bloom, *The Visionary Company: A Reading of English Romantic Poetry* (Ithaca: Cornell University Press, 1971), vii–viii.

4. Ibid., 18.

5. Northrop Frye, "Towards Defining an Age of Sensibility," in *Eighteenth-Century Literature: Modern Essays in Criticism,* ed. James L. Clifford (New York: Oxford University Press, 1959), 311–18.

6. See chap. 3, p. 63, n.22.

7. *The Prose Works of William Wordsworth,* 1:118, 120.

8. I have adopted the language of the 1850 Preface on this occasion. In 1800 Wordsworth writes: "Is there then, it will be asked, no essential difference between the language of prose and metrical composition? I answer that there neither is nor can be any essential difference" (1:134).

9. See Curran, *Poetic Form and British Romanticism,* 30.

10. Coleridge, for example, notes that the second line of Gray's sonnet ("And reddening Phoebus lifts his golden fire") "is a bad line, not because the language is distinct from that of prose; but because it conveys incongruous images, because it confounds the cause and the effect, the real *thing* with the personified *representative* of the thing; in short, because it differs from the language of GOOD SENSE!" (*Biographia Literaria,* ed. J. Shawcross [London: Oxford University Press, 1967], 2:58).

11. *Poems of Mr. Gray,* ed. William Mason; cited by Golden, 39.

12. This point is made by Donald Greene in "The Proper Language of Poetry: Gray, Johnson, and Others," in *Fearful Joy,* ed. J. Downey and B. Jones (Montreal and London: McGill-Queens University Press, 1974), 65–84. Greene's article expresses agreement with Johnson and Wordsworth against Gray.

13. *Lives of the Poets,* 3:435.

14. Ibid., 1:189–90.

15. A number of critics, however, have explored the various ways in which the *Lyrical Ballads* are grounded in eighteenth-century poetic norms. See, for example, Mary Jacobus, *Tradition and Experiment in Wordsworth's Lyrical Ballads (1798)* (Oxford: The Clarendon Press, 1976); Robert Mayo, "The Contemporaneity of the *Lyrical Ballads,*" *PMLA* 69 (1954), 486–522; and Charles Ryskamp, "Wordsworth's *Lyrical Ballads* in their Time," in *From Sensibility to Romanticism,* 357–72.

16. There has been a good deal of discussion as to the originating circumstances of *The Recluse* and of the lines that eventually became the "Prospectus." The manuscript evidence is inconclusive, but my own inclination would be to agree with Wordsworth's editors, de Selincourt and Darbishire, and his biographer, Moorman, that the lines date from early 1798, when the poet was living at Alfoxden. (See *The Poetical*

Works of William Wordsworth, ed. Ernest de Selincourt and Helen Darbishire [Oxford: The Clarendon Press, 1957], 5:372; Mary Moorman, *William Wordsworth: A Biography* [Oxford: The Clarendon Press, 1957], 1:359–68.) As M. H. Abrams suggests in *Natural Supernaturalism: Tradition and Revolution in Romantic Literature* (New York: W. W. Norton, 1971), the "Prospectus" is at the center of Wordsworth's "program for poetry" (pp. 19–32 et passim); and considering its importance in his development, as well as its stylistic contiguity with *Tintern Abbey,* I find it difficult to believe that the "Prospectus" could have been written after the July 1798 date of *Tintern Abbey.* However, some critics have recently argued that the "Prospectus" was probably begun in January 1800. (See, for example, Jonathan Wordsworth, "On Man, on Nature, and on Human Life," *RES* New Series xxxi, no. 121 [1980], 17–29).

17. *The Poetical Works of William Wordsworth,* 5:31–35. All citations from Wordsworth's poetry are to this edition and will hereafter be included in the text.

18. *The Poetry and Prose of William Blake,* 656.

19. "Esthétique du Mal," *The Collected Poems of Wallace Stevens* (New York: Alfred A. Knopf, 1973), 326.

20. I am indebted to Paul Fry for this insight.

21. See *Natural Supernaturalism,* chap. 1.

22. *The Collected Poems of Wallace Stevens,* 381.

23. See chap. 3, pp. 74–75.

24. I am focusing on Wordsworth's antithetical relationship to Gray, but of course there were positive models that Wordsworth could have looked to in developing a reconstituted blank-verse pastoral along demotic lines, the most important of them being Robert Southey's *Botany Bay Eclogues* (1797–1799). For Southey's influence on Wordsworth, see Stuart Curran, *Poetic Form and British Romanticism,* 197–99, and Mary Jacobus, *Tradition and Experiment in Wordsworth's Lyrical Ballads (1798),* 167–72.

25. See James K. Chandler, "Wordsworth and Burke," *ELH,* 47 (1980) 4:741–71. Chandler's argument is incorporated in his book, *Wordsworth's Second Nature* (Chicago and London: University of Chicago Press, 1984).

26. See chap. 4, pp. 159–60.

27. See also Book 8, lines 120–293, of *The Prelude,* where Wordsworth dismisses "all Arcadian dreams" in terms that are very similar to the passage quoted above from "Home at Grasmere."

28. *The Prose Works of William Wordsworth,* 2: 45–47. Further references to the *Essays on Epitaphs* will be cited from this edition in the text.

29. Leon Guilhamet, *The Sincere Ideal: Studies on Sincerity in Eighteenth-Century English Literature* (Montreal and London: McGill-Queen's University Press, 1974), 277.

30. Laurence Lerner, "What Did Wordsworth Mean by 'Nature'?" *Critical Quarterly* 17 (Winter 1975): 291–308.

   31. "The name of the song is called *'Haddocks' Eyes'* " [said the White Knight].

"Oh, that's the name of the song, is it?" Alice said, trying to feel interested.

"No, you don't understand," the Knight said, looking a little vexed. "That's what the name is *called.* The name really *is 'The Aged Aged Man.'* "

"Then I ought to have said 'That's what the *song* is called'?" Alice corrected herself.

"No, you oughtn't: that's quite another thing! The *song* is called *'Ways And Means':* but that's only what it's *called,* you know!"

"Well, what *is* the song then?" said Alice, who was by this time completely bewildered.

"I was coming to that," the Knight said. "The song really is *'A-sitting on A Gate':* and the tune's my own invention."

Lewis Carroll, *Complete Works* (London: The Nonesuch Press, 1966), 224.

Bibliography

Abrams, M. H. *Natural Supernaturalism: Tradition and Revolution in Romantic Literature.* New York: W. W. Norton, 1971.

Adorno, Theodor W. "Lyric Poetry and Society." Trans. Bruce Mayo. *Telos* 20 (Summer 1974):56–71.

Alpers, Paul. "What Is Pastoral?" *Critical Inquiry*, 8:3 (Spring 1982):437–60.

Aristotle. *Selections.* Ed. Philip Wheelwright. New York: Odyssey Press, 1951.

Arnold, Matthew. *English Literature and Irish Politics.* Vol. 9 of *The Complete Prose Works of Matthew Arnold.* Ed. R. H. Super. Ann Arbor: The University of Michigan Press, 1973.

Bateson, F. W. *English Poetry: A Critical Introduction.* London: Longmans, Green, 1950.

Benjamin, Walter. *Illuminations.* Ed. Hannah Arendt. New York: Schocken, 1969.

Blake, William. *The Poetry and Prose of William Blake.* Ed. David V. Erdman. New York: Doubleday, 1970.

Bloom, Harold. *The Anxiety of Influence.* New York: Oxford University Press, 1973.

———. *A Map of Misreading.* New York: Oxford University Press, 1975.

———. *The Visionary Company: A Reading of English Romantic Poetry.* Ithaca: Cornell University Press, 1971.

Brady, Frank. "Structure and Meaning in Gray's *Elegy.*" In *From Sensibility to Romanticism.* Ed. Frederick W. Hilles and Harold Bloom. New York: Oxford University Press, 1965.

Bronson, Bertrand H. "On a Special Decorum in Gray's *Elegy.*" In *From Sensibility to Romanticism.* Ed. Frederick W. Hilles and Harold Bloom. New York: Oxford University Press, 1965.

———. "Personification Reconsidered." *ELH* 14 (1947):163–77.

Brooks, Cleanth. *The Well-Wrought Urn: Studies in the Structure of Poetry.* New York: Harcourt, Brace and World, 1947.

Burke, Edmund. *Reflections on the Revolution in France.* Ed. Conor Cruise O'Brien. New York: Penguin Books, 1978.

Burke, Kenneth. *A Grammar of Motives and A Rhetoric of Motives.*

Cleveland and New York: The World Publishing Company, 1962.

Carroll, Lewis. *Complete Works*. London: The Nonesuch Press, 1966.

Chandler, James K. "Wordsworth and Burke." *ELH* 47: 4 (1980):741–71.

———. *Wordsworth's Second Nature*. Chicago and London: University of Chicago Press, 1984.

Coleridge, Samuel Taylor. *Biographia Literaria*. 2 vols. Ed. J. Shawcross. London: Oxford University Press, 1967.

Crabbe, George. *Poems*. Ed. Adolphus William Ward. 3 vols. Cambridge, England: Cambridge University Press, 1905.

Crane, R. S. *The Languages of Criticism and the Structure of Poetry*. Toronto: University of Toronto Press, 1953.

Curran, Stuart. *Poetic Form and British Romanticism*. New York: Oxford University Press, 1986.

Dante. *Inferno*. Trans. Allen Mandelbaum. Berkeley: University of California Press, 1980.

———. *Purgatorio*. Trans. Allen Mandelbaum. Berkeley: University of California Press, 1982.

Davenant, William. *Gondibert*. Ed. David F. Gladish. Oxford: The Clarendon Press, 1971.

de Man, Paul. *Blindness and Insight: Essays in the Rhetoric of Contemporary Criticism*. 2d ed. Minneapolis: University of Minnesota Press, 1983.

Donne, John. *Selected Prose*. Ed. Evelyn Simpson. Oxford: The Clarendon Press, 1967.

Downey, James, and Ben Jones, eds. *Fearful Joy: Papers from the Thomas Gray Bicentenary Conference at Carleton University*. Montreal and London: McGill-Queen's University Press, 1974.

Dryden, John. *Poems: 1649–1680*. Ed. Niles Hooker and H. T. Swedenberg, Jr. Vol. 1 of *The Works of John Dryden*. Berkeley: University of California Press, 1956.

———. *Selected Poetry and Prose*. Ed. Earl Miner. New York: Modern Library, 1969.

Eliot, T. S. *The Complete Poems and Plays: 1909–1950*. New York: Harcourt, Brace and World, 1971.

———. *Selected Essays*. New York: Harcourt, Brace and World, Inc., 1964.

Ellis, Frank. "Gray's Elegy: The Biographical Problem in Literary Criticism." *PMLA* 66 (1951):971–1008.

Empson, William. *Seven Types of Ambiguity*. New York: New Directions, 1966.

———. *Some Versions of Pastoral*. New York: New Directions, 1974.

Fisher, J. "James Hammond and the Quatrain of Gray's *Elegy*." *MP* 22 (1935):301–10.

———. "Shenstone, Gray, and the 'Moral Elegy.' " *MP* 34 (1937): 273–94.

Friedrich, Werner P. *Dante's Fame Abroad: 1350–1850.* Chapel Hill: University of North Carolina Press, 1960.

Frye, Northrop. "Towards Defining an Age of Sensibility." In *Eighteenth-Century Literature: Modern Essays in Criticism.* Ed. James L. Clifford. New York: Oxford University Press, 1959.

———, ed. *Romanticism Reconsidered.* New York and London: Columbia University Press, 1966.

Gay, John. *Poetry and Prose of John Gay.* 2 vols. Ed. Vinton A. Dearing and Charles E. Beckwith. Oxford: The Clarendon Press, 1974.

Golden, Morris. *Thomas Gray.* New York: Twayne Publishers, 1964.

Goldsmith, Oliver. *Collected Works of Oliver Goldsmith.* 5 vols. Ed. Arthur Friedman. Oxford: The Clarendon Press, 1966.

Gosse, Edmund W. *Gray.* London: Macmillan, 1882.

Gray, Thomas. *The Complete Poems of Thomas Gray.* Ed. Herbert W. Starr and J. R. Hendrickson. Oxford: The Clarendon Press, 1966.

———. *Correspondence of Thomas Gray.* 3 vols. Ed. P. Toynbee and L. Whibley. London: Oxford University Press, 1971.

———. *Gray and Collins: Poetical Works.* Ed. Austin Lane Poole. London: Oxford University Press, 1974.

———. *Gray's Poems, Letters and Essays.* Ed. John Drinkwater and Lewis Gibbs. London: Dent, 1966.

———. *The Poems of Gray, Collins and Goldsmith.* Ed. Roger Lonsdale. London: Longmans Group, 1969.

Greene, Donald. "The Proper Language of Poetry: Gray, Johnson, and Others." In *Fearful Joy: Papers from the Thomas Gray Bicentenary Conference at Carleton University.* Ed. James Downey and Ben Jones. Montreal and London: McGill-Queens University Press, 1974.

Greg, W. W. *Pastoral Poetry and Pastoral Drama.* 1906. New York: Russell and Russell, 1959.

Guilhamet, Leon. *The Sincere Ideal: Studies on Sincerity in Eighteenth-Century English Literature.* Montreal: McGill-Queens University Press, 1974.

Hamburger, Käte. *The Logic of Literature.* Trans. Marilynn J. Rose. Bloomington: Indiana University Press, 1973.

Havelock, Eric. *A Preface to Plato.* Cambridge, Mass.: Harvard University Press, 1963.

Hazlitt, William. *The Complete Works of William Hazlitt.* 21 vols. Ed. P. P. Howe. New York: AMS Press, 1967.

Hegel, G. W. F. *Aesthetics: Lectures on Fine Art.* 2 vols. Trans. T. M. Knox. Oxford: The Clarendon Press, 1975.

———. *The Phenomenology of Mind.* Trans. J. B. Baillie. New York: Harper & Row, 1967.

Horace. *The Odes and Epodes.* Trans. C. E. Bennett. Cambridge, Mass.: Harvard University Press, 1968.

Hough, Graham. *The Romantic Poets.* London: Hutchinson's University Library, 1953.

Jack, Ian. "Gray's *Elegy* Reconsidered." In *From Sensibility to Romanti-cism*. Ed. Frederick W. Hilles and Harold Bloom. New York: Oxford University Press, 1965.

Jackson, Gabriele Bernhard. "From Essence to Accident: Locke and the Language of Poetry in the Eighteenth Century." *Criticism* 29:1 (Winter 1987):27–66.

Jackson, Wallace, and Paul Yoder. "Wordsworth Reimagines Thomas Gray: Notations on Begetting a Kindred Spirit." *Criticism* 31:3 (Summer 1989):287–300.

Jacobus, Mary. *Tradition and Experiment in Wordsworth's Lyrical Ballads (1798)*. Oxford: The Clarendon Press, 1976.

Johnson, Samuel. *Johnson on Shakespeare*. Ed. Arthur Sherbo. Vol. VII of *The Yale Edition of the Works of Samuel Johnson*. New Haven and London: Yale University Press, 1968.

———. *Lives of the Poets*. 3 vols. Ed. G. B. Hill. New York: Octagon Books, 1967.

———. *Poems*. Ed. E. L. McAdam, Jr. Vol. VI of *The Yale Edition of the Works of Samuel Johnson*. New Haven and London: Yale University Press, 1964.

Keats, John. *Letters of John Keats*. Ed. Robert Gittings. London: Oxford University Press, 1970.

———. *Poetical Works*. London: Oxford University Press, 1972.

Kermode, Frank. *English Pastoral Poetry*. London: G. Harrap, 1952.

Ketton-Cremer, R. W. *Thomas Gray*. Cambridge, England: Cambridge University Press, 1955.

Lerner, Laurence. *The Uses of Nostalgia: Studies in Pastoral Poetry*. New York: Schocken, 1972.

———. "What Did Wordsworth Mean by 'Nature'?" *Critical Quarterly* 17 (Winter 1975): 291–308.

Lewis, Wilmarth S. *Rescuing Horace Walpole*. New Haven: Yale University Press, 1978.

Lucretius. *De Rerum Natura (The Way Things Are)*. Trans. Rolfe Humphries. Bloomington: Indiana University Press, 1969.

MacDonald, Alastair. "Gray and His Critics: Patterns of Response in the Eighteenth and Nineteenth Centuries." In *Fearful Joy: Papers from the Thomas Gray Bicentenary Conference at Carleton University*. Ed. James Downey and Ben Jones. Montreal and London: McGill-Queens University Press, 1974.

Marx, Karl. *Capital: A Critique of Political Economy*. 3 vols. Trans. Samuel Moore and Edward Aveling. New York: International Publishers, 1979.

Marx, Karl, and Friedrich Engels. "Manifesto of the Communist Party." Trans. Samuel Moore. In *Marx and Engels: Basic Writings on Politics and Philosophy*. Ed. Lewis S. Feuer. New York: Doubleday, 1959.

Mayo, Robert. "The Contemporaneity of the *Lyrical Ballads*." *PMLA* 69 (1954): 486–522.

Miles, Josephine. *Eras and Modes in English Poetry*. Berkeley: University of California Press, 1957.

Milton, John. *The Poems of John Milton*. Ed. John Carey and Alastair Fowler. London: Longmans Group, 1968.

Moorman, Mary. *William Wordsworth: A Biography*. 2 vols. Oxford: The Clarendon Press, 1957.

Newman, W. M. "When Curfew Tolled the Knell," *The National Review* 127 (September 1946):244–48; reprinted in *Twentieth Century Interpretations of Gray's Elegy*. Ed. Herbert W. Starr. Englewood Cliffs, N.J.: Prentice-Hall, 1968.

Nietzsche, Friedrich. *On the Genealogy of Morals*. Trans. Walter Kaufmann. New York: Random House, 1969.

Oates, Whitney J. *Aristotle and the Problem of Value*. Princeton: Princeton University Press, 1963.

Ovid. *Metamorphoses*. Trans. Arthur Golding. 1567. New York: Macmillan, 1965.

Panofsky, Erwin. *Meaning in the Visual Arts*. Garden City, N.Y.: Doubleday, 1955.

Peckham, Morse. "Gray's 'Epitaph' Revisited." In *Twentieth Century Interpretations of Gray's Elegy*. Ed. Herbert W. Starr. Englewood Cliffs, N.J.: Prentice-Hall, 1968.

Perret, Jacques. "The Georgics." In *Virgil*. Ed. Steele Commager. Englewood Cliffs, N.J.: Prentice-Hall, 1966.

Poggioli, Renato. *The Oaten Flute: Essays on Pastoral Poetry and the Pastoral Ideal*. Cambridge, Mass.: Harvard University Press, 1975.

Pope, Alexander. *Pastoral Poetry and An Essay on Criticism*. Ed. E. Audra and Aubrey Williams. Vol. I of *The Poems of Alexander Pope*. Ed. John Butt. London and New Haven: Methuen and Yale University Press, 1961–69.

——. *The Rape of the Lock and Other Poems*. Ed. Geoffrey Tillotson. Vol. II of *The Poems of Alexander Pope*. Ed. John Butt. London and New Haven: Methuen and Yale University Press, 1961–69.

Puttenham, George. *The Arte of English Poesie*. Ed. Gladys Doidge Willcock and Alice Walker. 1589. Cambridge, England: Cambridge University Press, 1936; reprinted 1970.

Reed, Amy L. *The Background of Gray's Elegy: A Study in the Taste for Melancholy Poetry 1700–1751*. New York: Columbia University Press, 1924.

Richards, I. A. *Practical Criticism*. New York: Harcourt, Brace and World, 1929.

Ryskamp, Charles. "Wordsworth's *Lyrical Ballads* in their Time." In *From Sensibility to Romanticism*. Ed. Frederick W. Hilles and Harold Bloom. New York: Oxford University Press, 1965.

Schorer, Mark, Josephine Miles, and Gordon McKenzie, eds. *Criticism: The Foundations of Literary Judgment*. Rev. ed. New York: Harcourt, Brace, and World, 1958.

Shepard, Odell. "A Youth to Fortune and to Fame Unknown." *MP* 22 (1923): 347–73.

Starr, Herbert W. " 'A Youth to Fortune and to Fame Unknown': A Reestimation." In *Twentieth Century Interpretations of Gray's Elegy.* Ed. Herbert W. Starr. Englewood Cliffs, N.J.: Prentice-Hall, 1968.

———, ed. *Twentieth Century Interpretations of Gray's Elegy.* Englewood Cliffs, N.J.: Prentice-Hall, 1968.

Stevens, Wallace. *The Collected Poems of Wallace Stevens.* New York: Alfred A. Knopf, 1973.

Sutherland, John H. "The Stonecutter in Gray's 'Elegy.' " In *Twentieth Century Interpretations of Gray's Elegy.* Ed. Herbert W. Starr. Englewood Cliffs, N.J.: Prentice-Hall, 1968.

Trapp, Joseph. *Lectures on Poetry.* 1742. Menston, England: The Scolar Press, 1973.

Virgil. *Georgics.* Trans. Smith Palmer Bovie. Chicago: University of Chicago Press, 1956.

Waller, Edmund. *The Poems of Edmund Waller.* Ed. G. Thorn Drury. New York: Greenwood Press, 1968.

Warren, T. H. *Essays of Poets and Poetry, Ancient and Modern.* London: John Murray, 1909.

Wasserman, Earl R. "The Inherent Values of 18th-Century Personification." *PMLA* 65 (1950): 435–63.

Wilkinson, L. P. *The Georgics of Virgil.* Cambridge, England: Cambridge University Press, 1969.

Williams, Anne. *Prophetic Strain: The Greater Lyric in the Eighteenth Century.* Chicago and London: University of Chicago Press, 1984.

Wimsatt, W. K. *Day of the Leopards.* New Haven and London: Yale University Press, 1976.

———. "The Structure of the 'Concrete Universal' in Literature." In *Criticism: The Foundations of Modern Literary Judgment.* Ed. Mark Schorer, Josephine Miles, and Gordon McKenzie. New York: Harcourt, Brace, and World, 1958.

Winters, Yvor. *Forms of Discovery: Critical and Historical Essays on the Forms of the Short Poem in English.* Denver: Alan Swallow, 1967.

Wordsworth, Jonathan. "On Man, on Nature, and on Human Life." *RES,* new series, xxxi, no. 121 (1980):17–29.

Wordsworth, William. *The Poetical Works of William Wordsworth.* 5 vols. Ed. Ernest de Selincourt and Helen Darbishire. Oxford: The Clarendon Press, 1957.

———. *The Prose Works of William Wordsworth.* 3 vols. Ed. W. J. B. Owen and J. W. Smyser. Oxford: The Clarendon Press, 1974.

Wright, George T. "Eliot Written in a Country Churchyard." *ELH* 18 (1976):227–43.

Index

HENRY WEINFIELD is Special Lecturer in English and
Humanities at the New Jersey Institute of Technology. He
is the author of several collections of poetry, including *Sonnets
Elegiac and Satirical* and *In the Sweetness of the New Time*,
and has written critical articles on a variety of topics in
English and American poetry. He is currently translating the
collected poems of Stéphane Mallarmé.